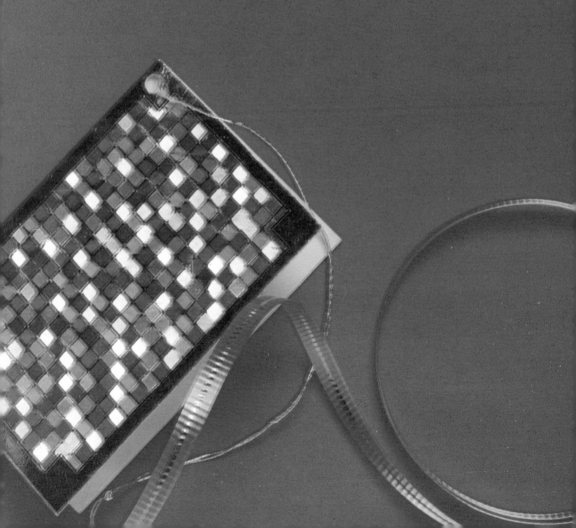

Creative
Handicraft
Gifts

Creative Handicraft Gifts

Edited by
Caroline Oliver

Contributors:
Valerie Janitch
Katie Dyson
Sheila Richardson
Eve Harlow

Galley Press

Contributors:
Valerie Janitch
Sheila Richardson
Eve Harlow
Katie Dyson

The Publishers would like to thank the following people and
organisations for their kind assistance in the preparation of
this book:
David Constable–Candle Makers Supplies; Copydex Ltd;
Cosmic Crayon Co; Dylon International; Elna Sewing
Machines Ltd; Emu Wools Ltd; French Wools Ltd; Harbutt's;
Lister & Co; Patons & Baldwins; Robert Glew & Co;
Sellotape Ltd; W H Smith & Sons Ltd; H G Twilley Ltd;
F W Woolworth & Co Ltd.

Photographs by Gover Grey Photography Limited.

This edition published 1979 by
Galley Press
In association with Cathay Books
59 Grosvenor Street, London W1

ISBN 0 904644 77 4

Produced by Mandarin Publishers Limited
22a Westlands Road
Quarry Bay, Hong Kong

Printed in Hong Kong

Quick Conversion Table

IMPERIAL	METRIC
1 inch	25 millimetres
2 inches	50 millimetres
3 inches	75 millimetres
4 inches	10 centimetres
5 inches	13 centimetres
6 inches	15 centimetres
8 inches	20 centimetres
12 inches	30·5 centimetres
18 inches	45 centimetres
24 inches	61 centimetres
36 inches	91 centimetres
48 inches	122 centimetres
2 yards	2 metres
3 yards	2·75 metres
6 yards	5·5 metres
9 yards	8·5 metres

Note: This table is an approximate guide only. Do not mix Imperial and Metric measures.

Contents

Making Things for Children

Enlarging patterns

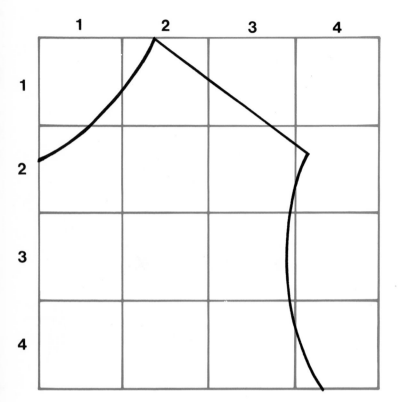

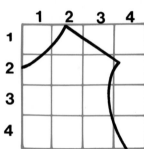

The important thing to remember when making your own patterns from the ones in this book is to make sure that you are working to the correct scale (indicated on each pattern). Seam allowances are included in the patterns. Before you start you will need: dressmaker's squared paper (if metric squared paper is used it is useful to remember that 5 centimetres equal 2 inches), or large sheets of brown wrapping paper, with one inch squares drawn on (use a yardstick and set square to do this accurately).
ruler
sharp pencil
1. Number the squares along the top and side side of the pattern in the book. Mark corresponding numbers on the dressmaker's

squared paper. Make sure there is sufficient length and width of paper for each pattern. If not, tape pieces together.
2. Start from the top left corner and work downwards and across. Make an accurate full-size pattern by marking dots on the squared paper to correspond exactly with places where the pattern crosses the lines of the graph in the book.
3. Connect dots on the pattern to copy curves and use a ruler to draw in any straight lines.
4. Transfer any cutting instructions and details from the original graph and write what each piece of pattern is clearly—skirt, bodice front etc.
5. Now cut out the patterns you have drawn and they are ready for use.

Good stitches to know

A selection of stitches, some to make sewing work quicker, others to be used for decoration.

Three useful stitches for decoration

1. Chain Stitch

Stitches must be even. Make a stitch along the sewing line. Loop thread under needle point and pull needle through. Insert needle point next to exit of last stitch and bring needle out further along sewing line, looping thread under point. Use this stitch for decorative embroidery on clothes.

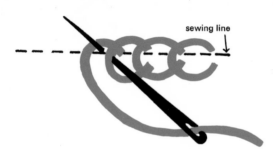

sewing line

2. Lazy-daisy Stitch

Once practised, this can be worked quickly freehand. Mark the daisy shape with tiny pencil points. Bring thread out at centre of daisy, stitch down into fabric from edge of "petal" and back up into centre on right side. Continue this way until daisy is completed. Use this stitch for all types of embroidery and especially for decorative embroidery on knitted baby clothes.

3. Knot a Fringe

Wind wool or thread on to card ¼ inch deeper than proposed length of fringe. Cut one edge. Fold one piece (two for thicker garment) of wool in half. Pull through garment hem with crochet hook (use needle threader if working on fine fabric). Pull ends of thread through loop until knot is firm. Use for making fringe on knitted or crochet things; on sewn play tunics, ponchos or capes.

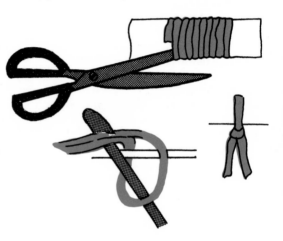

Short cuts with the sewing machine

1. Shirring Elastic

A gentle way of adding gathers to sleeve edges. Wind shirring elastic by hand on to bobbin, adjust upper tension and sew as for normal straight stitching. The shirring elastic will automatically gather the fabric.

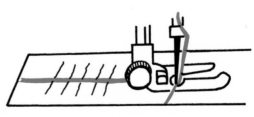

2. Speedy Gathers

A quick way of making neat gathers on skirts and particularly sleeve heads. Set the machine to a fairly wide zigzag. Cut two

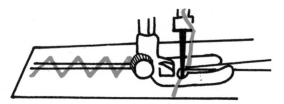

lengths pearl cord the same length as area to be gathered. Run cord under machine foot as you sew the zigzag stitch. The stitching will move along the cord so you can pull up fabric to required length.

3. Appliqué Work

Sew on appliqué with normal straight machine stitch. Trim edges neatly. Then sew all round edge with satin stitch. Use machine embroidery twist for smartest results. Put tracing or writing paper under fine fabrics while machining to give body to stitches and stop fabric from pulling.

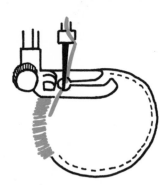

Six smocking stitches

Use these in any colour combination for effective patterning. For best effect, the stitches should not be sewn too deeply into the gathered pleats. Skim the tops of the gathers.

Note to left-handed people: Work all these stitches in reverse and study illustrations through mirror to get correct needle and thread positions. If instructions say "start at left", you should start at the right, and vice versa.

1. Single Cable

A good firm stitch for the top of a piece of smocking. Start from left. Bring thread out at left of pleat 1. Insert needle point on right-hand side of pleat 2. Stitch through back of pleat, bringing thread out parallel to first stitch and slightly above it on left of pleat 2. Make the next stitch downwards so thread comes out on a line with first stitch.

2. Trellis Stitch

Stitch this in the same way as single cable. Work along the pleats going 5 "steps" up and down to make a V pattern. The next row down and up turns this into a diamond shape. Thread should lie above needle when sewing downward steps and below needle when sewing upward ones.

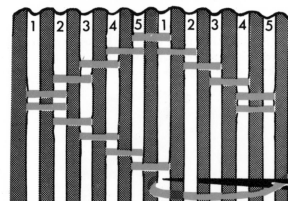

3. Vandyke Stitch

A good stitch for the base of a block of smocking. Work from right to left. Bring thread out on left of pleat 2. Stitch into right of pleat 1. Bring thread out on left of pleat 2, Take needle up and stitch into right of pleat 2 about ⅛th inch or slightly less above. Bring needle out horizontally on left of pleat 3. Take thread down and stitch into right of pleat 3. Bring needle out on left of pleat 4. Make the stitch more open at base of smocking by taking 2 or 3 steps up and 2 or 3 down at a time.

Open Vandyke.

4. Diamond Stitch

The first row makes the top of the diamond and the second completes it. Work from left to right. Bring thread out on left of pleat 1. Take thread across horizontally. Stitch through pleat 2 from right to left, bringing thread upwards, diagonally to right. Stitch from right to left of pleat 3. Take thread over

horizontally and stitch from right to left of pleat 4, bringing thread out below stitch. Sketch shows how to complete diamond shapes.

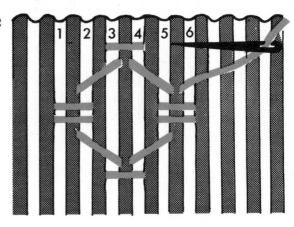

5. Outline Stitch

Begin with this stitch or use it before several rows of Vandyke stitch. Work from left to right. Bring thread out on left of pleat 1. Stitch diagonally downwards into right of pleat 2. Bring needle up and out on left of same pleat, in line with upper part of first stitch. Repeat the process, always taking thread diagonally down to right and pointing needle diagonally up to left.

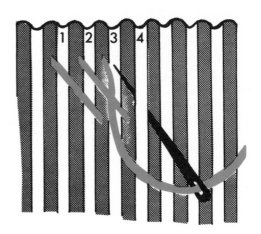

6. Feather Stitch

Work from right to left. Bring thread out on right front of pleat 1. Keep thread in front of needle. Take needle slightly down and stitch from right of pleat 1, through to left of pleat 2,

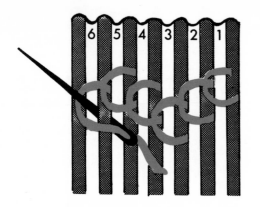

looping thread under needle. Hold thread down with left thumb so that it comes below thumb. Insert needle slightly below from right of pleat 2 to left of pleat 3. Loop thread under needle point. Continue working 3 stitches downwards and 3 upwards. When stitching a line of 3 upwards, hold thread down with left thumb so it comes above thumb while making the stitch. This stitch is particularly effective when a contrasting colour is worked just under the row.

Knitting and Crochet

Knitting needle and crochet hook sizes

Equivalent American knitting needle sizes are given in brackets, throughout the knitting patterns, after the British sizes. Continental equivalents will be found in the chart below New International size crochet hooks are quoted in the crochet patterns, followed by the American equivalents in brackets. British sizes will be found in the chart below.

Size note

Where more than one size is given follow 1st figures for 1st size and figures in brackets in order for other sizes. Where only one set of figures is given, read for all sizes.

Note

Where terms or materials may be different for overseas readers, an equivalent is given in parenthesis after the British term or material.

Crochet Hook Chart

Continental (New International Size)	American	British
2·50 mm	B/1	12
3·00 mm	D/3 or C/2	10/11
3·50 mm	E/4	9
4·00 mm	F/5	8
4·50 mm	G/6	7
5·00 mm	H/8	6
5·50 mm	H/8	5
6·00 mm	I/9	4

Knitting Needle Chart

British	American	Continental
3	10	$6\frac{1}{2}$ mm
5	8	$5\frac{1}{2}$ mm
7	6	$4\frac{1}{2}$ mm
8	5	4 mm
9	4	$3\frac{1}{2}$ mm
10	3	$3\frac{1}{4}$ mm
11	2	3 mm
12	1	$2\frac{1}{2}$ mm

Abbreviations

Colours

M: main shade mc: main colour
C: contrast

Knitting

k:	knit
p:	purl
sts:	stitches
st st:	stocking stitch
g st:	garter stitch
alt:	alternate
foll:	following
inc:	increase
dec:	decrease
rep:	repeat
beg:	beginning
rem:	remain (ing)
ins:	inches
cont:	continue
tog:	together
SKPO:	slip 1, knit 1, pass slip stitch over
SK2tog.PO:	slip one, K2 tog, pass slipped stitch over
m 1:	make 1
pw:	purlwise
K21N:	K twice into stitch, i.e. first into front, then into back of stitch
patt:	pattern
tbl:	through back of loop
m st :	moss stitch
C 6f:	cable 6 front, i.e. slip next 3 sts on to cable needle and leave at front, k 3, then k sts from cable needle
C 6b:	as C 6f, but leave sts at back
sl:	slip
C 4b:	slip next 2 sts on to a cable needle and leave at back of work, k 2, then k 2 sts from cable needle
C 4f:	slip next 2 sts on to a cable needle and leave at front of work, k 2, then k 2 sts from cable needle
T2R:	k into front of second st on left hand needle, k first st slipping both sts off needle together
T2L:	k into back of second st on left hand needle, k first st slipping both sts off needle together
T2RP:	k into front of second st on left hand needle, p first st slipping both sts off needle together
T2LP:	p into back of second st on left hand needle, k first st, slipping both sts off needle together
C4BP:	slip next 2 sts on to a cable needle and leave at back of work, k 2, then p 2 sts from cable needle
C4FP:	slip next 2 sts on to a cable needle and leave at front of work, p 2, then k 2 sts from cable needle
y fwd:	yarn forward
yrn:	yarn round needle

Crochet

(American abbreviations in brackets)

ch:	chain
dc (sc):	double crochet (single crochet)
h tr (hdc):	half treble (half double crochet)
tr (dc):	treble (double crochet)
d tr (tr):	double treble (treble)
tr tr (d tr):	triple treble (double treble)
sl st:	slip stitch
yrh:	yarn round hook
sp:	space
gr:	group
dec:	decrease
inc:	increase
ML:	make a loop by inserting hook into next dc (sc), yarn over hook, and draw up a one inch loop on index finger of left hand, draw yarn through st, as in dc (sc), yarn over hook and draw through loops on hook
dec 1:	decrease 1 by inserting hook into next st, draw through a loop, insert hook into next st, draw through a loop, yarn over hook, draw through 3 loops on hook

Making Things for Your Home

Making a Start

There are very few basic essentials. Most of the remainder come in handy occasionally and perfectly good substitutes can be found around the house.

Scissors: You will need a good pair of cutting-out scissors, plus two small pairs, if possible, so that you can keep one specially for fine sewing and embroidery, and use the other for cutting paper and other jobs which require small, pointed blades.

Sewing Equipment: Pins, needles, thimble, thread . . . and a block of beeswax. This latter might sound a bit old-fashioned, but some of the old ideas are often the best, and drawing your thread through wax really does prevent it breaking and knotting.

A sharp craft knife: This is essential. The best kind has a long blade which snaps off in tiny bits, so that you can keep renewing the tip. It is well worth paying a little extra for a knife with a self-locking device to prevent the blade slipping.

Metal-edged rule: This is necessary for cutting against with the blade of a knife.

A pair of compasses: These are very useful for drawing patterns. They need not be expensive as long as they are accurate, and not too stiff to use.

A set square (T-square)*:* This does ensure complete accuracy in drawing out patterns. Alternatively, an absolutely square piece of cardboard will do.

Adhesives: It is vital to use the right one. *Fabric adhesive* sticks many more materials than the name implies. It is clean, quick-drying and reliable. *Clear all-purpose adhesive* gives a stronger bond, and is necessary when fabric adhesive is not strong enough. *Wallpaper paste* can be very useful for certain jobs: it spreads easily and does not leave a mark. Mix it a little stiffer than directed for paperhanging. *Dry stick adhesive* is by no means essential, and is expensive to use for everything. Occasionally it is very useful however and is worth having to hand. Tough, *woven fabric tape* in a variety of colours is invaluable and if you have never encountered *double-sided tape* before, you will be amazed at its versatility!

Illustration on page 14:
Flower shower

Hall

The first impression guests have of your home is when they walk through the hall. So make this room as attractive as possible.

Create a subtle, flattering light with the paper lampshade. To brighten a dull corner, arrange some colourful paper asters in a pretty vase. For a desk or telephone table, make the elegant set of table lamp, jotter and waste-paper bin in an attractive fabric.

Gold-Embossed Desk Set

A sophisticated set for a desk or telephone table. Simple lines and a strong, bold choice of covering are designed to have distinct masculine appeal – but if you use the same fabric as for your curtains or covers, you'll have a truly individual set stamped with your own personality.

Method

To make the *lampshade*:
Measure round the outer edge of one ring and add 1 inch. Cut a piece of bonded parchment this length by $7\frac{1}{4}$ inches. If necessary, adjust the depth to suit the pattern of fabric being used. Cut a strip of fabric $\frac{1}{4}$ inch longer than the length of parchment and to the same depth. Iron the fabric on to the parchment, overlapping $\frac{1}{4}$ inch at one end, making sure it has adhered firmly all over.
Using double thread oversew one edge of the fabric-covered parchment all round one ring; do not finish stitching the overlap. Oversew the other edge round the second ring. Stick the overlap with double-sided tape or fabric adhesive, and finish the stitching at top and bottom.
Stick braid round the top and bottom edges as illustrated.

To cover the *waste-paper bin*, measure round the outside of the bin and add 1 inch. Then cut a strip of fabric this length by the depth of the bin. Stick smoothly round bin and join overlap with double-sided tape or fabric adhesive.
Stick wide braid round the top of the shade and narrow braid round the bottom, as illustrated.

Materials

$\frac{3}{4}$ yard of 36 inch wide non-fraying fabric
2×8 inch diameter lampshade rings, one with inner lamp fitting
Bonded lampshade parchment
Cylindrical metal waste-paper bin (about 7 inches in diameter and $8\frac{1}{2}$ inches high)
A jotting pad (about $6\frac{1}{2}$ inches by 5 inches)
Heavy cardboard
$1\frac{1}{2}$ yards of $\frac{3}{8}$ inch wide gilt braid for the lampshade
$\frac{3}{4}$ yard of $\frac{7}{8}$ inch wide gilt braid
$\frac{3}{4}$ yard narrow gilt braid
Fabric adhesive
Strong adhesive tape
Double-sided tape
The instructions given are for the articles illustrated but the directions can easily be adapted to different measurements to make the items larger or smaller.

Gold-embossed desk set

18

To make the *jotter*, cut two pieces of heavy
card $\frac{1}{2}$ inch wider than the jotter pad and
about $\frac{3}{8}$ inch deeper. Also cut a narrow strip
to the same width and about $\frac{1}{8}$ inch deeper
than the spine of the pad.
Place these three pieces together touching
each other, (as diagram 1).
Stick tape over the two joins (indicated by
broken lines).
Cut a piece of fabric $\frac{3}{4}$ inch larger all round
than the card. Mitre lower corners by cutting
away a triangle (as diagram 2), and slash at
centre joins. Cover the outside of the card in
three stages, beginning with the lower
section, by bringing the surplus fabric round
to the inside and sticking smoothly: fold over
at centre so that the fabric is stretched
round the spine, then mitre remaining
corners and stick surplus fabric round as
before. Finally, stick fabric inside the spine.
Cut another piece of fabric fractionally
smaller than the cover, and stick to the
inside.
Stick back of pad to inside back of cover.

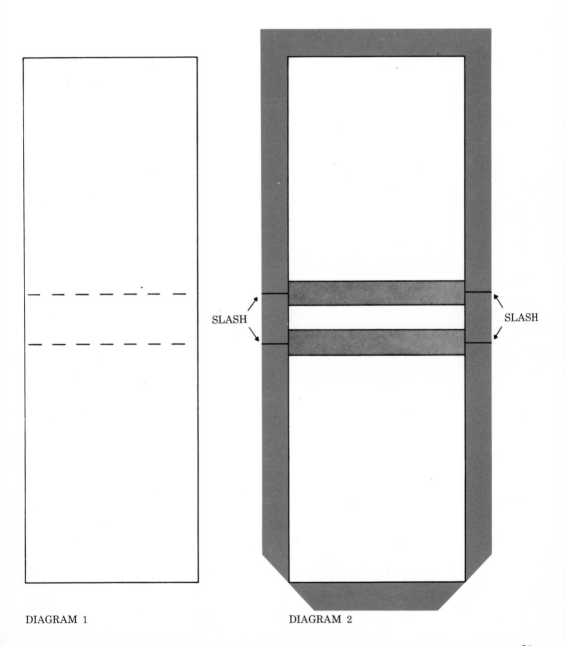

DIAGRAM 1   DIAGRAM 2

SLASH   SLASH

Green cut Paper Lampshade

This sophisticated hanging lampshade is perfectly designed for those areas where a subdued downward light is required – in hallways for instance or over a side table. The fascinating three-dimensional effect is very easy to do. All you need is a sharp knife, a metal-edged rule – and a steady hand!

Method

Cut a piece of the squared paper 7¾ inches deep by 18 inches long. Starting ½ inch from the top edge, and ½ inch in from the side, draw the top row of 10 hexagon shapes right across the paper, following the diagram. Draw seven rows of 10 shapes in this manner. The second row of hexagons starts 1¼ inches in from the side and ¼ inch down (see diagram).
Cut a piece of cartridge (construction) paper to the same size as the squared paper. Pin the squared paper over the cartridge (construction) paper securely. Prick through the squared paper, marking the ends of the solid lines. There will be six prick marks for each hexagon shape. Remove the squared paper and begin to cut and score each shape firmly and accurately (see diagram 2). Using a sharp pointed blade, and the tip of a blunt knife, cut the 4 solid lines of each shape and score the 3 broken lines. Curve the cartridge (construction) paper round – rather more than it will be when made up and gently push all the little 'windows' in. Oversew the top and bottom edges of the lampshade to the rings. Trim the overlap and stick the join. Finish off by sticking a ¾ inch deep collar of paper round the top and bottom of the lampshade to cover the oversewing stitches.

Materials

Coloured, heavy cartridge (construction) paper
2 × 5 inch diameter lampshade rings, one with inner lamp fitting
¼ inch squared paper
All-purpose adhesive
Sharp-bladed knife

Green-cut paper lampshade

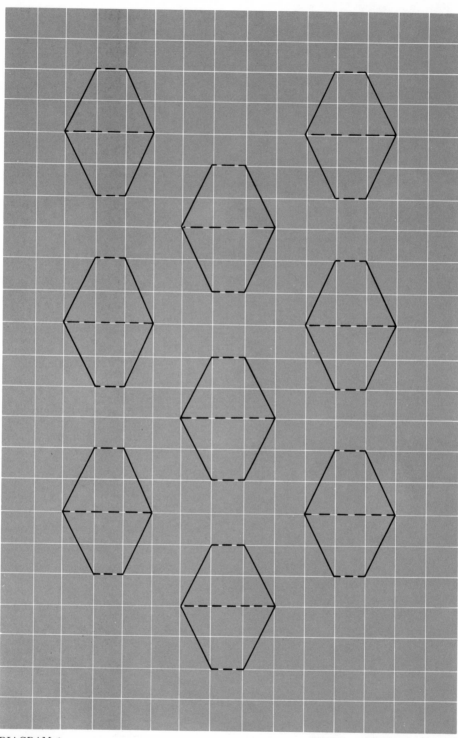

DIAGRAM 1

SCALE: 1 SQUARE=$\frac{1}{4}$ INCH

DIAGRAM 2

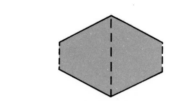

ACTUAL SIZE OF EACH 'WINDOW'

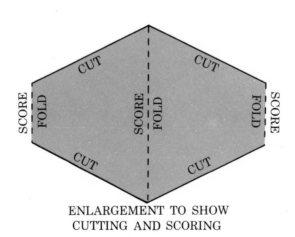

ENLARGEMENT TO SHOW
CUTTING AND SCORING

All-The-Year Asters

Shade your gathering of larger-than-life
asters from delicate pink through mauve, to
deep purple. Just look at a summer flower
bed for colour inspiration.

Method

Hook over the tip of a length of florists' wire
and wrap a scrap of cotton wool round it,
moulding it into a firm ball a little bigger
than a large pea. Cut a 3 inch diameter circle
of bright green crepe paper, place it centrally
over the cotton wool, bring the edges down
all round, and secure tightly with fine wire or
thread (diagram 1).
Cut two 9 inch long strips, 3 inches wide, in
yellow crepe with grain widthways (diagram
2). Fold in half lengthways, as indicated by
broken line. Cut a close $\frac{1}{4}$ inch deep fringe,
along the folded edge of each piece, open out,
turn over, and re-fold along the line of the
previous fold – but do not crease. Stick the
two strips together along the lower edge, then
wind the double strip round and round the
green centre – the cut edges level with it –
sticking along the base.
Cut two 12 inch long strips, 3 inches wide,
for the petals, grain as shown by arrows
(diagram 3). Cut each piece down to within
$\frac{1}{4}$ inch of the lower edge all the way along to
form a fringe. Stick strips together along the
lower edge, as before. Wind this double strip
round and round the centre, keeping
absolutely level and sticking the lower edge
of the petals $\frac{1}{4}$ inch above the lower edge of
the yellow.
Fix a garden stake to the wire with adhesive
tape, for the stem.
Trace the large and small leaf patterns,
following the black and coloured lines

Materials

Crepe paper in different shades – bright
   green, deep leaf green, yellow and pink,
   mauve etc. for petals
Florists' wire
18 inch long thin garden stakes
Cotton wool
Fine wire or thread
Adhesive tape
Fabric adhesive

All-the-year asters

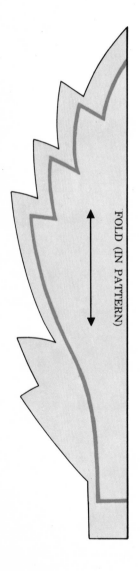

FOLD (IN PATTERN)

respectively. Cut two large and three small shapes in leaf green (grain as arrows).

Cut an 18 inch long strip, $\frac{1}{2}$ inch wide in green crepe with the grain running across. Stick one end round the base of the petals, wind round once, and then bind in the bases of the three small leaves evenly round the flower, securing with a little adhesive. Continue to wrap the strip round the base of the flower, then slowly twist it round and down the stem – binding in the two large leaves as you go. Secure the end of the strip with tape.

Open out the petals and curl gently, but firmly, stroking them between the ball of your thumb and blade of your scissors – or a blunt knife. Curl the leaves slightly in the same way.

1

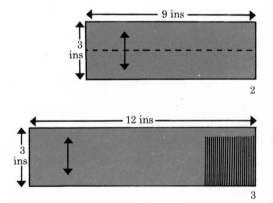

9 ins

3 ins

2

12 ins

3 ins

3

Living Room

Decorative touches add character to this room. For the walls, you can make the straw-daisy plaque or harvest trio, both of which feature dried flowers.

Smarten up a writing-pad by making a soft velvet case for it. Cover matchboxes and arrange them in interesting shapes. And, to keep happy memories, make a Victorian photograph album or a frame for individual photographs.

The coffee and cream coasters both look attractive and protect your table from unsightly rings.

Victorian Family Photograph Album

Make a truly personal photograph album to hold happy family memories. Moiré was used for the album which is illustrated, but almost any fabric can be used, plain or patterned, trimmed with lace or embroidered braid.

Method

Measure the album leaves and add 1 inch to each measurement. Cut two pieces of heavy cardboard to these dimensions. Place a leaf centrally on one piece of cardboard, and mark the position of the holes. Punch holes in the cardboard, then mark and punch corresponding holes in the second piece of cardboard. Score the inside of the front cover piece of cardboard only, to correspond with the leaves, so that the cover opens easily. Stick wadding to the outside of each piece of cardboard and trim the edges neatly. Place each piece of cardboard, wadding down, on the wrong side of the fabric; cut fabric 1½ inches larger than the measurements of cardboard. Mitre the corners by cutting away a triangle (diagram 1), and fold the edges neatly over to the inside and stick. Neaten corners with adhesive tape (diagram 2). Cut pieces of fabric 1 inch smaller than the covers all round and stick neatly to inside, covering raw edges of outer covering fabric. Pierce holes through covering, then assemble leaves between covers, fixing with ribbon or cord tied at the back. Stick trimming round the edges of the front to form a frame, using clear or fabric adhesive. Make a mock bow of velvet ribbon to trim the corner as illustrated.

Materials

Refill photo album leaves
Fabric for the cover
Wadding
Gilt or an alternative trimming
½ yard narrow ribbon or cord
¼ yard narrow velvet ribbon
Heavy cardboard
White adhesive tape (or to match fabric)
Fabric adhesive
Double-sided tape or clear all-purpose adhesive

INSIDE COVER

DIAGRAM 1

INSIDE COVER

DIAGRAM 2

For the living room: photograph album, photograph frame, random-shaded lampshade, wall plaque, harvest trio

Oval Velvet Photograph Frame

With its distinctly Victorian air, this padded velvet frame will make an elegant setting for your favourite pictures. Choose a glowing shade of velvet to tone with the colour scheme of your room.

Drawing an accurate oval is very difficult – unless you know the secret. Here is how it is done. Follow the instructions to learn the process, then adjust the measurements to make larger or smaller frames.

Materials

A piece of velvet 9 inches deep by 6 inches wide
Stiff cardboard
Wadding
Clear plastic or acetate (optional)
Fabric adhesive
A pair of compasses
Ruler

Method

Begin by drawing the inner oval (diagram 1) on your cardboard. Rule a 4-inch vertical line (A–B) in the centre of the card. Mark the centre (C) and then quarters (D and D). With compasses point on centre D, draw 2-inch diameter circles. With centre C, rule E–F 2 inches long, at right angles to A–B. With centre E and radius $2\frac{3}{8}$ inches, draw arc G–G. With centre F, draw a similar arc, H–H.

To draw the outer oval (diagram 2), mark points J $\frac{1}{4}$ inch from A and B on your inner oval. With centre J, draw $3\frac{1}{2}$-inch diameter circles. With centre C, rule K–L (through E–F), $3\frac{1}{2}$ inches long, at right angles to A–B. With centre K and radius $4\frac{1}{4}$ inches, draw arc M–M. With centre L, draw a similar arc, N–N.

Cut round the outer oval, then carefully cut out the inner oval. Place the larger oval frame on a piece of cardboard for the back of the frame and draw round both ovals (it is only necessary to mark the inner oval if you want to be able to remove the photograph. If you wish it to remain in the frame permanently, ignore diagram 3 and the directions for cutting a back opening).

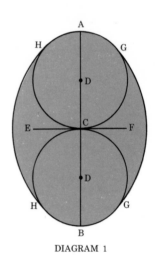

DIAGRAM 1

32

Cut round the outer edge of the back, but do not cut the inner oval. To make the back opening, 'frame' the marked inner oval as diagram 3. Mark centre of oval O. With centre O, rule P–Q 4½ inches long, and R–S, 3¼ inches long. With centres P, Q, R and S, rule lines, each 1½ inches long. Then join the ends as shown. Cut this shape out carefully with a sharp knife, and put to one side. Stick a piece of wadding to the front oval frame, trimming level with the edges of the inner and outer ovals. Place the front, wadding down, on the wrong side of the velvet, brushing with a little adhesive to hold it in place. Cut out the inner oval, ½ inch inside the edge of the cardboard to allow ½ inch turning. Snip this surplus velvet all the way round, to form tiny tabs. Bring these smoothly up, one by one, and stick to the back of the frame. Cut round the outer oval, ¾ inch outside the edge of the cardboard. Stick transparent plastic or acetate to the back of the frame, if required to protect the picture. If you do not wish to remove the photograph, stick this, too, into position. Now stick the back oval to the front frame. Snip the surplus velvet into tabs as before, and stick them round the outer edge of the back. If you have made a back opening, cut your photograph to size and fit into the opening, then replace the cardboard shape. Cut a piece of paper slightly smaller than the frame and stick over the back. (To remove photograph, cut round back opening with a knife and replace by sticking a slightly larger piece of paper over it, or using adhesive tape.)

Cut a 6-inch long strut, as diagram 4. Score broken line at top, and stick to back so that the frame stands at the correct angle.

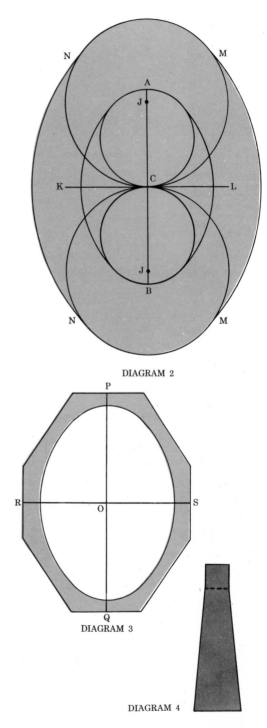

DIAGRAM 2

DIAGRAM 3

DIAGRAM 4

Harvest Trio

A charming set of miniatures inspired by the sun-ripened fields at harvest-time – quick and easy to make and sure to attract compliments.

Method

Cut a barley head about 4 inches long, trimming away the 'whiskers' at the top. Cut sprays of oats and heavy grass slightly longer. Tie the stalks together in a bunch with raffia.
Stick the spray to a coaster diagonally, across the grain of the wood, using either double-sided tape or clear adhesive, spreading out the heads attractively. Trim the stalks neatly.
Decorate all three mats in a similar way, to make up a set. Fix picture hangers to the backs of the mats ensuring they are positioned so that the plaques will hang at the correct angle.

Materials

3 round wooden coaster mats (about 4 inches diameter)
Wheat or barley heads, oats and grasses or other dried plants
Natural raffia or matching thread
3 self-adhesive picture hangers
Double-sided tape or all-purpose clear adhesive

Straw-daisy wall plaque and harvest miniatures

Straw-Daisy Wall Plaque

This unusual wall decoration really could not be simpler to make. Choose an attractive basketwork table mat and some everlasting or dried flowers. If you do not grow everlasting flowers (helichrysums) yourself, then any colourful dried flowers would be as attractive. Florists are now stocking more and more varieties as the popularity of this form of decoration grows.

Materials

A round woven straw table mat (about 7–8 inches diameter)
Everlasting (dried) flowers
Self-adhesive picture hanger
Clear all-purpose adhesive
Tiny pins

Method

Fix the picture hanger to the back of the mat, marking the front to show the way the mat will hang.
Arrange the flower-heads on the mat, moving them around until a satisfactory composition has been achieved. Alternate light and dark flowers so that they contrast and complement each other.
Stick the flowers into position one at a time, using plenty of adhesive, and anchoring each head to the mat with one or two tiny pins, driven through the petals at an angle, the heads pushed down until they are out of sight.

Random Shaded Wool Lampshade

The subtle colour combinations available in the range of random shaded knitting wools (yarn) can be used to great effect on many things other than knitted garments. This simple, but attractive lampshade, for example, is just a matter of winding the wool (yarn) round and round the rings – let the colours do the rest.

Method

Measure round the outer edge of one ring and add 1 inch. Cut a strip of covering material this length by the depth required. Using double thread, oversew one long edge of the parchment round one ring: do not finish stitching overlap. Oversew the other edge to the second ring. Trim the overlap, if necessary and stick the join neatly. Finish the stitching at top and bottom.
Hold a tape measure round the top edge of the lampshade and mark every $\frac{1}{4}$ inch. Repeat round the lower edge.
Secure one end of the wool (yarn) at one marked point with your thumb and then begin to wind the wool (yarn) evenly making sure it is neither too loose nor too tight. Work round and round the shade crossing over the top and bottom edge each time at the next marked point. Continue right round the shade, then secure the end of the wool (yarn).
To make the trimming, cut two $\frac{1}{2}$ inch wide strips of the basic lampshade covering material to the same length as the original piece for the shade. Wind wool (yarn) evenly and closely round and round this strip so that the material is completely covered. Turn the end under and stick round the edge of shade, overlapping about $\frac{1}{4}$ inch.

Materials

2 lampshade rings, one with lamp fitting (about 8 inches diameter)
Coloured lampshade covering (or iron thin fabric on to adhesive parchment)
1 oz. random shaded double-knitting wool (knitting worsted)
Clear all-purpose adhesive

Velvet-Striped Writing Case

It is surprisingly easy to create sophisticated effects by using interesting combinations of textures. Here an unbleached lining canvas has been striped with soft velvet in a glowing colour to make an elegant writing case. Choose the colour of the writing paper first, then key the cover fabrics to that. The measurements given are for a standard 8 inch by 6 inch pad but you can adjust them to fit any size.

Method

Measure the writing pad and add $\frac{1}{2}$ inch to each measurement. Cut two pieces of heavy cardboard to this size, and another strip the same depth, but only 1 inch wide for the spine.

Place these three pieces of cardboard side by side, the spine in the centre, touching each other, with the top and bottom edges absolutely level. Tape together as shown in diagram 1, where broken lines indicate edges of card under tape – inside of case.

Cut a piece of canvas 1 inch larger all round than the cardboard. Cover the outside of the case in three stages. Beginning by sticking the canvas *to one side only* (marked A in diagram 2), the cardboard should be exactly centred on the canvas. Mitre the corners by cutting away a triangle, (diagram 2), and slash at centre joins. Bring the surplus fabric round to the inside and stick down smoothly. Fold in the canvas at centre so that the fabric is stretched round the spine and stick the canvas to the spine. Then stick the canvas to the second main piece of cardboard. Mitre the corners, and bring the surplus fabric to the inside, as before.

Cut four strips of velvet ribbon, one of each

Materials

Writing pad (8 inch by 6 inch)
Matching envelopes
$\frac{1}{2}$ yard × 24 inch wide lining canvas
1 yard × $1\frac{1}{2}$ inch wide velvet ribbon
$\frac{5}{8}$ yard × 1 inch wide velvet ribbon
$\frac{3}{8}$ yard × $\frac{5}{8}$ inch wide velvet ribbon
1 yard × $\frac{3}{8}$ inch wide velvet ribbon
Heavy cardboard
Thin cardboard
Strong adhesive tape
Fabric adhesive

Velvet-striped writing case, coffee and cream coasters, straw-daisy plaque, matchboxes

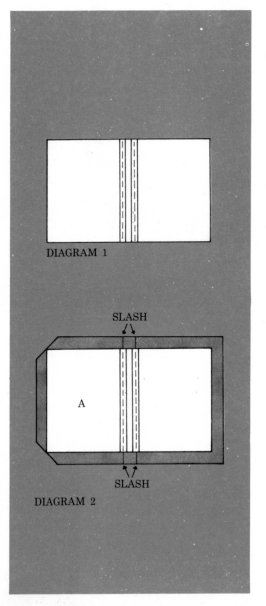

DIAGRAM 1

SLASH

A

SLASH

DIAGRAM 2

of the different widths, and each 2 inches deeper than the depth of the writing case. Stick these to the cover as illustrated, 1 inch apart and overlapping equally, top and bottom. Turn the ends over neatly and stick to the inside of the case. Stick a 1 inch wide length of velvet ribbon down the spine.

Cut two pieces of the narrowest ribbon, each 2 inches deeper than the depth of the case. Open up the case and fix the two pieces to the left-hand inside cover. Turn the ends under and stick very securely into position, leaving the ribbon loose enough to slip the envelopes underneath.

Cut a piece of canvas to the overall width measurement of the inside of the case plus 2 inches and to slightly less than the depth. Stick this neatly into place inside the case, under the ribbon loops.

Cut a piece of thin cardboard exactly the same size as the writing pad. Place this behind the pad. Cut a 6 inch length of the widest velvet ribbon, fold it diagonally round a corner of the pad to form a triangle, and stick the ends neatly to the back of the card behind the pad. Finish the remaining three corners in the same way and then stick the cardboard to the right hand inside cover very securely.

Coffee and Cream Coasters

There is nothing more cheering than a mug of steaming hot coffee – and nothing more distressing than a ring on a polished table-top. Pretty coaster mats made in contrasting shades of coffee and cream will protect your furniture.

Method

Cut a 4 inch diameter circle in linen or felt.
Bind the raw edge of the linen.
Stitch a circle of brown daisies round the edge of the linen mat, over the binding, or individual cream daisies in the centre of the felt mat, as illustrated.

Materials

Cream linen
Brown felt
Cream binding (for linen)
Brown and cream lace daisies or similar trimming

Matchbox Magic

Matchboxes assume a very elegant character when grouped in intriguing shapes and smartly covered. Use up odd scraps of pretty fabrics – or use vinyl for the kitchen – to make the most inexpensive, yet personal, presents. Half the fun is inventing different arrangements of the boxes.

Materials

Boxes of matches
Fabric or self-adhesive vinyl to cover
Narrow ribbon
Stiff cardboard
Fabric adhesive

Method

Group two, three or four boxes on a piece of stiff cardboard (diagram 1 shows the different positions of the boxes illustrated). When a pleasing arrangement has been achieved, draw round the outline of the grouped boxes making sure that they do not move. Cut out the shape with a sharp knife or scissors. Place the shape on another piece of cardboard, draw round it and cut out a second piece.
Using just a smear of adhesive, stick each piece of cardboard to the wrong side of the fabric and then cut out, leaving $\frac{1}{2}$ inch surplus fabric all round. Mitre the corners and clip into the angles (diagram 2). Fold the excess fabric over and glue it down to the cardboard.
Cut a $2\frac{1}{2}$ inch length of ribbon for each drawer. Fold the ribbon in half lengthways and glue cut ends inside the boxes so that a looped end protrudes as illustrated. Replace the matches in the boxes.
Glue the matchboxes into position on the wrong side of one piece of covered cardboard. Glue the second piece of covered cardboard on top and press down firmly. Leave the boxes under a weight until quite dry.

Matchbox magic

DIAGRAM 1

DIAGRAM 2

CLIP   CLIP

44

Kitchen

Tempt all your family to help you in the kitchen by making them gay aprons in tough denim or practical PVC.

Quick notes and shopping lists can be pinned on a decorative wall board, and rubber bands kept on a tidy wall dispenser. There is also an attractive hanging rack for herbs and spices.

Hanging Spice Rack

A bamboo or woven straw table mat can be turned into a charming hanging rack for herbs and spices. Any thin wood will do for the inside as long as it can be cut with a sharp craft knife and joined with $\frac{1}{2}$ inch steel pins – $\frac{1}{8}$ inch balsa is particularly suitable.

Method

Cut pieces of wood as follows, and sandpaper smooth:

1 piece, 11 inches long by 2 inches wide – A
2 pieces, 11 inches long by 1$\frac{1}{2}$ inches wide – B
2 pieces, 2 inches square – C
2 pieces, 6 inches long by 1 inch wide – D
1 piece, 12 inches long by 1 inch wide – E
1 piece, 12 inches long by $\frac{3}{4}$ inch wide – F

Stick and pin the two ends C to the base A (diagram 1). Stick and pin the two sides B between (diagram 2).
Fold the mat in half and stick the two ends together. Stick this joined edge level with the front of the rack, overlapping equally at each end, then take the mat down over the front, under the base and up the back, sticking securely all the way – so that the folded edge extends about 2$\frac{1}{2}$ inches above the rack. Strengthen with pins through the mat into the wood at each side.

Materials

A bamboo or straw table mat 12 inches × 18 inches
Thin wood
Decorative transfer motifs
Self-adhesive labels
All-purpose adhesive
Tiny steel or panel pins

For the kitchen: rubber band dispenser, hanging spice rack, reminder board

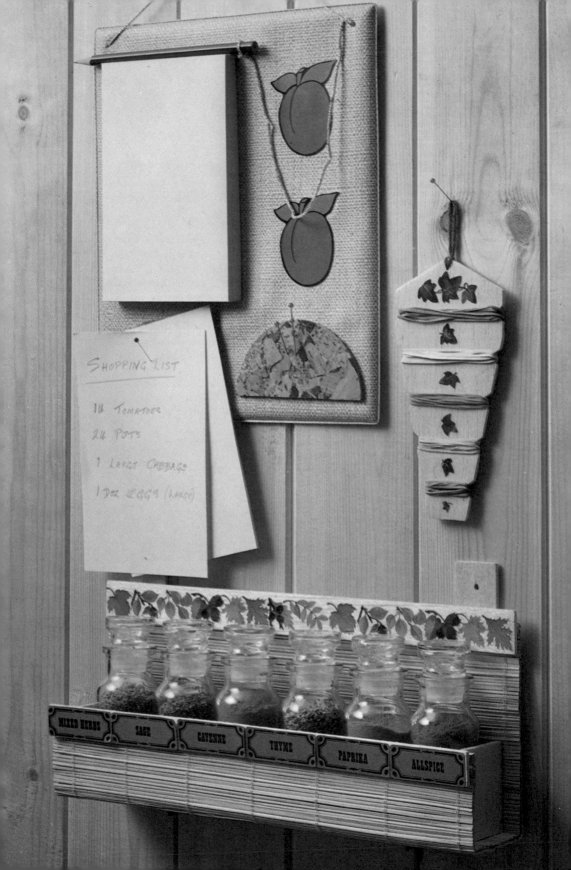

SHOPPING LIST

1lb TOMATOES

2lb POTS

1 LARGE CABBAGE

1 DZ EGGS (LARGE)

MIXED HERBS   SAGE   CAYENNE   THYME   PAPRIKA   ALLSPICE

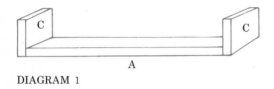

C   C

A

DIAGRAM 1

Stick the two 6 inch strips D behind the mat,
positioning as illustrated, so that the lower
edges are level with the base of the rack,
and extending about 1½ inches above. Pin at
the base to strengthen and drill a hole at the
top of each, to hang.
Stick strip E along the top edge at the back
of the mat, and strip F along the front.
Decorate the back strip with transfer motifs,
and stick herb and spice labels the front.

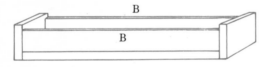

B

B

DIAGRAM 2

48

Kitchen Reminder Board

It is essential to be able to make a hasty note or shopping list in the kitchen – and to have somewhere to pin a reminder or a recipe. This quick-to-assemble board combines both functions.

All kinds of decoration are possible – sticky seals, motifs cut from self-adhesive vinyl or washable wallpaper or transfer would be suitable.

Method

Make holes in the two top corners of the hard table mat and thread cord through to hang, knotting the ends securely at the back. Cut the cork mat in half, and stick each piece near the base, as illustrated. Stick the pad securely above.

Cut a groove near the end of the pencil and tie a length of cord round it. Fix the other end through the top hole and secure it at the back. Decorate the board with motifs to match the kitchen scheme.

Materials

Hard table mat (about 9 inches by 10 inches)
Jotting pad (about 6 inches deep by 4 inches wide)
4 inch diameter circular cork mat
Pencil
Decorative motifs
Cord to hang
Clear all-purpose adhesive

Togetherness in the Kitchen

Really practical and straightforward aprons
for the whole family: 'His' and 'Hers' are
tough denim with a nautical air – 'It' has a
smaller version in wipe-clean PVC (vinyl)
(which can, of course, be lengthened as
necessary). The halter neck adjusts to size
automatically – just by pulling the ties.
If you do not want to rule squares, and have
no graph paper, you can simply measure out
the pattern, following the measurements
indicated by the squares on the chart:
X shows you where to place the point of your
compasses for the lower curve.

Method

Rule a sheet of paper into one-inch squares,
use graph paper or measure (see above) out
patterns for the aprons and pockets, following
the diagram. Follow the lefthand straight
line for the centre front fold of the aprons.
Cut His apron in dark denim, with a pocket
in the light shade, 9 inches deep by 14 inches
wide. Cut Hers in light denim, with the
pocket as shown on the pattern in the dark
shade. Cut Its apron and the pocket in PVC
(vinyl).
Bind each apron across the top (A–A), down
the straight sides (below B) and round the
lower edge, and all round the pocket except
across the top, with narrow binding. Then
bind the curved sides between A and B with
wide binding, allowing the same amount as
the narrow to show on the right side. Bind
the top edge of the pocket in the same way.
Pin the pocket in position and top-stitch
securely into place, double-stitching firmly at
the top corners.
Thread the cord through channels formed by
wide binding at each side, looping it across
the top and knotting cut ends to prevent
fraying.

Materials

¾ yard each 36-inch wide light and dark
   denim (His and Hers)
An 18-inch square of PVC (vinyl) (Its)
½-inch wide bias binding
1-inch wide bias binding
2 yards piping or lacing cord (for each)

Aprons for all the family

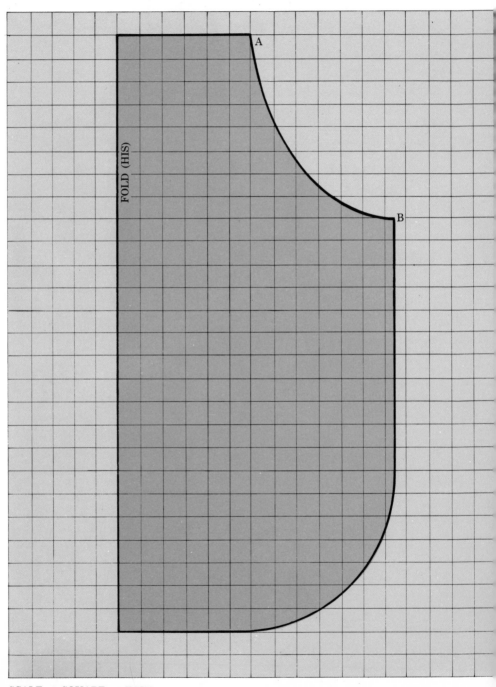

FOLD (HIS)

A

B

SCALE: 1 SQUARE=1 INCH

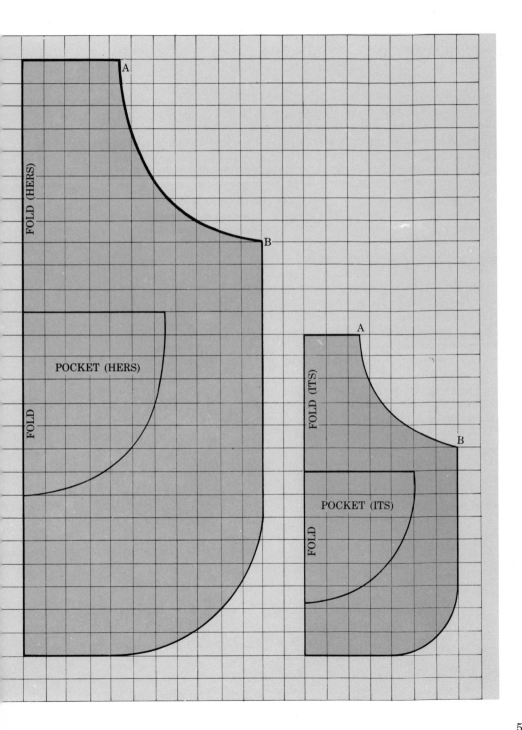

FOLD (HERS)

A

B

POCKET (HERS)

FOLD

FOLD (ITS)

A

B

POCKET (ITS)

FOLD

53

Rubber Band Dispenser

Use thin wood or ply – balsa is quick and easy to cut, using a sharp craft knife and a metal rule. Painted or decorated, this is a useful item to hang anywhere where a quick choice of the right-sized rubber band is needed.

Method

On a sheet of $\frac{1}{4}$ inch squared graph paper, draw out the shape following diagram 1. Rule five horizontal lines 1 inch apart as indicated. Cut this out to use as your pattern. Place the pattern on the wood and mark round the outline carefully. Cut out. Replace the paper pattern on the wood shape and mark the horizontal lines on the edges of the wood.

Cut out a notch ($\frac{3}{8}$ inch wide by $\frac{1}{4}$ inch deep) on the edge of a piece of paper, following the pattern in diagram 2. Placing the edge of the paper level with the edge of the wood, mark and cut a notch at each marked point.

Make a hole at the top of the wood shape, as indicated. Sandpaper all over until smooth. Paint, stain or varnish and decorate as desired. Make a loop of cord at the top to hang. Fit graduated elastic bands into the notches.

Materials

A piece of wood 6 inches deep by 3 inches wide by about $\frac{3}{8}$ inch thick
Cord to hang
Paint, stain or varnish
Decorative motifs
Assorted rubber bands
Sharp craft knife
Metal rule

Rubber band dispenser

DIAGRAM 1   SCALE: 1 SQUARE=$\frac{1}{4}$ INCH

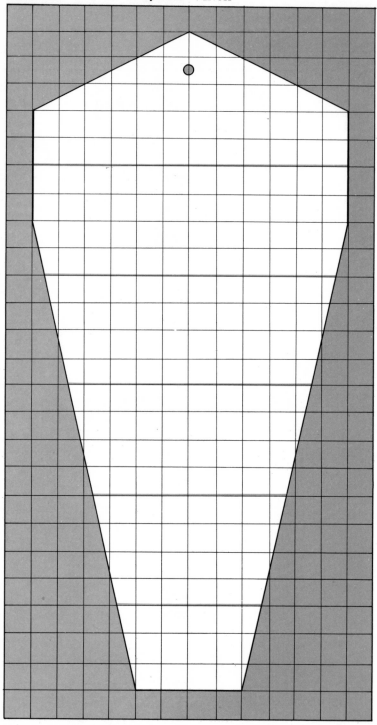

DIAGRAM 2 PATTERN FOR CUTTING NOTCH

Dining Room

Make some pretty paper roses for a year-round summery look.

For the dining table, you can make decorative mats. There are informal luncheon mats and braid place mats – match the braid to your colour scheme.

At breakfast, keep eggs warm in the amusing grandma and grandpa egg cosies.

Scandinavian Luncheon Mats

If you have never embroidered before, begin
with cross-stitch. It is quick, easy, and gives a
really professional result.

This versatile design, rather Scandinavian in
feeling, can be adapted to articles of any size.
It can be used in stripes for a cushion, as a
border for a tablecloth – or for motifs to
decorate a wide variety of home accessories.
In these two examples, which show
contrasting colour schemes, an even-weave
linen-like dress fabric with about 20 threads
to the inch has been used – and six strands
of stranded embroidery cotton to give a bold
effect. If you use a more finely woven fabric,
use fewer strands – and remember your
stitches will come up smaller. Each cross has
been embroidered over two threads: to make
your crosses larger on a finger fabric,
embroider over three threads in each
direction.

Method

Cut fabric to size, then begin by embroidering
the double line of single stitches at the outer
edge. Then count the number of crosses in
this line and centre either a large or small
motif, depending on the number of motifs
which will fit into the complete line (see my
two examples): embroider this the correct
distance from the outer border, then complete
the remaining motifs above and below.
Follow with the decorative inner
borders each side of the motifs, and finish
with another row of single crosses. To
balance the luncheon mats, work another
double line at the opposite edge. And on the
light, putty-coloured mat, the edge has been
hem-stitched by hand, using three strands of
the mid-brown used in the outer border.

Materials

Even-weave fabric
Stranded embroidery thread in five different
shades

Scandinavian luncheon mats

58

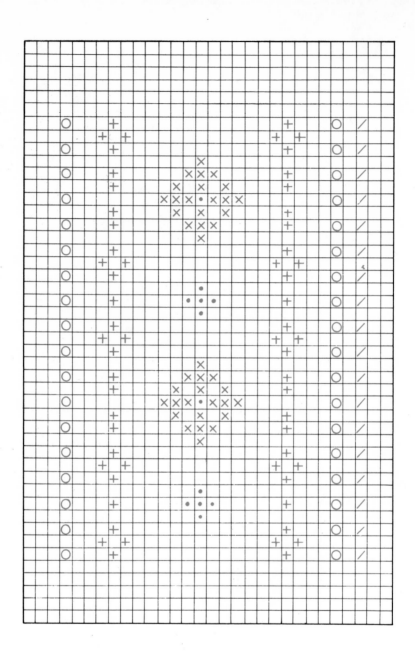

Summer Roses

A bunch of paper roses in sunshine colours to brighten the dullest winter's day. Shade them from red through orange and yellow or simply make them in a single colour – it is just as effective.

Method

To make one rose
Trace the petal shape and cut it out in thin cardboard to use as a pattern. With the grain of the paper running vertically, (see arrows) cut five petals out of two layers of crepe paper, deep red on top, orange behind. Place the dull surfaces of the paper facing so that the shiny side is outside. Cut out five more pairs of petals, this time just a little larger than the cardboard pattern and with orange on top and yellow behind.
Using solid stick adhesive, stick each pair of petals together at the tip, sides and base. Now 'cup' the lower half of each petal as follows: holding the petal, place your thumbs in the middle and gently stretch the crepe paper so that it forms a cupped, petal shape. Turn the petal over and cup the upper half from the back, so that the tip of the petal curls over backwards.
Cut a length of florist's wire and hook the end. Wrap a scrap of cotton wool over the hook and mould it into a ball about the size of a pea. Cut a 2 inch diameter circle of yellow crepe paper (or use green) and place it centrally over the cotton wool ball. Bring the crepe edges down and secure tightly close under the cotton wool with fine wire or thread.
Now take a red and orange petal and roll it lengthways round the yellow tip of the wire, quite tightly. Stick the base of the petal

Materials

Crepe paper in deep leaf green, red, orange and yellow.
Florists' wire
Thin garden canes, 18 inches long
Cotton wool
Fine wire or thread
Adhesive tape
Solid adhesive in stick form
Fabric adhesive

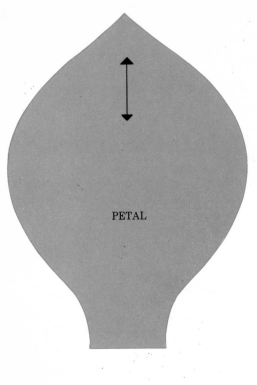

PETAL

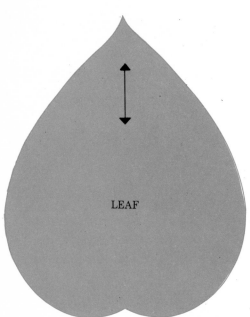

LEAF

round the wire close under the tip. Follow with another red and orange petal, exactly opposite the first and then stick the three remaining red and orange petals round the stalk, each new petal half overlapping the previous one and the lower edges always level. Continue in the same way with the five orange and yellow petals. Wire the base to hold the petals securely then re-cup and curl where necessary before pushing the petals together with your hands.

Fix a garden cane to the wire with adhesive tape for the stem.

Trace off the leaf shape and make a cardboard pattern.

Cut out two shapes in doubled green crepe paper (grain as arrows). Stick each doubled leaf together as for the petals, inserting a 6 inch length of wire straight down the centre of each. The rest of the wire extends from the bottom of the leaf for a stem.

Cut a strip of green crepe paper, 18 inches long and ½ inch wide, the grain running across. Stick one end of the strip round the base of the petals, wind it round several times to secure and then gradually twist it round and down the stem, binding in first one leaf and then the second. Secure the end of the strip with adhesive tape. Cup and curl the leaves slightly in the same way as for the petals.

Braid and ribbon mats

Braid and Ribbon Mats

Attractive place mats give distinction to the simplest meal and whether it is 'just the family' or a formal dinner party, it is important to set your table with style. By making sets of place mats in a linen-like woven fabric and decorating them with braids and ribbons, you can ring the changes with your table settings as often as you like. A set of six mats can be made from $\frac{1}{2}$ yard of 36 inch wide fabric.

Method

Cut the fabric to size, following the thread. Draw three or four threads about $\frac{5}{8}$ inch from the edge, all the way round. Zig-zag the inner edge on the sewing machine – or hem-stitch, by hand – and then pull away the remaining outer parts to form a fringe.
Cut the ribbon or braid into strips to fit the mat, allowing $\frac{1}{2}$ inch at each end to turn under. Pin or tack into position, making sure it is absolutely flat, then hem-stitch neatly all the way round.
The braids used for the mats illustrated are 2 inches wide (the single stripe), $1\frac{1}{2}$ inches (silk embroidery on black ribbon), $1\frac{1}{4}$ inches (two-colour woven) and 1 inch (the daisies).

Materials

For each mat
A piece of woven fabric, 9 inches by 12 inches
$\frac{1}{4}$ yard of braid or ribbon for *each* stripe

Grandma and Grandpa Egg Cosies

Whether you are seven or seventy, it is cheering to find Grandma and Grandpa thoughtfully keeping your eggs warm when you're late for breakfast!

Method

Rule a sheet of paper into half-inch squares or use dressmaker's squared graph paper which shows half-inch markings. Draw the cosy pattern following the diagram.
Cut the shape twice in flesh felt for each cosy: cut a 1¼ inch diameter circle for Grandpa's nose.
Oversew the two cosy pieces all round the curved edge, leaving lower edges open. Turn to right side.

To make *Grandma*, stitch embroidered ribbon round the base of the cosy, join the ribbon at centre back. Stitch lace level with the top edge of the ribbon.
Cut a piece of cardboard 6 inches deep and wind double-knitting wool (knitting worsted) round it fifteen times for the hair. Tie the loops temporarily on both sides, slide off the cardboard and tie loosely at the centre. Stitch centre to centre top of cosy, towards the front. Then bring the loops down, catch securely over side seam and remove ties. Wind wool (yarn) round the cardboard again fifteen times, and tie as before. Stitch centre behind centre of first piece, then catch loops across back of head, removing ties as before. Wind wool (yarn) ten times round a 4 inch deep piece of cardboard: slide off, tie a knot, and stitch securely to top of head.
Embroider mouth as indicated on the pattern in stem stitch.

Materials

A piece of flesh-coloured felt 9 inches by 6½ inches
A scrap of black felt
Grey double-knitting wool (knitting worsted) (Grandma)
Beige textured knitting yarn (Grandpa)
6 inches of embroidered ribbon (Grandma)
6 inches of ⅜ inch wide guipure lace (Grandma)
9 inches of 1 inch wide white ribbon (Grandpa)
2½ inches of 1½ inch wide tartan ribbon (Grandpa)
2 × ⅝ inch diameter brass curtain rings (Grandma)
1 × 1 inch diameter brass curtain ring (Grandpa)
Tiny gilt beads, fine chain or gold cord (Grandpa)
Pearls or beads (Grandma)
Red stranded embroidery thread (Grandma)
Fabric adhesive

Position curtain rings for eye glasses and sew into place at the centre and at each side.
Trace eye pattern and cut out in black felt: stick in the centre of each ring.
Stitch beads over seam at each side, just below hair, for ear-rings.

To make *Grandpa,* stitch white ribbon round the lower edge of the cosy, folding the ribbon back 1½ inches at each side of the centre front, so that the cut ends are level with the seams. For the neck bow, fold 2 inches of ribbon into three widthways; gather the centre and pull it up tight. Then fold a ½ inch strip into three, wrap round gathered centre, trim ends and join at back. Stitch securely over centre front of collar.
Gather nose circle all round outer edge: put a scrap of cotton wool in the centre and draw up tightly. Stitch to face (from behind) at X.
Cut a piece of cardboard 3 inches deep; wind textured yarn round it about twenty times (according to thickness) for the moustache. Slide off carefully and tie at the centre. Stitch securely just below the nose.
Cut a piece of cardboard 1 inch deep by 4 inches long, and wind yarn round it about 100 times for the hair. Thread a needle with matching thread and catch end securely over the side seam, 2¾ inches above the lower edge. Place the cardboard across the back of the head, distributing the yarn evenly over 3 inches and catch the loops along the top edge of the card securely across the back of the head. Slide cardboard out gently, then catch a few lower loops at the front of the face at each side, and the remainder lightly across the back of the head.

Stitch a curtain ring into position for a monocle, with a chain or string of tiny beads to hold it to the side seam. Trace the eye pattern off and cut two in black felt. Stick them to the face, centring one inside the monocle.

Grandma and grandpa egg cosies

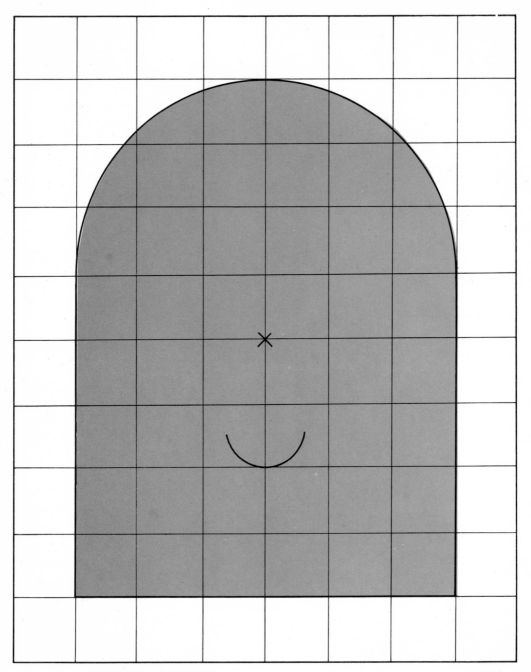

SCALE: 1 SQUARE=$\frac{1}{2}$ INCH

Bedroom

You can make the bedroom look very pretty with this selection of makes. Pamper yourself with a patterned breakfast set and tray cloth.

To decorate a bedroom chair, make the rosebud gingham cushion; for the dressing table, there is a frilly lace lampshade and a matching set of wastepaper basket, tissue-box cover and picture frame. Add charm to the walls with an elegant Edwardian silhouette.

Rosebud Gingham Cushion

Cushions are one of the most delightful ways to dress a room – and you can reflect your own personality and taste in the way you use trimmings. The instructions here are for a basic cushion but they can be easily adapted to make cushions of different shapes and sizes. Use the different design ideas in this book for trims and decoration; Scandinavian cross-stich embroidery, for example; the nursery wall hangings; stripes of woven or embroidered braids. You can also try interesting textural effects such as velvet ribbons on canvas, as used for the writing case.

Materials

2 × 14 inch squares of check gingham
1½ yards of 1 inch deep cotton fringe
Embroidered rosebud motifs
2 × 14 inch squares of fine cotton for the inner cushion
Filling

Method

Cut the fabric to size and stitch the fringe to the right side of one piece ¼ inch in from the edge, with the outer edge of the fringe towards the centre of the cushion. Stitch the trimming into position on the front of the cushion. With right sides facing, join the front and back of the cushion on three sides following the stitching line of the fringe. Trim seams, clip corners and turn to right side.
Make up the inner cushion in the same way, omitting fringe and decoration. Stuff firmly, then turn in raw edges and slip-stitch together. Fit inner cushion inside cover, turn in edges of remaining side, and slip-stitch neatly. Alternatively, insert a zip or touch-and-close fastening, so that the cover can be removed more easily.

For the bedroom: rosebud gingham cushion, embroidery and lace lampshade, Edwardian silhouette

Embroidery and Lace Lampshade

Perfect for a dressing table, this frilly lace shade looks delicately fragile. Yet it is the simplest thing to whisk off the cover, wash it out and slip it back into place when dry.
The directions and quantities given are for 3 inch wide lace, but you can, of course, use a narrower lace, in which case you will require a longer length – or a wider lace, when you will need less. To adapt the instructions to the lace of your choice, just divide the width of your lace into twenty-four to calculate the number of strips (about 6½–7 inches long) you will need.
And if you cannot find a lace that combines embroidery, use separate strips embroidered flowers or ribbon. Although the directions are for a 6 inch deep, 7 inch diameter shade, the design can be used for any cylindrical lampshade of different proportions.

Materials

2 × 7 inch diameter lampshade rings, one with lamp fitting
1½ yards of 3 inch wide embroidered frilled nylon lace
White nylon net
White lampshade parchment
Narrow round elastic
Double-sided tape (or all-purpose adhesive)

Method

Measure round the outer edge of a ring and add 1 inch. Cut a strip of parchment this length by 6 inches deep.
Using double thread, oversew one long edge of the parchment round one ring: do not finish stitching overlap. Oversew the other edge round the second ring. Trim overlap, if necessary, and stick with double-sided tape or adhesive. Finish stitching at top and bottom of join.
To make the cover, cut a piece of net 8 inches deep by 25 inches long. Cut the 1½ yards of lace into eight equal 6¾ inch lengths.
Leaving ¼ inch of net clear along top, bottom and both side edges, stitch the strips of lace side-by-side to cover the net (see diagram). Right sides facing, join the two short side edges of the net. Turn and stitch a ½ inch hem

all round the top and bottom edges.
Turn to the right side. Thread narrow elastic
through the top and bottom channels and fit
the cover over the shade with upper and
lower edgings overlapping equally. Draw up
the elastic so that the cover fits the shade.

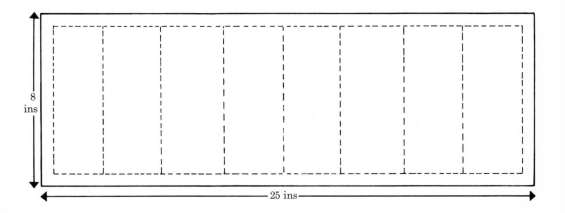

8
ins

25 ins

Flowered Breakfast Set

Certain to cheer the dullest morning, this
gay breakfast set is not just pretty –
it is practical too.

Method

Draw the pattern for the *tea cosy* as follows.
Draw a 9 inch diameter circle and mark the
centre, point A. Rule a straight line from the
top edge of the circle to the bottom, through
A (see diagram 1). Mark point B 2½ inches
below A, and draw line C–D at right-angles
to A–B. Mark point E ¾ inch from the edge of
the circle (point F), and draw line G–H
parallel to C–D. Now extend line E–F ¼ inch
to point J (1 inch above point E), and draw
line K–L, 6 inches long, centre J and parallel
to G–H. Then join K–G and L–H. Finally,
with the point of your compasses at A, draw
an arc between points K and L. Cut out,
omitting the shaded section at the base, so
that it looked like diagram 2.
Draw a 5 inch diameter circle for the base.
Allowing ½ inch turnings all round, cut out
the cosy pattern four times and the base
circle twice from the printed cotton. If you
are using the design of the fabric for special
effect, it is a good idea to cut out all three
items in the set first, cutting the linings of
the cosies and the base pieces from the
remaining fabric.
Cut the cosy pattern twice more, and the base
circle once, in doubled wadding. This time
cut same size as the pattern, without
allowing turnings.

Materials

½ yard of 48 inch wide printed cotton
Washable wadding
½ yard of ¾ inch wide double-edged broderie
  anglaise
½ yard of ¾ inch wide frilled broderie anglaise
1½ yards narrow broderie anglaise or guipure
  lace
½ yard of ½ inch wide white tape or binding
Narrow round elastic

Flowered breakfast set and tray cloth

To make up the tea cosy

Tack a layer of double wadding to the wrong side of each lining piece for the cosy and to the base circle lining. Mark the edge of the pattern shape on the wrong side of the two outer cosy pieces, then place each piece onto the linings, with right sides facing. Stitch all round, leaving the straight lower edges open. Trim seams, clip curves and corners and turn both to the right side. Turn in the raw edges and tack.

Pad and stitch the base pieces in the same way remembering to leave a section unstitched to turn to right side. Use slip-stitch to close the section. Oversew to join the straight lower edges of each half of the cosy to the base, with corners meeting. Stitch the tape or binding to the wrong side of the double-edged broderie anglaise, forming a channel. Join the short ends to make a circle. Thread elastic through and draw up the circle so that it holds the top of the cosy together, as illustrated.

To make the egg cosy

Rule a sheet of paper into half-inch squares (or use graph paper), as diagram 3. Draw line A–B (4 inches long), then A–C and B–D (each 1¾ inches). Mark point E (4 inches above A–B) and, with the point of your compasses at F, draw an arc to join E–D, and with the point at G, join E–C.

Allowing ½ inch turnings all round, cut out the pattern in cotton four times. Cut the pattern out twice more in single wadding without turnings.

Tack the single layer of wadding to the wrong side of each lining piece. With right sides facing, join all round the top edge, leaving the lower edge open. Trim and clip seam.

Mark the edge of the pattern shape on the right side of one outer cosy piece, stitch frilled broderie anglaise along this line, with the scalloped edge of the broderie anglaise towards the centre (diagram 4). Allow a little extra at the top of the cosy. Place the second outer cosy piece on top of this trimmed piece, right sides facing and, following the previous stitching line, stitch all round, but leaving lower edge open. Trim and slip seam and turn the cosy to right side. Fit the padded lining inside the cosy outer. Turn in the edges neatly and slip-stitch to close.

To make the *napkin*

Cut a 12 inch square of printed cotton. Neaten the edges with zig-zag stitch, or by turning a narrow hem. Trim with narrow broderie anglaise.

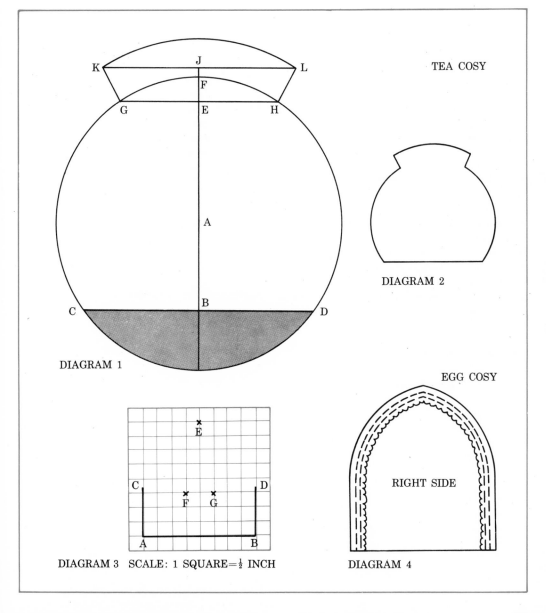

TEA COSY

DIAGRAM 1

DIAGRAM 2

EGG COSY

RIGHT SIDE

DIAGRAM 3   SCALE: 1 SQUARE=$\frac{1}{2}$ INCH

DIAGRAM 4

Edwardian Silhouettes

This artistic looking collage is easier to do than it looks at first sight. The colour scheme and decoration can be based on the figure shown here or the basic outline can be trimmed in different ways.

Method

Cut the cardboard and background paper to size. Stick the green paper on the mount leaving a 1½ inch border all round.
Trace the outline of the silhouette and cut out the shape very carefully. Place the paper pattern flat onto the black paper and draw round the outline with a white pencil. Cut out very carefully. Stick the figure and the parasol in the centre of the background and draw in the parasol handle and ferrule using a felt pen. Cut scraps of lace for the collar, cuffs, hem and parasol. Trim and stick into position. Stick ribbons and flowers in an attractive arrangement. Stick gilt braid all round the edge of the mount for a frame. Fix the picture hanger to the back.

Materials

Stiff dark grey-green cardboard, 13 inches by 10 inches for mount
Lime green cartridge (construction) paper, 10 inches by 7 inches for background
Thin black cartridge (construction) paper
Artificial flowers in assorted colours
Narrow white lace edging
Scraps of ribbon
1½ yards gilt braid
Fabric adhesive
Self-adhesive picture hanger

Edwardian silhouette collage

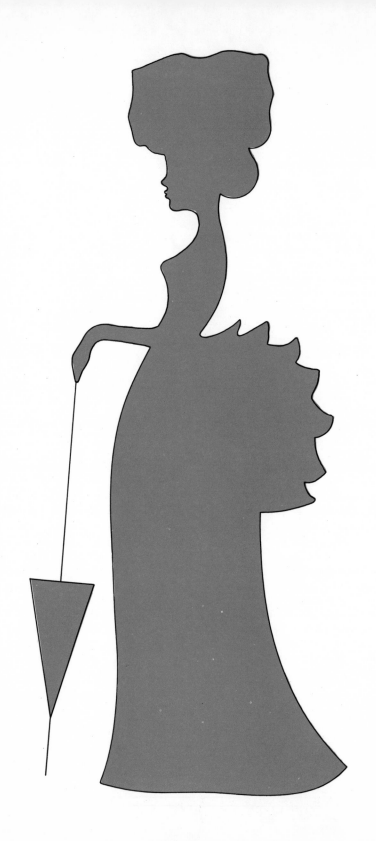

Breakfast Tray Cloth

If you can darn, you can make this pretty tray cloth – and it is much more fun than mending socks. Choose a yarn to match the colours of the flowered breakfast set. An even-weave embroidery linen may be used, but an evenly woven dress fabric, with the large selection of colours available, is a less expensive alternative.

Method

Cut your fabric to size, following the thread. Draw three or four threads about ¾ inch from the edge, all the way round. Zig-zag the inner edge on the sewing machine – or hem-stitch, by hand. Pull away the remaining outer threads to form a fringe. Now draw a single thread about ⅜ inch from the inner edge of the fringe, *along one side only*. Thread your needle with three strands of contrasting knitting yarn. Bring the needle up from the wrong side, ⅜ inch from one end of the drawn thread line and 'darn' along it, weaving over six threads and under one – until you reach the other end. Stop ⅜ inch from the end and draw a thread at right-angles to continue down the next side in the same way. Repeat until all four sides are 'darned'.

Now draw a thread, in the same way, eleven threads in from this first border and weave a similar border inside the first one. Then weave a third border, five threads in from the second one.

Finally, working on the outer, first, border only, weave in and out all the way round, see diagram. Take the wool backwards and forwards under each existing stitch, forming a wavy line held in place by the first row of straight stitches.

Materials

A piece of even-weave fabric, about 26 threads to the inch, 18 inches by 24 inches (or to fit your tray)
4-ply random-shaded knitting yarn (or use strands from 3 different coloured yarns)
A medium tapestry needle

Photograph on page 79

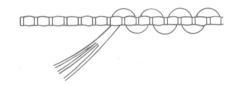

Dressing Table Set

Dress up your bedroom with this sophisticated set in a softly toning velvet. The 'velvet' is a quick cheat – self adhesive velour – the lazy way to a luxury finish. Amounts for the braids and trims vary according to the size of the articles. The quantities given were used for the articles illustrated.

Method

Measure round the outside of the bin and add 1 inch to the measurement. Cut a strip of velour to this measurement by the depth of the bin. Peel off the paper backing and stick the velour round the bin smoothly. Stick the fringe round the top edge as shown.

For the tissue box cover:
Measure the length and width of the box top and add $\frac{1}{4}$ inch to each measurement. Measure each of the sides in the same way, adding $\frac{1}{4}$ inch to each measurement. Cut pieces of cardboard for the top and the four sides to these dimensions.
Remove the perforated opening from the top of the box and measure its position. Place it on the cardboard cut for the top and draw round it. Cut out the shape with a sharp pointed knife.
Fix the sides and ends of the box top using adhesive tape and secure the four corners in the same way.
Cut pieces of velour to the same measurements as the cardboard pieces. Do not attempt to cut a hole in the velour for the box top. Simply stick the velour in position and then cut out the hole with a sharp knife, working from inside.
Stick narrow trimming round the edge of the

Materials

1 yard of 18 inch wide self-adhesive velour paper
Cylindrical metal waste-paper bin (about 7 inches diameter and $8\frac{1}{2}$ inches high)
Box of paper tissues
Heavy cardboard
$\frac{3}{4}$ yard fringe (and braid if fringe is plain), for bin
$\frac{1}{2}$ yard narrow embroidered trim, for box
$1\frac{1}{4}$ yards wider matching braid
$\frac{1}{2}$ yard gilt braid, for frame
$\frac{1}{4}$ yard narrow embroidered trim
Adhesive tape
Fabric adhesive

Dressing table set

top opening and then stick wider braid over
joins, round the top and down the sides.

For the frame:
Cut two circles of cardboard $4\frac{1}{2}$ inches in
diameter and then cut a smaller circle in the
centre of one, $2\frac{1}{2}$ inches in diameter. Cut a
piece of velour into a circle $4\frac{1}{2}$ inches in
diameter, and stick it to the frame. On the
wrong side, cut out the smaller circle in the
velour. Stick embroidered trimming round
the edge of the smaller circle.
Fit a photograph behind the frame and hold
it in position with tape. Stick the back of the
frame to the front round the outer edge.
Trim with gilt braid. Make a strut by
cutting a piece of cardboard 4 inches deep by
$1\frac{1}{4}$ inches wide. Score one end $\frac{5}{8}$ inch from the
end. Stick the strut into position on the back
of the frame.

Nursery and Playroom

Here are several bright colourful items to make for the children's room. There are two collages – one

showing the Owl and the Pussycat and one called Toadstool Cottage. Young children will love the pixie ring mobile.

On a more practical note, which mothers will appreciate, there is a cuddly rabbit pyjama case and gay tidy bags – one for a boy and one for a girl.

The Owl and The Pussycat

This colourful wall hanging in collage uses a woven table mat for the background. Here is the romantic owl with his pussycat friend sailing away in their beautiful pea-green boat and not forgetting to take some honey and plenty of money!

Method

Make a ¾ inch hem along the two long edges of the mat. If fabric is being used, bind all four edges first. Using 1 inch to 1 square graph or dressmaker's squared paper, copy the squared diagram. Trace off the separate pieces to use as patterns to be cut out in felt as follows.

Trace the outline of the owl, following the broken lines at his base and cut out the shape in brown felt. Cut the wings in dark brown felt and stick them at each side of the body. Trace the chest and forehead in three sections, following the broken lines to join them. Cut the largest shape in deep beige, the middle one in light beige and the smallest shape in stone colour. Stick the three shapes into position on the owl's body, one on top of the other.

Cut two 1¼ inch diameter circles in bright yellow felt for the eyes and stitch yellow guipure lace round the edges. Stick a large white lace daisy and a small black one in the centre of each eye. Stick the eyes into place with the orange beak between.

Trace the cat's body, following the broken lines at the top and the bottom and cut out in pale grey felt. Cut the head separately in the same colour. Trace off the cat's white front, following the upper broken line. Edge the front with white lace and stick down on to the body.

Materials

A woven table mat or a piece of blue fabric about 18 inches by 12 inches.
Matching binding if fabric is used
2 thin garden canes about 20 inches long
¾ yard of narrow card
Coloured felt
Braid, beads, buttons, sequins, flowers and lace to trim
Stranded embroidery thread, black
Fabric adhesive

For the nursery: collages and mobile

Trace the features off onto thin paper and
tack the paper in position on the head.
Embroider the mouth through the paper and
mark the position of the nose and eyes with
tacking stitches. Tear the paper away gently.
Narrow black braid, cut in half, can be used
for the eyes or embroider them in stem
stitch. If you decide to use embroidery, work
before removing the paper.
Stick the head to the top of the body. Catch
beads at each side to hang as illustrated.
Cut out the boat in bright green felt. Stick
the boat into position over the bases of the
owl and the pussycat, following the diagram
and your pattern. Trace and cut out the honey
jar and the money, embroidering the latter
and tying a scrap of wool round the top.
Stick these two pieces inside the boat.
Embroider the cat's whiskers and stick
flowers behind her ear. The boat can be
trimmed with a band of braid and wide and
narrow braid can be used for the waves of
the sea.
The crescent moon is cut in yellow felt and
the sequin stars are stitched into place with
a tiny glass bead in the centre.
Finally, thread the canes through the
channels at top and bottom and fix the cord
at the top to hang the wall hanging.

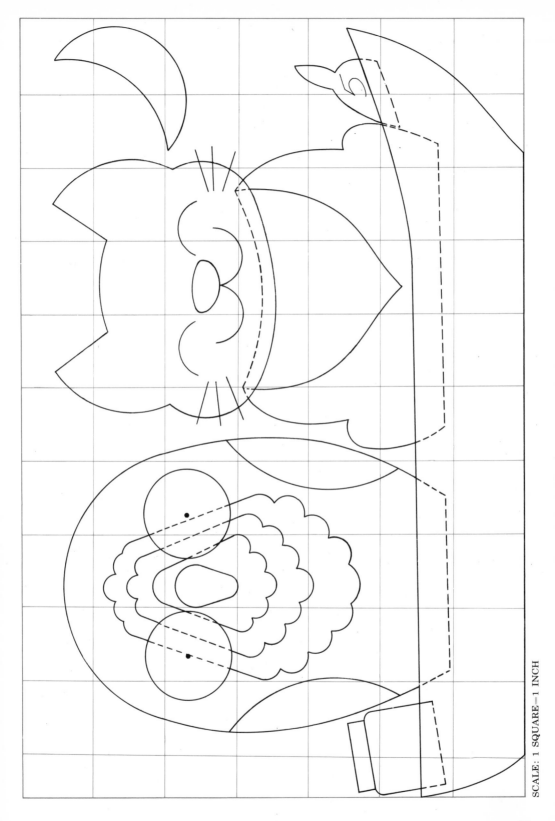

SCALE: 1 SQUARE=1 INCH

Pixie Ring Mobile

Five little pixies jigging merrily around make a perfect mobile for the nursery.

Method

Trace off and cut out separate paper patterns for one hand, the jerkin and the trousers, following the broken lines for the hand and trousers. Cut a 3 inch diameter half-circle for the hat.

Cut the hand shape out twice in flesh coloured felt and the jerkin and trousers twice each in gay coloured felt. Cut out the hat shape once in a felt to match either the jerkin or the trousers.

Stitch two small coloured beads down the centre of one jerkin piece for front buttons. Place the back jerkin piece flat and stick a hand at each end of the sleeve as shown in the diagram. Stick one trouser piece to the jerkin back putting adhesive on the upper part only and positioning as shown.

Cut a piece of pipe cleaner 4 inches long and bend it into the shape of the coloured line in the diagram. Stick it into position.

Stick the second trouser piece over the first and finally the front of the jerkin. Spread adhesive all over sleeves and across top and down each side.

To make the head, pierce a small hole in a table tennis ball with a long needle and then paint the ball flesh-coloured. When the paint is dry, push the ball down over the protruding pipe cleaner.

To make the hair, cut a piece of cardboard about 4 inches deep and wind the brown wool (yarn) round it about 15 times. Slide the loops off the cardboard and tie tightly in the middle. Cut the ends and spread out the wool (yarn) into a circle. Stick the wool (yarn) to

Materials

5 table tennis balls
Felt squares in bright colours
Flesh-coloured poster paint
Flesh-coloured felt
Black poster paint, ink or small adhesive labels
Pipe cleaners
Brown double knitting wool (knitting worsted), about 4 yards
Large and small coloured beads
9 inch diameter lampshade ring
1 small brass curtain ring
$\frac{7}{8}$ yard braid trimming
Black sewing thread
Black button thread
Fabric adhesive
Clear all-purpose adhesive
Tracing paper

Detail of pixie in pixie ring mobile

the ball, the tied centre at the crown and trim
the ends neatly. Paint in the eyes. Form the
hat into a cone and stick the straight edges
together. Smear a little adhesive round the
brim of the hat and stick the hat onto the
hair. Make four more pixies in the same way.
To make up the mobile, knot the end of a
piece of black sewing thread and catch it
firmly to the top of a hat. Slide a large bead
to rest on top of the hat and then tie the
other end of the thread to the lampshade
ring, about 6 inches above the figure.
Fix the remaining pixies equally around the
circle in the same way.
Cut four 15 inch lengths of black button
thread. Loop each one through the curtain
ring and knot about $1\frac{1}{2}$ inches above the cut
ends of each pair. Then tie each doubled
thread at quarterly intervals round the ring.
Glue braid round the ring to neaten.

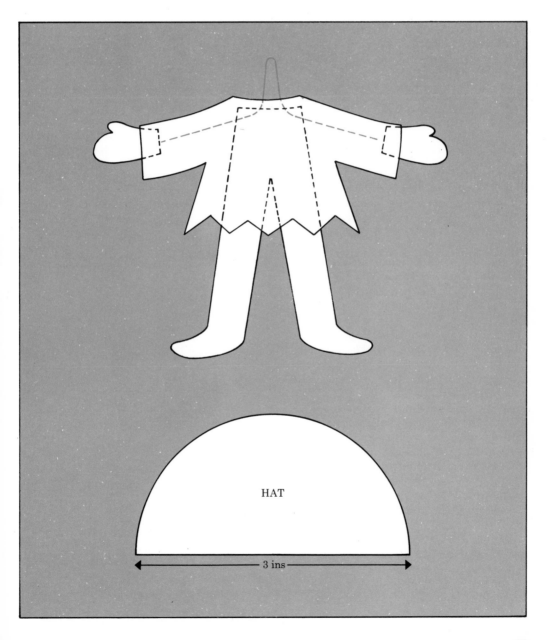

HAT

3 ins

Bunny Pyjama Case

A small child's pyjamas will tuck away tidily inside this friendly little bunny.
He is simple to make, too – all squares and circles! Make him in a soft, fleecy fabric with a slight stretch to give him a cuddly, rounded shape.

Method

On a sheet of squared graph or dressmaker's paper, (1 square = 1 inch), draw a pattern following the diagram. Use compasses to draw all the curves – the small x shows where to place the point of the compasses in each case.
Cut the body piece out once, the head, ear, upper foot and sole twice each, and the paw four times, all in cotton jersey, fleece side up. Cut out the ear twice more in pink fabric. Then cut the ear twice more in buckram, a little smaller all round than the pattern, tapering the sides slightly so that it is only about 1 inch wide across the base. Cut out the sole twice more in stiff cardboard, and a little smaller than the pattern.
Right sides facing, fold the body piece as indicated by the vertical broken line between notches on the pattern, so that the edges overlap for the centre back opening. Tack at the top and join the seam below the point x. With the right side of the fabric inside, join the lower edge, and run gathering threads round the front and back edge at the top.
With right sides facing, join the two head pieces, leaving the lower edge open between notches. Join to front and back of body, drawing up the gathers to fit, and distributing them evenly round the neck. Turn the *head only* to the right side, and

Materials

¼ yard of 48 inch wide fleece-surfaced cotton jersey
Pink felt about 5 inches by 7 inches for the inner ears
Checked gingham 10 inches × 12 inches
½ yard of ½ inch wide ribbon for trouser straps
Scraps of pink and black felt for features
White wool (yarn)
Stiff cardboard
Buckram
Filling
Narrow round hat elastic
Fabric adhesive (optional)

Bunny pyjama case

94

stuff. Then oversew the lower edges securely together. Turn body to right side.

Gather the curved edge of the upper foot. With right sides facing, pin round the curved edge of the sole, distributing gathers evenly, then draw up to fit and stitch. Stick cardboard stiffening to the wrong side of the cole, turn in raw edges and slip-stitch together. Stitch straight edge securely to lower edge of body front, over-lapping slightly at one side. Repeat with second foot.

With right sides facing, join two paw pieces all round the curved edge. Turn to right side and stuff. Turn in raw edges and slip-stitch together, gathering slightly. Stitch to the body along side fold, positioning 1 inch below head. Repeat with second paw.

With right sides facing, join a fleece ear and a pink ear piece, leaving the lower edge open. Clip seam and turn to right side. Slip buckram inside, turn raw edges inside and slip-stitch together. Catch the two corners of the ear together and stitch each ear securely to the top of the head.

For the rabbit's hair, wind double-knitting wool (knitting worsted) about thirty times round a $2\frac{1}{2}$ inch deep piece of cardboard. Tie the loops tightly on one edge, slide off and stitch to the top of the head between the ears. Trace off the nose and eye pattern and cut out in felt. Stick or appliqué them to the face.

To make the rabbit's baggy trousers, cut two pieces of gingham 5 inches deep by 12 inches wide. Join the short sides, turn the top edge under and stitch, to form a narrow channel. Join the back and front for 1 inch only in the middle of the lower edge. Turn under a narrow hem for each trouser leg and gather. Fit on the rabbit and draw each up round the back of each foot. Thread elastic through the top channel and draw up to fit round the body. Stitch ribbon at each side for shoulder straps, catching to the top of the body close to head.

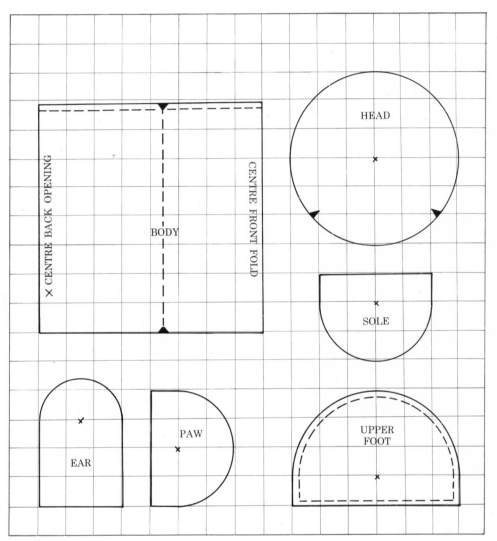

CENTRE BACK OPENING ×

BODY

CENTRE FRONT FOLD

HEAD ×

SOLE ×

EAR ×

PAW ×

UPPER FOOT ×

SCALE: 1 SQUARE=1 INCH

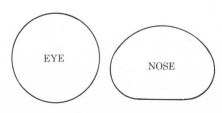

EYE

NOSE

Toadstool Cottage

This charming wall-hanging for the nursery
has been worked on a rather coarsely woven
table mat but any fabric with a distinctive
weave would be as effective. Add to the basic
pattern from your own collection of pretty
scraps.

Method

Turn a hem about 1 inch deep on both short
edges. If using fabric, bind all four edges first.
Copy the toadstool design onto squared
paper, (1 square equals 1 inch). Trace off the
separate outlines as follows and cut out the
patterns in felt.
Following the broken lines at the top, trace
the mushroom stalk and cut out in cream felt.
Trace the door following the broken lines at
the bottom and cut out in brown. Short
pieces of black braid can be stuck on for door
hinges and a small curtain ring stitched on
for a door knocker. A wooden bead has been
used for the handle. Stick the completed door
onto the stalk with the grey door step over
the lower door.
The small window is cut in pale blue felt and
edged with a narrow strip of black braid cut
lengthways.
The lattice is simply criss-crossed lines of
embroidery cotton. The bell-pull is made from
small gilt beads threaded onto thread and
left hanging free.
Cut the mushroom cap in red felt and cut the
window in pale blue. Stick into position, at a
slight angle, with a scrap of lace each side
for curtains. You can stitch equidistant
threads of embroidery cotton up and down
(double at the centre) and from side to side,
'darning' through the vertical threads.
Cut the window shape out again in another

Materials

Woven table mat or a piece of green fabric
   18 inches by 12 inches.
Matching binding (for the fabric only)
2 thin garden canes about 14 inches long
¼ yard narrow cord
Coloured felt squares
Braid, beads, buttons, flowers, lace, curtain
   ring, to trim
Black stranded embroidery thread
Fabric adhesive

Toadstool cottage

98

LEAF

colour for shutters, and then cut the piece in half. Snip a diamond shape out of each shutter as illustrated. Stick the shutters in position. Cut a window box in dark brown felt and fill it with lace and artificial flowers. Border the top curve of the window with broad braid. Cut different sized spots in cream felt and stick them at random over the red roof. Trace the chimney following the broken line and cut out in grey felt. Stick the chimney behind the roof.

Place the stalk and roof on the background fabric, the roof overlapping the stalk as shown, with the base of the stalk $3\frac{1}{2}$ inches from the bottom edge. Stick both pieces down firmly.

Cut the waterbutt and hanging basket in dark brown felt and trim the waterbutt with two bands of narrow braid. Stick both into position and embroider two threads to hang the basket from the roof.

Cut shapes in grey and beige felt for the path. Stick some green braid round the bottom of the stalk and dot gaily coloured flowers over the braid. Put a few flowers into the basket and arrange the rest over the foreground. Trace the leaf pattern from the diagram and cut out in green and gold felts. Stick a group of leaves in the upper corners of the hanging, as illustrated.

Finally, thread the canes through the channels at top and bottom to support the hanging. Knot the cord at the top.

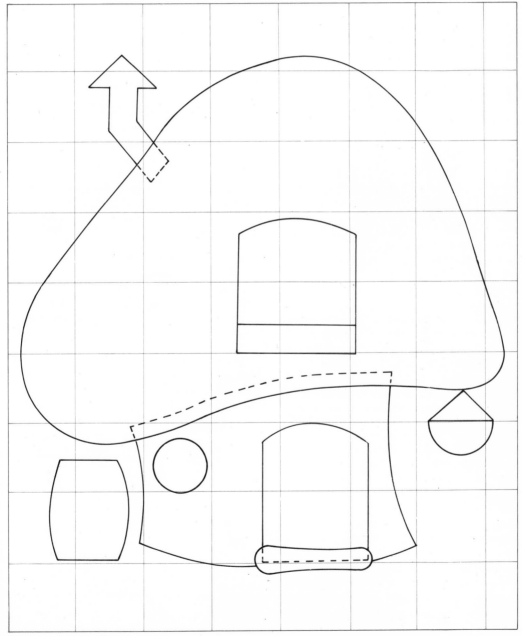

SCALE: 1 SQUARE=1 INCH

Boy's Tidy Bag

Hang these gay tidy bags in the children's rooms and perhaps pyjamas and nighties will disappear neatly inside each morning! The collage designs would make attractive circular pictures to match.

Method

To make the bag, turn and press a 4 inch hem onto the right side along each selvedge (see diagram). Stitch each end of the turning, taking $\frac{1}{4}$ inch seam, as indicated by dotted line. Fold the hessian in half along the line coloured on the diagram, right sides facing and join the side seams as far as the lower edge of the selvedge edge, finishing off very securely. Trim seams and turn bag and hems to right side.

Cut two pieces of pelmet buckram 12 inches by $3\frac{1}{2}$ inches and fit one inside each top hem. Fix buckram to the facing by glueing or catch selvedge neatly to the inside of the bag. Cut the piping in half, binding each end securely and stitch to the front and back with ends 6 inches apart, to form handles. To work the collage designs trace off and then cut each piece separately following the coloured line to complete the shape where indicated on the pattern. Follow the directions carefully for the order in which to work.

The Boy:
Cut the whole head, extending the neck as indicated by coloured line, in flesh felt: embroider the mouth in stem stitch and cut the eyes in black felt. Stick them into position. Cut the hair in brown felt and stick over the top of the head. Cut a circle of deep yellow felt for the hat, and stick this behind the head.

Materials

For each bag:

15 inches of 36 inch wide hessian
$\frac{3}{4}$ yard thick piping cord
Stiff pelmet buckram
Coloured felt squares
Broderie anglaise
Lace, ribbon, trimmings, as illustrated
1 yard lace or ric-rac braid
Red stranded embroidery thread
Black stranded embroidery thread
Fabric adhesive

Boy's tidy bag

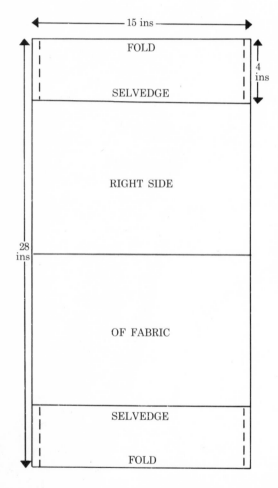

15 ins

FOLD

SELVEDGE

4 ins

RIGHT SIDE

28 ins

OF FABRIC

SELVEDGE

FOLD

Cut the suit top in mid-blue felt, cutting the centre front opening level with the inside edges of the collar. Cut a rectangle of striped ribbon or fabric as indicated and stick this behind the suit top, as illustrated. Cut the two collar pieces in white felt and stick into position. Cut the hands in flesh felt and stick the wrists behind cuffs. Now stick this body over lower edge of neck, as pattern.

Cut the trousers in deep blue felt, extending the top edge and the legs as shown by coloured lines. Stick trousers behind the lower edge of the suit top. Cut the boots in black felt, and stick over the lower edges of the trousers.

Stick the whole figure to centre front of the bag. Surround the figure with a 9 inch diameter circle of ric-rac braid or other decorative trimming.

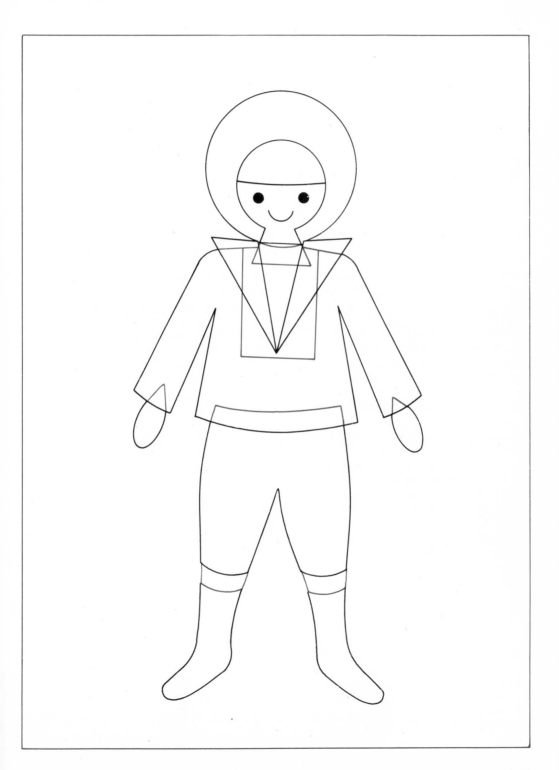

Girl's Tidy Bag

Method

To make the bag, see page 102.

To work the collage designs trace off and then cut each piece separately following the coloured line to complete the shape where indicated on the pattern. Follow the directions carefully for the order in which to work.

The Girl:
Cut a circle of flesh felt for the face: embroider the mouth with two straight stitches and cut the eyes in black felt and stick into position. Cut the hair in brown felt, following the coloured line indicating the lower edge, and then cutting up the vertical coloured line under the chin. This makes it easier to cut away the face section round the hairline. Stick hair over the face section. Cut the hair-bow and the bodice (to edge of face) in lilac felt: stick bow behind hair, and bodice over lower hair. Cut the sleeves and the whole skirt, in deep pink felt. Cut the hands in flesh, and stick behind cuffs as indicated. Cut the pinafore in broderie anglaise and stick over skirt. Trim the lower edge of the pinafore with white guipure lace, the neck and cuffs with white, and stick tiny coloured motifs over the sleeves. Stick coloured lace behind lower edge of skirt so that it is just visible below the hem. Cut the legs in black felt and stick behind skirt. Now assemble the upper and lower sections of the body and the two sleeves, and stick them to the centre front of the bag. Surround the figure with a 9 inch diameter circle of lace flowers or other decorative trimming.

Materials

For each bag:

15 inches of 36 inch wide hessian
¾ yard thick piping cord
Stiff pelmet buckram
Coloured felt squares
Broderie anglaise
Lace, ribbon, trimmings, as illustrated
1 yard lace or ric-rac braid
Red stranded embroidery thread
Black stranded embroidery thread
Fabric adhesive

Girl's tidy bag and owl and pussycat collage

Bathroom

Give a wicker wastepaper basket a new lease of life
with a pretty padded covering. For decoration, an
arrangement of dried flowers in an old-fashioned
glass storage jar looks most attractive.

Daisy Linen Basket

Underwear and stockings wait, ready for the washtub, in this flower-patterned linen basket. It is made from an inexpensive waste-paper basket but with a pretty padded top and wipe-clean lining, it has become a dainty bedroom or bathroom accessory.
The basket illustrated was 10 inches deep with a top 10 inches in diameter.
The directions given can be adapted to any size of basket.

Method

Measure the depth, the outside top edge of the basket and the diameter of the base. Add $1\frac{1}{2}$ inches to the measurements. Using these measurements, cut a strip of plastic for the sides and cut a circle for the base.
With right sides facing, join the two short edges of the plastic strip for the side seam. Turn the top edge over $\frac{1}{4}$ inch to the wrong side and tack. Run a gathering thread round the lower edge, distributing the gathers evenly round the circle. Draw up gathers to fit the circle cut for the base, and stitch into position right sides facing. Trim the seam, fit the lining into the basket. Bring the top edge of the lining over the edge of the basket and catch plastic into place invisibly.
For the lid, measure the diameter of the top basket and add 1 inch to the measurement. Cut two circles of fabric to this measurement. Then cut two circles of wadding and a circle of cardboard to the same diameter as the top of the basket. Stick a circle of wadding to each side of the cardboard.
Pin the lace frill to the right side of one fabric circle, the outer edge of the frill towards the centre of the circle. Stitch the frill $\frac{1}{2}$ inch from the raw edge of the fabric

Materials

Straw waste-paper basket
Plastic sheeting for lining
Fabric for lid
Wadding
Stiff cardboard
$1\frac{1}{2}$ yards of 1 inch wide frilled lace
Fabric adhesive

Daisy linen basket

110

(see diagram). Right sides facing, pin the two
fabric circles together then stitch, following
the stitching line of the frill. Leave room to
fit the padded cardboard inside. Trim the
seam, then turn to the right side and pin
opening before slip-stitching into place.
Gather remaining lace frill and draw up
tightly, forming it into a rosette. Catch
together underneath and stitch securely to
the centre of the lid.

Flower Shower

Instead of bath salts, fill an old-fashioned apothecary jar with dried everlasting flowers and foliage for the prettiest of bathroom decorations.

Method

Shape a piece of Plasticine into a small mound about 1 inch high and approximately 1½ inches across the base. Press shells into the Plasticine to cover the sides of the mound. Stand the jar behind the Plasticine mound so that you can judge the height of the flower display. Cut lengths of foliage, grass and oats. Press these into the top of the mound. Fill in the lower section with flower heads, pressing the stalks into the Plasticine firmly. When the arrangement is completed, make sure that the inside of the jar is quite dry and clean and then drop a little adhesive inside the jar. Pick up the flower arrangement carefully, holding it by the top and lower it on to the adhesive. Leave to dry.
Sprinkle a few silica gel crystals into the jar to prevent moisture forming and seal the top of the jar.

Materials

Glass storage jar, about 6 inches high
Everlasting flowers and foliage
Small sea shells
Plasticine, stone coloured or white
Clear all-purpose adhesive
Silica gel crystals (obtainable from chemists or drugstores)

Photograph on page 111

Sewing Materials

It is always difficult to keep sewing materials tidy.
The tape measure châtelaine is an unusual idea
for keeping all you kit together. For pins, make the
Easter bonnet pin-cushions. If you are a keen
knitter, you will need a knitting granny to look
after all your materials.

Tape measure châtelaine

Tape Measure Châtelaine

Here is an idea for a complete sewing kit, attached to the ends of a tape measure. Wear the tape measure around your neck while working and everything you need is conveniently to hand.

Try to find a tape measure that has a hole at each end or, if necessary, make the holes and finish them off with an eyelet.

Method

Pin cushion
Cut two 3 inch squares of contrasting felt for the pin cushion. Oversew together round three sides, stuff firmly and oversew the remaining side. Oversew back again in the opposite direction as before.

Thimble case
Cut two circles 2 inches in diameter from contrasting colour felt. Oversew round two-thirds of the circle as before. Stitch a press fastener inside the opening to close.

Thread holder
Cut two 2 inch squares of contrasting colour felt for the thread holder. Oversew two opposite sides as illustrated.

Scissors case
Trace the pattern for the scissors case from the outline given. Place your own scissors on the pattern and adjust the dimensions and adapt the shape as necessary. Cut the whole shape out of felt twice for the back and cut the front, lower section out once. Cut the back shape out again in buckram or cardboard, slightly smaller than the pattern. Stick the buckram lightly between the two back pieces and tack the front section into

Materials

Coloured felt squares
Trimmings
Buckram or cardboard
Filling
Narrow cord
Small press fastener
Fabric adhesive
Tape measure
Scissors
Thimble
Skein of assorted threads
Needles and pins

116

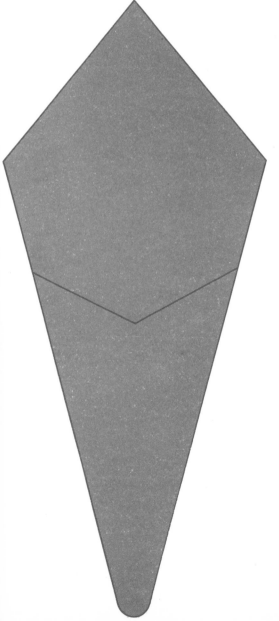

position. Oversew all round the edge with contrasting thread and then oversew back again in the opposite direction, crossing the first row of stitches.

To assemble the châtelaine, knot one end of the cord and stitch the knot to one corner of the pin cushion. Cut the cord off about three inches away, thread through the hole in the tape measure and knot the other end. Stitch the knot to the thimble case. Repeat with the scissors case and thread holder. Trim each item as illustrated.

Knitting Granny

Every busy woman needs a knitting granny. She looks after sock needles, crochet hooks, stitch holders . . . and all those other small items which tend to get lost at the bottom of the work basket.

You need a cardboard inner tube – and if you want your granny to hold full-length knitting needles, look for a longer tube!

Method

First close one end of the tube as follows. Cut a circle of cardboard the same diameter as the tube, and stick it to the centre of a circle of fabric about $\frac{3}{8}$ inch larger all round. Snip the excess fabric into tiny tabs all round, then place cardboard over end of tube and stick the tabs round the edge of the tube, to hold the end securely into position.

For the face, measure the circumference of the tube and add $\frac{1}{2}$ inch to the measurement. Cut a strip of flesh felt this length by 3 inches deep. Embroider the mouth in the centre, about $\frac{3}{4}$ inch above the lower edge. Stitch curtain rings above for spectacles with a bar across the centre. Stick or embroider a tiny circle of black felt in the centre of each line for eyes. Stick the felt round the top, open, end of the tube, level with the edge, ends overlapping at the back. Make a skein of wool (yarn) for the hair by winding grey double-knitting wool (knitting worsted) 20 times round an 8 inch deep piece of cardboard. Tie the loops at each end, slip off the cardboard and tie loosely in the centre. Catch the centre to the felt at front of tube, above the face, then take the sides round to the back and stitch firmly into position to cover the rest of the 'head'. Cut a piece of fabric to cover the remainder of the tube, and

Materials

Cardboard inner tube
Printed dress cotton
Flesh-coloured felt
Scrap of black felt or embroidery thread
White nylon net
Grey knitting wool (yarn)
Lace, ribbon, etc. to trim
$2 \times \frac{1}{2}$ inch diameter curtain rings
Red stranded embroidery thread
1 cocktail stick
2 small wooden beads
Scrap of contrasting wool (yarn)
Narrow round hat elastic
Cardboard
Stiff paper
Small piece of foam sheet or a large cork
Fabric adhesive

Easter bonnet pin cushions and knitting granny

118

stick into position. To make the arms, trace
the pattern shape and cut out twice in stiff
paper. Cover one side of each arm with
fabric, cutting it level with each straight
edge, but leaving surplus along each side,
snipping it into tabs and sticking to the back
as for the base. Trace the hand and cut twice
in flesh felt, then stick a hand under the end
of each arm as indicated. Stick the top of each
arm level with the neck, then stick the
lower part to the body (leaving the hands
free), so that the elbow area stands away
from the body slightly.
Trim the neck, wrists and lower edge with
lace, ribbon and a flower as shown. Wind
coloured wool (yarn) into a small ball. Cut
the cocktail stick in half and fix a bead to
each blunt end: push points through the
wool (yarn), then place between granny's
hands. Stick securely into position.
Roll up a strip of foam – or use a large cork –
to close the open end of tube.
Cut a 9 inch diameter circle of double net for
the mob cap. Cut a 6 inch diameter circle of
paper and tack it to the centre of the double
net. Catch elastic to the net in a circle, just
outside the edge of the paper – use a running
stitch working alternately each side of the
elastic. Draw up the elastic to fit round the
top of the head.

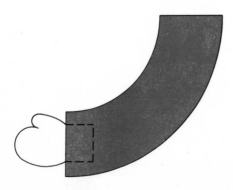

Easter Bonnet Pin Cushions

You may not find many occasions to *wear* anything quite so fancy as these pieces of millinery – but as pin-cushions, they will be in use all the time.

Method

Brown boater:
Cut two circles of felt 4 inches in diameter and a strip 8 inches long by 1 inch deep. Then cut a 2½ inch diameter circle from the centre of one large circle: this circle will form the top of the boater. Cut a piece of stiff cardboard slightly less than 4 inches in diameter. With tiny stitches, oversew one long edge of the side strip round the edge of the small top circle. Join the two short ends where they meet. Oversew the other edge of the side strip round the inner edge of the large circle from which the top was cut. Stuff the crown of the hat very firmly, then place the cardboard on top of the stuffing, with the second felt circle on top of that. Oversew together all round the outer edge of the brim. Catch lower edge of crown through to underside of brim, to hold the shape neatly. Trim with a band of narrow ribbon and a large daisy.

Green cocked hat:
Follow the instructions for the boater, but cut the side strip 1½ inches deep. Cut the card 2¼ inches in diameter. Fit the card inside over the stuffed crown.
Trim the outer edge of the brim with lace edging and catch it to the crown at each side. Trim with two flowers.

Violet toque:
Follow instructions given for making the boater, but cut the two circles 3 inches in diameter with a 2½ inch diameter top circle. Cut an 8 inch side strip, 1½ inches deep. Cut card slightly less than 3 inches in diameter. Trim with 1¼ inch wide lace, gathering it into a wide bow at the back, and add a bunch of tiny forget-me-nots in front.

Materials

For one hat:
Piece of felt (about 8 inches by 6 inches)
Stiff cardboard
Filling
Flowers, ribbons, lace, beads etc. to trim
Fabric adhesive

Patio and Out-of-Doors

For outdoor parties, you can make very attractive
candles, with decorated pottery bases.

*Oriental candles and pottery candle
bases*

Oriental Candles

Candles with an expensive, hand-made look can cost as little as the cheapest plain variety – plus the cost of a packet of children's wax crayons. Be sure to buy good quality crayons; not only are the colours more subtle, the results are far more satisfactory.

Materials

Coloured crayons
A white candle

Method

The basic method is simple. Peel some of the paper covering from the crayon. Warm the end of the crayon in a flame and dab it on the surface of the white candle, rather as you would use sealing wax. Cover the whole surface of the candle with random spots of contrasting colour. Then fuse the crayon spots to the candle by partially melting it in the flame of a candle (although this gives a slightly blackened effect) or a gas flame. Move the candle slowly in the flame and allow the wax to melt sufficiently for the colours to run into each other.
Try decorating a plain purple candle with heavy blobs of gold crayon or cover the whole surface of a pale pink candle with spots of carnation pink and violet, running them into each other. Stripe the lower half of a blue candle with deep blue and green, fusing them together. The variations are endless – and great fun!

Pottery Candle Bases

These pretty candle holders are so simple to make that even children can learn to do it. They would enjoy the fun – and have results they can be proud of.

Materials

Self-hardening modelling clay
Poster paints and clear varnish or enamel
  paints

Method

Roll a lump of clay to about the size of a table tennis ball. Press it down on a smooth surface to make a firm, flat base. Press the base of a candle well down into the centre of the clay, so that it is firmly gripped. Shape the sides of the holder round it.

Remove the candle and gently smooth the surface of the clay all over with water, so that it is quite wet. If you want to incise a design or decorate the surface in any way, do so now. The rounded tip of a blunt cooking knife was pressed into the clay at random all over the outside of the gold candle holder. Leave the holder in a warm, but not hot, place to dry.

When quite dry and hard, paint it with poster colours, finishing with a coat of varnish, or use enamel.

Pink and purple poster paints were used for one of the candles illustrated, streaked blue poster paint over very wet green for another and gold enamel for the third.

Page 126: A selection of handicraft gifts including knitting, decorating china, candlemaking, fabric painting, embroidery, fabric craft, beadwork.

Make Your Own Handicraft Gifts

Patchwork

Patchwork is one of the most delightful crafts in the world and, if you like fine sewing, you will love patchwork. Although there are dozens of exciting patchwork patterns on record and most of them originated by the early American settler women, if you are just a beginner, you will want to try an easy pattern first. Next to the square, the pentagon shape is the simplest to work with because the angles are wide which makes joining up easier. The patchwork pig and the perfumed ball are all made with pentagon shapes and the stuffed cat is made up of square and rectangular patches stitched together at random.

Perfume ball

illustrated on page 131

Materials
Scraps of cotton or silk fabric in toning colours and matching patterns ($\frac{1}{4}$ yard of each of six different fabrics will make about 20 perfume balls).
Matching thread
Stiff paper for backing
Stiff card for templates
Loose lavender or potpourri
2 yards satin baby ribbon
Sharp knife
Ruler with metal edge
Pencil
Protractor

Preparing for patchwork The shape used here is a pentagon, a five-sided shape. You can trace off the pentagon shapes given here to make templates or, for greater accuracy, draw your own. The more accurate your template, the

better your finished patchwork. Two templates are required for patchwork – one is used for cutting out the fabric pieces and the other is used to cut out backing papers.
To make the perfume ball illustrated, the fabric template measures $1\frac{1}{2}$ inches along each side of the shape and includes $\frac{1}{4}$ inch turnings. The backing template measures 1 inch along each of the sides.

Fabric template Draw a horizontal line exactly $1\frac{1}{2}$ inches long. Place the protractor so that the 90 degrees line is exactly on the left end of the line and mark with a pencil dot the angle of 72 degrees (diagram 1). Join the dot and the

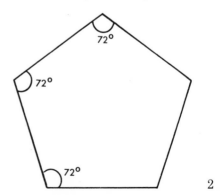

1

left side of the horizontal line and make this line exactly $1\frac{1}{2}$ inches long. Turn the card and place the 90 degree line of the protractor on the end of the line and again mark 72 degrees (diagram 2).

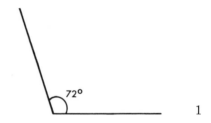

2

Continue, always working on the left side of the line and to the left and making the line 1½ inches long. Thus you will draw a pentagon shape. Cut out the completed shape very carefully with a very sharp pointed knife and using a metal edged rule.

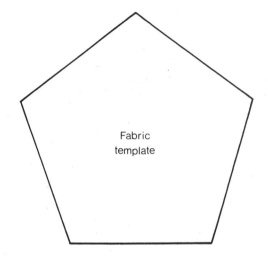

Fabric
template

Backing template Draw a pentagon as above but make each line 1 inch long. Cut the template out of stiff card.

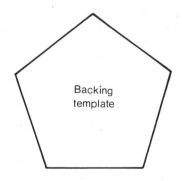

Backing
template

Cutting out fabrics and backing papers Press all the creases out of the fabrics and lay them on a flat surface. Place the template on the wrong side of the fabric and draw round the shape with a sharply pointed soft pencil. Cut out 12 pentagon shapes, two from each

of six different fabrics for the best effect or all from different scraps of fabric. It is important that the same *type* of fabric should be used throughout. If different kinds of fabric are used, the seams are liable to break open. Using the smaller template, draw and cut out 12 paper shapes. They must be very accurately cut or the patchwork will not lie flat.

Making and joining patches Pin a backing paper to the wrong side of a fabric shape, centring it (diagram 3).

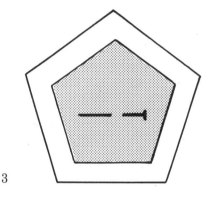

3

Fold the turnings to the wrong side and baste to the backing paper (diagrams 4 and 5). When all the backing papers have been basted to the fabric shapes, place two patches together, right sides facing, and oversew together using tiny stitches

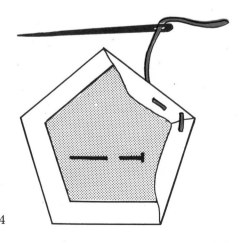

4

(diagram 6). Do not tie a knot at the end of the thread – lay the end along the tops of the patches and oversew over it.

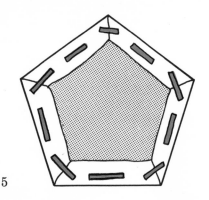

5

Push the needle through the fabric only, at right angles to the edge so that the stitches are neat. To fasten off, work back about four stitches.

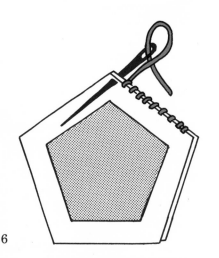

6

Several patches can be joined together continuously but remember to strengthen the corners with two or three stitches. When 11 patches have been joined, remove the backing papers very carefully by cutting the basting stitches and turn the ball to the right side. Stitch the final patch into position along two sides only, keeping the backing paper in position for the moment.

Finishing the perfume ball Fill the ball with lavender quite tightly and then stitch the remaining three sides of the last patch. Just before the last stitches are made, fold and stitch a cluster of ribbon loops (diagram 7) and push the ends into the ball. Close off the last patch, securing the ribbon ends. Make a 6 inch hanging loop and stitch this into the middle of the small cluster of ribbon loops.

7

Note: Although the foregoing is the technique for patchwork, when flat pieces of work are being done, the finishing off technique is different.

Finishing off flat patchwork When all the patches are joined, press the patches on the wrong side with a warm iron, keeping the backing papers in position. Take out the paper shapes and baste all round the edge of the work to keep the turnings of the edge patches secure. Press again to remove any marks made by the basting. Mount on to lining or on to the main article with slip stitches. Large areas of patchwork will need to be caught down to the lining at regular points.

Perfume ball, patchwork cat, patchwork felt pig

Patchwork felt pig

illustrated on page 131

Felt is much easier to use in patchwork because backing papers do not need to be used.

Materials:
1¼ inch pentagon template
Pink felt
Black felt
Kapok filling
Matching threads

Cut out 12 pentagon shapes in pink felt and two in black for the ears. Stitch 11 together into a ball. Turn the pig right side out and then stitch the last patch in so that the seams of this patch show on the right side. This patch is the pig's snout. Stuff the pig with kapok quite tightly and close the last patch. Cut four circles of pink felt ½ inch diameter. Embroider two black nostrils on the top one. Glue the circles one on top of the other. Glue to the pig's snout. Gather one edge of the two black ear pieces and stitch to the top of the pig's head. Cut four strips of black felt, 3 inches long by ½ inch wide and roll them up to make feet. Secure with stitches and then glue and finally stitch the feet to the underside of the body. Cut a thin 2 inch strip of black felt for the tail. Draw it up on a piece of black cotton to curl it and stitch in place.

To make other patchwork animals, try green felt for a frog and add two long arms and legs. Make an owl using light and dark brown felt or a cat using black and white. A rabbit or a panda could also be made on the pentagon ball shape.

Felt balls can be made using the same basic instructions. Cut the pentagon shape with 2½ inch sides and cut 12 shapes from felt using bright, primary colours. Push a bell into the middle of the ball as you are stuffing it.

Patchwork cat

illustrated on page 131

This charming patchwork cat is very easy to make and uses a quick random patchwork technique.

It is made from square and rectangular pieces of fabric, cut out with pinking shears and joined, overlapping, with machine zigzag stitch. If a swing needle machine is not available, overlap the patches ¼ inch, baste together and join with straight machine stitching, worked on the right side.

Materials
Scraps of cotton fabric
Kapok filling
Scraps of blue and black felt
Anchor stranded embroidery thread, crimson

Make up two pieces of patchwork 11 inches wide by 12 inches deep using method already described under 'Perfume ball'. Draw out and cut a paper pattern on graph paper and draw a face. Cut out two cat shapes using the paper pattern. On one piece embroider the mouth in stem stitch. Cut out the eyes, pupils and nose from felt. Glue them in position. Stab stitch to secure. Add sequins. Make up a strip of patchwork pieces 3¼ inches wide by 47 inches long. Using ½ inch seams, join the strip to one cat piece, matching raw edges and right sides facing. Join the second side of the cat to the strip, leaving a gap of 4 inches under the body for inserting the filling. Stuff the cat and close the opening with neat oversewing.

Papier mâché

Papier mâché is a most fascinating craft and can be an inexpensive way of making gifts. The amusing savings pig, the tumbler dolls, the Easter egg and the comfit bowl were made using a layering technique.

Materials
Newspaper
Tissue paper
Paste
Gesso glue
Paints

Making the paste Some papier mâché enthusiasts use diluted white glue or wallpaper paste but a simple flour and water paste works just as well. Mix a small quantity of plain white flour to a thick paste with cold water. Add common salt to the mixture (about 1 tablespoon to $\frac{1}{2}$ lb. flour). This preserves the paste for several days while you are working on the project. Keep the paste in the refrigerator or a cool place. Pour boiling water on to the paste, stirring all the time. The paste will thicken again and become translucent. Dilute to the consistency of thick cream.

Preparing the paper Newspaper is best for papier mâché – magazine pages are usually too thick to absorb the paste. Tear up a quantity of newspaper first into strips and then into pieces about 1 inch square.

The technique In the layering technique, the newspaper is first dipped into the paste, the excess removed with the fingers of the other hand and then applied in layers to the surface of a prepared mould. The mould is coated with an oil (such as cooking oil) so that the papier mâché shape can be removed easily when it has dried out.
Various objects can be used as moulds. For round shapes, balloons, inverted bowls, cups and some kinds of fruit can be used. The savings pig, for instance, was made on an inflated balloon. The fall-over dolls were made on blown eggs and the Easter egg was made on an orange. A melon is also a good shape for making a savings pig and cups make good moulds for papier mâché puppet heads. Pretty bowls, plates, dishes and trays can be made using the layering technique if a similar utensil is used for the mould. After oiling the mould carefully build the layers of papier mâché up on the *underside* or outside of the utensil.

Decorating papier mâché Papier mâché can be decorated with poster colours and then varnished afterwards, with modeller's enamel paints, with layers of coloured tissue added after the shape has dried or with various shapes cut out of cardboard. String, dipped in gesso, can be glued in curlicue designs on to the sides of bowls or on trays and painted in a contrasting colour when the gesso has completely dried. Sequins, beads and shells, glued to the surface of papier mâché are a quick and attractive form of decoration.

Savings pig

illustrated opposite

Materials
Newspaper
Flour and water paste
A balloon
1 inch curtain ring
Tissue paper
Gesso powder or paste
Enamel paints or poster paints
Transfers if desired
Scraps of felt for ears
All purpose adhesive
2 large bowls
1 pudding basin
Sharp knife

Inflate the balloon to about the size of a child's head. Knot the opening. Cover the balloon's surface with oil and then rest it on a bowl or basin so that about half of the balloon is above the bowl's rim (diagram 1). Tear up the newspaper

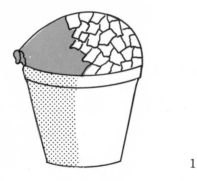

1

into 1 inch squares. Dip pieces of torn newspaper into the prepared paste and cover the entire surface of the balloon with layers of paper. When two complete layers have been applied, leave to dry overnight. Apply two more layers of newspaper then make the pig's snout as follows:

Stand the balloon on end in the basin, tied end down. Tear a long strip of newspaper about 1 inch wide, dip it into the paste and roll it up, adding more strips until you have a circular lump of papier mâché about 2 inches across. Place this in position on the balloon mould and paste small pieces of paper up the sides until it is firmly held. Smooth the snout underneath so that it blends into the pig's body (diagram 2). Cut open a curtain ring and push the cut ends into the snout. Leave to dry overnight. Work one more layer of paper all over the mould.

2

To make the feet, tear long strips of newspaper about 1 inch wide. Paste and then roll them up until you have stumps about ¾ inch in diameter. Balance each foot in position on the underside of the pig's body and paste small pieces of paper up the sides until the feet are held firmly, as for the snout. Leave to dry and then add three more layers of paper all over the pig. When the papier mâché is completely dry, stick a needle into the balloon through the knot and deflate it. Draw the balloon out through the hole carefully. Make a tail from a piece of tissue paper twisted and pasted. Leave it until dry and then insert the tail into the hole. Glue in position and secure with pasted paper pieces. Cut a hole in

Savings pig, tumbler dolls, Easter egg, comfit bowl

the pig's back using a sharp pointed knife, to put the coins in. Sandpaper over to smooth out any obvious lumps but if you have applied the newspaper evenly there should not be any. Paint mixed gesso all over the pig and leave to dry. Apply one layer of white tissue paper all over the gesso – this makes a good painting surface. Paint the pig with modeller's enamel paints or with poster paints. If poster paints are used, two coats of quick-drying varnish must be applied after the paint is dry. Designs can be painted or, for a quick yet professional-looking decoration, use transfers. Paint in black spots for eyes. Cut two floppy ears (diagram 3) from felt and glue them to the pig's head.

Trace same size

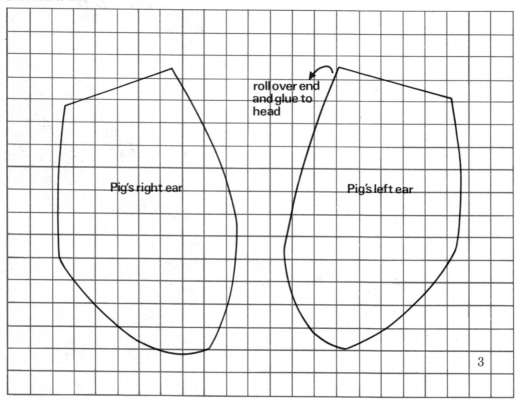

roll over end and glue to head

Pig's right ear

Pig's left ear

3

Tumbler dolls

illustrated on page 135

Tumbler dolls such as these are familiar in many mid-European countries and are usually made of wood. When they are knocked over, they spring upright again. These are made from egg-shells and papier mâché.

Materials
Three raw eggs
White tissue paper
Flour and water paste
Gesso powder or ready-mixed gesso paste
Modeller's enamel paints or poster colours
Lead shot

To prepare the eggs First, blow the eggs. This is done by making a small hole in the shell at both ends. Make a hole first with a thin sharp needle and then enlarge the holes with a thicker needle. Poke into one hole with a long needle to break up the yolk inside. Hold the egg between the thumb and forefinger and, bending over a ready saucer, blow firmly into one of the holes. At first, nothing seems to happen and then a single spot of egg yolk will drop out of the other hole. Persevere and the drops of egg will fall out quite quickly. As the egg empties, hold the egg more carefully and blow more gently or it will smash in your fingers. When all the egg seems to be out, wash the eggshell and leave to dry. You do not need to oil the shell in preparation for papier mâché because the shell mould remains inside the tumbler doll.

Making the tumbler doll Close the hole at the 'blunt' end of the egg with a piece of pasted paper. Enlarge the hole at the pointed end of the egg and drop in some all-purpose adhesive. Drop in three pieces of lead shot and leave the glue to set so that the lead shot is firmly held. Close this hole also with a small piece of tissue paper. Tear up tiny pieces of tissue paper, each about $\frac{1}{2}$ inch square and apply them to the surface of the egg with paste. Build up four or five layers and leave each layer to dry out before applying the next.

When the last layer is dry, apply a thin coat of mixed gesso and then decorate the eggs with paints. For an alternative design, paint the eggs to look like circus clowns.

Easter egg

illustrated on page 135

Oil a large sized orange all over and balance it on a large mug or cup. Apply eight layers of newspaper papier mâché and leave until quite dry. Using a sharp knife, cut lengthwise through the papier mâché and remove the whole orange. Cover the inside and the outside of the two halves with two layers of tissue paper pieces and if the surface is still not smooth enough, paint with mixed gesso. Decorate the egg with enamel paint or poster colours, afterwards finishing with two layers of quick drying varnish.

Place a gift inside the egg and tie the two halves together with ribbon.

Comfit bowl

illustrated on page 135

The comfit bowl is made on an upturned glass bowl, oiled with cooking oil. Apply newspaper papier mâché until eight layers have been built up and then two layers of white tissue paper for a smooth finish. Paint the bowl with modeller's enamels. It is better not to use poster colours for papier mâché dishes and trays.

For an interesting surface decoration on bowls such as this, cut out shapes in thin card and glue them to the surface of the bowl. Give the entire bowl two layers of thickly mixed gesso and sand down until smooth. Paint the shapes, which are slightly in relief from the surface, with contrast colours.

Papier mâché bowls and trays cannot be put into water but they can be cleaned with a damp cloth.

Decoupage

Decoupage is a centuries old craft, now enjoying a revival in popularity. The technique involves cutting out prints, pasting them on to suitable furniture or furnishings and varnishing the piece. Even if you cannot draw at all, you can create beautiful or amusing pieces of decoupage which will make wonderful gifts. It is possible to utilize furniture which has been cast aside, such as old sewing boxes, occasional tables, book racks or trays and with a little imagination, transform them into pieces which look every bit as good as those decorated items seen in exclusive decorator's shops. Alternatively, decoupage can be used to produce gay and modern accessories.

The cheese board illustrated was decorated with cut-outs from a sheet of gift wrapping.
The egg cups are made of wood, painted with white emulsion paint and then decorated with tiny cut-out flower sprays from a magazine advertisement.

Materials
Scissors Cutting out must be done very carefully and cuticle scissors are the best for the job. These have a curved blade and are about 3 inches long overall. Buy the very best you can afford – it is a worthwhile investment if you want to enjoy doing decoupage.

Paste Only a water soluble paste is suitable for decoupage. There are several available and they are usually white or translucent. Many **glues** are not water soluble and should not be used.

Varnish Professionals use good quality lacquers for the craft, leaving the surface to dry out for a whole day. Modern polyurethane varnishes dry in about half the time and produce a good hard finish. For decoupage, gloss varnish is better than matt as gloss enables the print to show through better. Spray varnishes can be used for the first two or three coats if you hesitate to use the liquid kind immediately, but they are not suitable for the whole job as the applied coat is so thin. It would need more than 100 coats to get the right finished effect.

Brushes Varnishing brushes must be the very best that can be obtained. The width of the brush, of course, depends on the size of the piece you are working on, but try to have one which requires the least number of strokes to cover the surface of the piece. Choose a brush with a soft bristle and if you insist on the best quality available, the bristles are less likely to fall out and fasten themselves into your decoupage. Nothing is more irritating than having to pick up a fine brush bristle which has fastened itself right in the middle of a beautiful piece of decoupage, and you can easily damage the surface trying to pick up the bristle.

Other equipment A bowl of warm water and a small sponge; baby buds or cottonwool on a toothpick; white blotting paper for removing excess water; solvent in a jar for the varnishing brush; a sharp blade; lintless cloth or old nylon tights; fine sandpaper; fine steel wool; wax polish.

Preparing the surface First, the

Decoupage cheese board, egg cups

surface of the item to be decorated must be absolutely smooth. Fill any dents with plastic wood or wood putty and when the filler has hardened, sand the entire surface, finishing off by rubbing down with steel wool. When the surface is quite smooth, paint or stain it. If you are working on natural wood and you like the colour, leave it as it is. If you are painting, water paints, oil paints or enamel can be used. Before painting, seal the surface with a commercial sealer, selected for the type of paint you are using. When the paint or stain is dry, rub down again with steel wool and dust off with a lintless cloth – old nylon stockings or tights are ideal.

Prints Ideally, the prints used should be on thin paper, otherwise they are difficult to cut out and it takes many more layers of varnish to cover them. Studios which specialize in decoupage produce books of delightful designs by such artists as Jean Pillement, Watteau and Boucher. These are printed on a suitable paper for the craft but if they are not easily available there are wonderful designs to be had from other sources. Gift wrapping papers are often well designed and can provide a good source of material. Greetings cards are sometimes suitable or illustrations from magazines and seed catalogues could be used. Search out old wallpaper sample books, visit your local crafts shop and look at their stock of prints and transfers, and most exciting of all, try old books – sometimes the engraved chapter headings and frontispiece pages can provide charming designs. Black and white prints can be hand-coloured and Derwent oil pencils are best for this. However, if you prefer to use black and white prints just as they are, they can look superb on a white painted background.
If you are planning to decorate an old item, first remove all the original finish.

Metal objects can be decoupaged, but every spot of rust must be removed and a rust inhibitor applied before painting. Any colour of paint can be used under decoupage but if white is used, note that it will turn ivory under the coats of varnish.

Cutting out To learn to cut out really well requires practice but you will find it is a most relaxing occupation. A good way to get the feel of cutting paper is to practise on cutting scallops. Hold the paper in your left hand (or right hand if you are left handed). Hold the scissors with the curved tips pointing away from you, third finger and thumb in the scissors. Rest the scissors on the index finger. The hand holding the scissors does not move, it merely opens and closes the blades. The paper is fed into the blades by moving the left hand. To practise cutting scallops, turn the hand holding the paper towards the right and at the same time, slowly close the scissor blades on the paper. Cutting out in this way gives the cut edge a 'feathered' look and makes pasting down far easier. Before actually cutting out a print, spray it first with a fixative, obtained from art shops. This gives the paper more body, helps to prevent it breaking up during pasting and also helps to preserve the colours from the varnish.
There are no absolute rules about cutting out; it is advisable to avoid long straight cuts – the paper should be moved gently during cutting to obtain a slightly serrated edge and inside corners should be crisp rather than rounded. But whether you prefer to cut round the outline first or whether you feel you would like to cut the inside portions of the design first is up to you.

Pasting down If you are pasting down small pieces of cut-out, it is easier to apply the adhesive to the back of the paper with a small brush. Spread the adhesive right to the edge of the piece or the edges will curl or bubbles will appear under the print. Place the print on the prepared surface and press it down, exerting pressure from the centre out towards the edges. Some excess adhesive may be forced out. Remove this carefully with a small sponge dipped in warm water and squeezed out. If you are pasting down larger pieces you may find it easier to spread adhesive on the surface of the object, then press the print down on to the adhesive. To remove excess adhesive from the small inside areas of the background use a baby bud stick or twist a piece of cotton wool round a toothpick. When all the cut-outs have been pasted down, check to see that all the edges are quite flat and that there are no air bubbles. Air bubbles can be dealt with if they do occur by carefully slitting the paper with a sharp blade and inserting more adhesive with a toothpick. Leave the pasted prints to dry out very thoroughly.

Varnishing The final stage of decoupage can seem the most tedious of all but the care with which you varnish and rub down can make all the difference in the world to your finished piece. First of all, spray the entire surface with fixative and rub the surface down with a lintless cloth. Apply the varnish with long smooth strokes and work on a flat surface. Leave the varnish to dry completely before applying the next coat. A finished piece can have as many as 30 coats of varnish. It is necessary to apply as many coats as this to give it the perfect finish which is typical of good decoupage. Sometimes, if

the prints are on very thin paper you can get away with as few as sixteen to twenty coats of varnish – but it very much depends on the use for which the item is intended. Trinket boxes, which are likely to be handled for instance, would be better with the full 30 coats. For a decorative kitchen wall plaque, a fewer number of coats might be sufficient.

In most homes, there is inevitably some dust in the air and if you can make a kind of tent from a large plastic bag or a sheet of Cellophane, this will provide some cover while the varnish is drying out.

After 10 coats have been applied or when you can no longer feel the edge of the paper cut-out with a finger tip, sanding down begins. Wrap a small piece of fine sandpaper round a matchbox and rub the surface all over in a circular motion. Dust the surface off, wash it clean with a dampened sponge and leave to dry. Now rub the surface again with the fine steel wool and wipe the surface clean. You are now ready for the next coat of varnish. Continue giving coats of varnish, rubbing down between coats, until the entire surface is quite flat and the prints are showing through with a dull, soft glow.

Give a final polish with good wax polish.

Some ideas for decoupage gifts: boxes of all kinds for trinkets, cigarettes, playing cards, stamps or handkerchiefs; tea trays and cocktail trays; small tables, wastebaskets, door finger panels, wall plaques, wooden household utensils, wooden or metal jewellery, shoe and belt buckles, paperweights.

Beltmaking

Belts make marvellous gifts and can be made from all kinds of materials. Ribbons and braids, for instance, mounted on belt stiffening, make colourful, gaily patterned belts; felt, trimmed with narrow braid and finished with eyelet fastenings, makes a charming peasant belt.

A sporty-looking link belt can be made from scraps of suede or leather and, of course, a belt worked in quick-stitch on canvas has a special cachet all of its own. Belts take comparatively little time to make and junk shops, you will find, are a treasure house for unusual buckles and clasps.

Ribbon and braid belts

illustrated opposite

It is advisable to choose the buckle first and to have it with you when you are choosing the ribbon or braid. Not only will you be able to make sure that you have chosen the best ribbon to enhance the buckle but you will also be able to check that the width of the ribbon fits the buckle bar.

Ribbons and braids are available up to quite wide widths. A 3 inch wide woven ribbon will make a superb belt used just as it is but do consider the narrower kinds. Sometimes, a ribbon or braid with a geometric design takes on a new

and exciting look if two or more narrow strips are mounted side by side.

The red and white ribbon belt illustrated is made up of three widths of diagonally striped $\frac{1}{2}$ inch wide ribbon with the middle strip reversed to make a chevron design.

If a single length of ribbon or braid is being used, buy a length to the waist measurements plus 6 inches. If narrower widths are being used mounted together to make a wide belt, multiply the waist-plus-six measurement by the number of lengths you are planning to use.

Materials
Embroidered ribbons or braids
Belt stiffening or other stiff interlacing
Backing material such as taffeta or silk
Fabric adhesive
Suitable buckle
Strong all-purpose adhesive

Cut a piece of belt stiffening or interfacing to the exact width of the ribbon and to the waist measurement plus 6 inches. Cut one end of the stiffening into a point (diagram 1) and then trim the two cut edges (A and B) back a further $\frac{1}{4}$ inch. Trim the other short end of the stiffening (C) $\frac{1}{4}$ inch.

Ribbon and braid belts, felt peasant belt

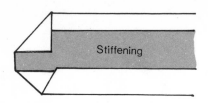

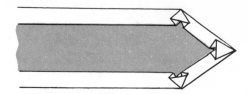

Cut a piece of lining fabric to the width and length of the belt, (waist-plus-six), plus 1¼ inches on both measurements. Place the stiffening down on the wrong side of the lining fabric and fold over the ⅝th inch turnings all round. Mitre the corners neatly and fold the lining over the pointed end of the belt as shown (see diagram 2). Glue the turnings down onto the stiffening using fabric adhesive but use very little or the adhesive may seep through and spoil the look of the inside of the belt. Place a weight on the pointed end and leave the belt to dry.

While the belt is drying, cut a point on the right hand end of the ribbon, clip into the point ¼ inch and turn under ¼ inch turnings. Turn the other short end of the ribbon under ¼ inch and press. To mount the ribbon, spread adhesive on the belt itself, not on the ribbon, taking the adhesive to within ⅛th inch of the edges. This is so that any excess adhesive can spread a little without spoiling the ribbon or the lining. Use the minimum amount of adhesive and spread it as evenly as possible.

Place the ribbon down onto the glued surface of the stiffening and press it firmly into position with the flat of the hand. Leave the belt to dry. When quite dry, slip the buckle onto the square end – this is the left hand side of the belt so make sure that the buckle is the right way up if it has that kind of shape – and fold the end of the belt under over the buckle bar for about 2 inches. Glue the belt over the buckle bar using all-purpose adhesive and leave to dry under a weight. Secure with oversewing stitches.

Felt peasant belt

illustrated on page 143

Materials
Strip of felt to the waist measurement less 2 inches and 3½ inches wide.
Narrow braid or ribbon, twice the length of the belt plus 9 inches.
Six eyelets
1 yard contrasting coloured silk cord

Place the strip of felt on a flat surface and fold in the short ends 1 inch on the top side of the fabric. Glue these ends down. Cut two pieces of the trim, 3½ inches wide and mount these along the cut edges of the folded ends.
Cut the remaining trim into two equal lengths and glue along both long sides of the belt and over the short end strips.
Turn ½ inch under at both ends to neaten.
Make three equidistant marks on both edges of the belt fronts, ¼ inch in from the edge and insert eyelets.
Lace the belt together with the cord.
If eyelets cannot be obtained, finish off the holes with closely worked buttonhole stitch, using a brightly contrasting thread.

Norweave belt

illustrated on page 147

Norweave embroidery, which as its name suggests came from Norway, is especially recommended for beginners in canvas work, or for those in a hurry, as

3 by 28 inches lining material
Matching thread for lining
3 press studs

Note The length of the belt can be adjusted by approx 1¾ inches which is the measurement of one pattern repeat (18 stitches).

Point shaping

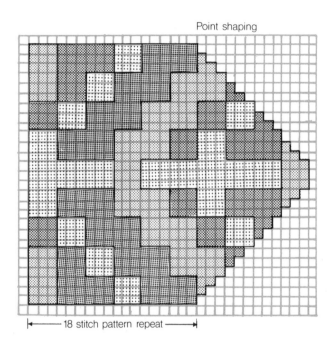

|← 18 stitch pattern repeat →|

you get fairly quick results. It consists of blocks of satin stitch worked over three horizontal and vertical double threads of canvas. It can be used for pictures, panels, cushions or anywhere where a bold design is suitable.

Materials

3½ by 28 inches of double thread canvas, 10 threads to the inch
2 skeins each Anchor Tapisserie Wool in dark, medium and light colours

Start working the design from the chart leaving 4 double threads unworked at each edge for turning in when making up. The satin stitch here is worked over three double threads each way. Try not to catch your wool on the raw edges of the canvas or it will fray and weaken.

To make up Press the completed embroidery lightly, with damp cloth and warm iron. Fold over turnings to wrong side of work and baste, neatening the point. Baste hems on lining to correspond and handstitch lining in position on wrong side of embroidery.

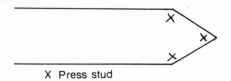

X Press stud

Sew press studs as indicated on diagram, making sure that the pattern matches when belt is fastened.

Suede belts

illustrated opposite

Smart suede and leather belts can be very simply made by cutting a strip of the material to the waist measurement plus six inches and fastening it to a beautiful buckle.

Decorating china and pottery

Old crafts are being revived and decorating china and pottery is one of the newest 'revivals'.

China painting

There are two ways of approaching painting china and pottery. The way you choose depends on whether or not the piece is going to be subjected to hard wear and constant washing up.

China subjected to hard wear
If the pieces are going to be used every day and washed up, such as cups and saucers, mugs and plates, the decoration must be more or less permanent and stand up to being immersed in detergent. For this kind of decoration a special cool-bake enamel is used, obtainable from craft shops. The enamel is simply painted on to the surface of the piece and each colour left to dry before the next is applied. When all the colours of the design are completed, the piece is placed in a cold oven which is set for 350°F, gas mark 4. When the oven reaches this temperature, turn off and leave to cool down. Under no circumstances should the oven be opened during the process. Open only when it has cooled completely. The piece of china should now be permanently decorated. However, it is wiser not to clean decorated china with steel wool or the design might be damaged!

China used as decoration
Pottery or china which is not intended for hard wear, such as flower pots, kitchen crocks, ornaments etc., can be decorated with modeller's enamels or with Polymer water colours. Once again, colours should be applied and left to dry thoroughly before the next colour is applied. Use any kind of brush which seems right for the job, – soft sable brushes, sizes 2 and 3 are ideal.

Stencilling pottery

Stencilling is great fun to do and, if you cannot draw, designs can be taken from books, posters, gift wrapping papers or greetings cards. You might look at the pottery section of your local museum too and study the traditional folk designs, adapting them to your pieces.
Choose designs which are simple in outline and avoid those with fine lines or sharp points. Inevitably a little paint floods under the stencil and while the effect can be quite attractive on a simple design, it can spoil a complicated one.

Materials
Pot or jar with unindented surface
Fast drying spray enamel
Stencil paper (available from art and craft shops)
Sharp crafts knife
Tracing paper
Rubber cement
Masking tape (available from art shops)
Newspaper

Trace off your selected design and glue

the tracing down on to the stencil paper with rubber cement. Cut out the stencil with the sharp point of the knife and tape the stencil to the china with masking tape. Mask the areas not to be

spray down on to it and, studying the manufacturer's instructions first, hold the spray can about 12 inches away from the piece. Spray in short bursts and avoid applying too much paint as it will

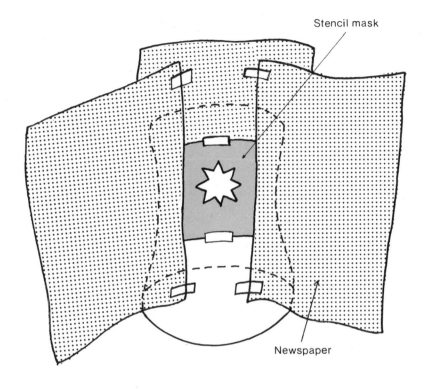

Stencil mask

Newspaper

stencilled with newspaper, taping it down firmly (see diagram).
Place the piece on the floor on several sheets of newspaper so that you can

bleed under the stencil edges.
Very messy edges can be cleaned up by scratching away after the paint is dry, using a sharp razor blade.

Collage

Collage is great fun to do because there are so few rules to follow. It is simply a technique of sticking different kinds of materials down on to a background. Basically, there are three types of collage: paper collage, which uses different kinds of paper; fabric collage where mostly fabrics are used, with perhaps some beads, sequins or buttons for additional texture, and lastly, three-dimensional collage where all kinds of materials can be utilized – nails, straw, raffia, string, pieces of glass, pasta, seeds, safety pins – practically anything which looks decorative and can be glued down. The collage picture 'Fish dinner' uses fabrics and buttons. You may want to try the fish picture for yourself and a diagram is given on page 153 from which you can make a paper pattern of the various pieces. However collage is such a personal craft that you will probably want to try something original yourself. Look for inspiration in magazines, books, posters or on gift wrappings or greetings cards or work freehand. Flower studies are delightful subjects for fabric collage and so are still lifes of fruit and objects. You might even try a portrait – it could be fun!

Essential equipment

A few tools are needed for collage: soft pencils, a ruler, some tracing paper, cardboard, large and small scissors, pins, a sharp craft knife and, of course, adhesives. Three kinds of adhesive are used, but you will need only two of them for the fish picture. For heavy fabrics and for adding trims, a fabric adhesive such as Copydex is used. For light fabrics and for paper, an adhesive such as Polycell is ideal and for three

dimensional objects, such as buttons, a clear all-purpose adhesive is used. You will need either Copydex or Polycell and a clear all-purpose adhesive.

Fabrics

Keep scraps of fabric in a separate bag just for collage pictures. It does not matter how small the piece, it will probably prove perfect somewhere in a design. It is not worthwhile buying remnants for collage but you may find that you can pick up interesting fabrics at junk sales or white elephant sales. Old garments, washed and with the good pieces cut away, can provide the collage enthusiast with some valuable colours and textures.

Firmly woven fabrics often make the best backgrounds but one cannot generalise about this. Loosely woven fabrics, such as tweeds, can give marvellous textural effects and, if such a material is being considered, it may be better to mount it on a non-woven interfacing first. Cut background fabrics at least 2 inches larger all round for turnings.

Loosely woven fabrics to be used in the design are best mounted on non-woven interfacing before cutting them out: other fabrics can either be cut out with a clean edge before mounting on the background, can be frayed or have the edges turned under. It depends on the fabric and the effect you are trying to achieve.

Method

Make a rough drawing of your picture on tracing paper first. When you are satisfied with the design, which should be kept to the simplest possible shapes,

Hand-decorated china

make another tracing which you can cut up for patterns. It is possible to cut into fabrics freehand, but beginners often find it easier to cut from paper patterns. If you decide to draw out your shape directly onto the back of the fabric before cutting out, remember that the design must be reversed or you will find that your shape is the wrong way round when you come to mount it. Place the background fabric flat on a table and arrange the various components of the design upon it. When you are satisfied that the colours and textures look right, start by glueing down the parts of the design which are in the background first, mounting the foreground units over them. Do not stick anything down until you are quite satisfied that an edge may not need to be tucked behind another piece for the best effect.

Mounting collage pictures

Small collage pictures, such as 'Fish dinner,' see page 154, can be mounted on cardboard. Cut the cardboard to the finished picture size. Spread all-purpose adhesive on the edges of the card on the wrong side. Spread adhesive about 2 inches from the edges. Place the fabric picture down on a flat surface, right side down. Place the prepared card on the wrong side of the fabric, with the prepared side uppermost. Fold the turnings over onto the glue, mitreing the corners neatly (diagram 1).

Glue the corners and leave to dry. For framing, mount the finished collage on another piece of good quality cardboard so that a neat border shows round the picture. 'Fish dinner' was simply mounted on card and two curtain rings were attached to the corners with small pieces of ribbon (diagram 2, page 154).

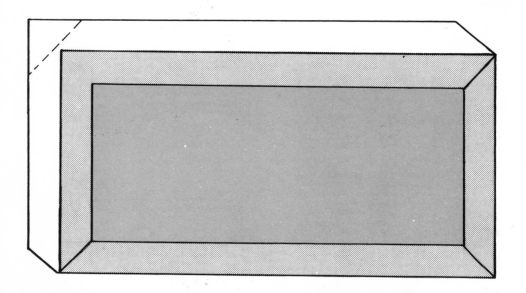

1

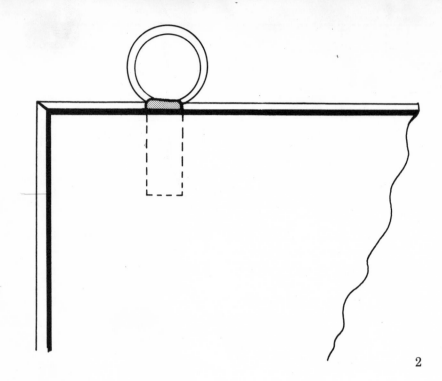

2

Fish dinner

The background fabric of the collage is a piece of blue poplin. On this, scraps of green and blue patterned organza are mounted for the sea effect. The small fish in the background are cut out of grey green velvet with sequin eyes and these, together with the darker clump of seaweed are mounted next. Pale blue nylon net goes next over the entire picture. The fish bodies are cut from a patterned cotton fabric which was chosen because it has a scaly effect and, in fact, this fabric inspired the whole picture. The fish heads are cut from velvet and the eyes are buttons of different sizes. The fish bubbles are small circles of interfacing material, chosen because it has a slightly transparent look.

Fish dinner collage

Tie-dye and Fabric painting

Tie-dyeing is an ancient craft, practised almost all over the world at different times. Modern cold-water dyes and fixes make tie-dyeing comparatively simple to do and a wide variety of gifts can be made from everyday, natural fabrics. Cushion covers, towels, tea cloths, bed linen, neckties, scarves, lampshades are all possible tie-dye projects.

Materials

Very little basic equipment is needed for tie-dye. The most important is a large utensil to use as a dye bath. Using cold water dyes, this can be made of metal, plastic, pottery or glass. Other equipment, depending on the tie you are using, might include string, pieces of stone, corks and rubber bands, and clothes pegs.

Basic technique

This consists of taking a piece of fabric and tying, folding, binding, knotting or sewing it so that when the fabric is dipped in the prepared dyebath, the colour penetrates only the untied areas of the cloth. Patterns appear on those areas which have been partially protected from the dye and complex patterns can be achieved by tying an area, then untying and retying and dyeing again in a different colour. Cold water dyes, which are intended for natural fabrics, produce a fast colour and the tie-dye pattern will therefore last. Man-made fibre fabrics use a special dye and this is not as fast. Fabrics which have special finishes should not be used as they resist dyes. Wool fabrics should be avoided as the garment's shape can be spoiled.

Quantities of dye As a rough guide, one small tin of cold water dye will dye approximately 6 ozs of dry fabric. A dress weighs about 1 lb. so if you were planning to dye this amount of fabric (about 2–3 yards) in two colours, you would need two tins of *each* colour.

Preparing the dye bath It is important to use a large enough dye bath – this is the secret of satisfactory dyeing. Make up the dye according to the manufacturer's instructions and add, as instructed, 1 sachet of cold water dye fix and four tablespoons of common salt for each tin of dye used.

Preparing the fabric If a soft effect is required, use the fabric dry; if the pattern is to be crisp, wet the fabric first. Tie the fabric in any of the ways illustrated on pages 157–165. Immerse the knotted fabric in the bath, leaving it for the recommended period of time. If a piece is to be dyed in two or more colours, the part which is not to be dyed can be protected by tying it up in a polythene bag.

'His' and 'Hers' guest towels

illustrated on page 159

Materials
Two cotton towelling squares
2 polythene bags
1 tin each of Dylon Cold Water dyes in Coral and French blue
2 sachets of cold dye fix.
8 tablespoons common salt

(continued on page 162)

 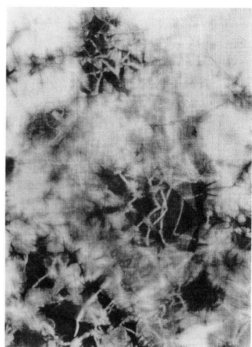

Marbling: Cloth screwed up into a ball and bound tightly.

Dyeing sample *wet* gives crisper resist. Dyeing sample *dry* gives softer resist.

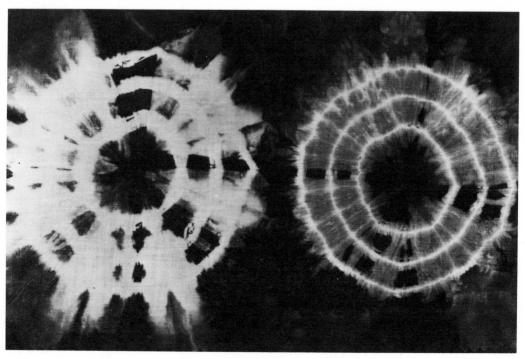

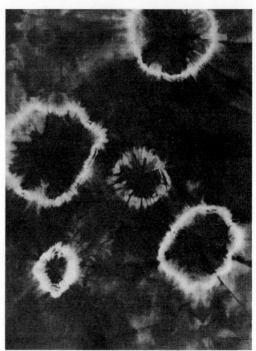

Clump: Small and large tufts picked up and bound.

Tritik (Stitching): Double rows of stitching are pulled up very tight and knotted off securely.

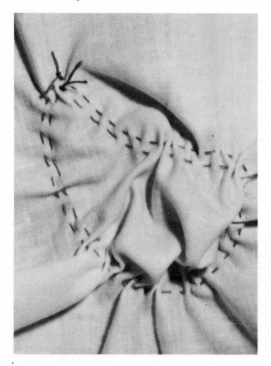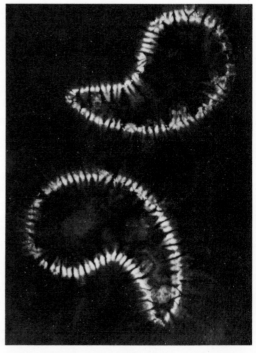

'His' and 'Hers' guest towels

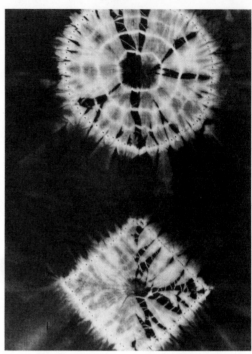

Safety-pin: Oval and Diamond picked up with safety-pin then bound. Oval with line binding, diamond with open binding.

Ruching: Cloth rolled round cord or doubled string and ruched.

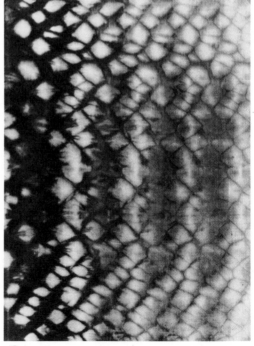

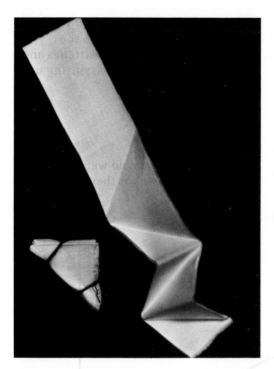

Triangle: Cloth folded into four lengthwise, then folded back into a right angled triangle and bound securely.

Knotting: Length with three knots.

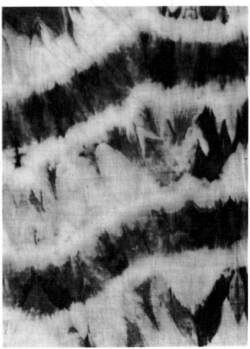

Draw the lettering on the towels with a soft pencil, copying the photograph. Using strong thread, knotted securely at one end, run small basting stitches over the pencilled lines. Leave a long length of thread. Damp the towelling and pull up the thread really tightly, binding the end of the thread round the bunched fabric. Put half the towel into the polythene bag (up to the diagonal line) and secure it very firmly by tying with

up to one hour, stirring occasionally. Rinse off excess dye. Remove the polythene bag, remove the stitches and wash the towel in hot suds, rinsing until the water runs clear.

Fabric painted gifts

illustrated opposite

Fabric paints using cold water dyes are comparatively new but they are

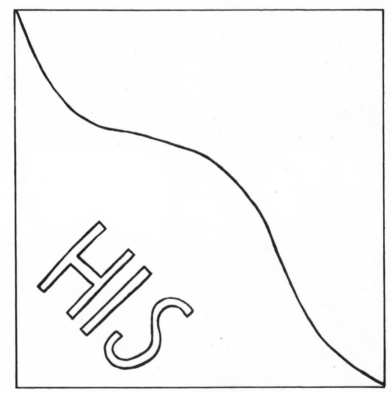

Guest towel, showing lettering position and diagonal line

string, to prevent the dye seeping in. Make up the French blue dye. Immerse the exposed area of the towel in the dye and leave for up to one hour, stirring occasionally. Remove from the dye-bath and rinse off excess dye. Put the dyed half of the towel into a polythene bag and seal tightly. Steep the other half of the towel in Coral dye for

fascinating to use and very easy. Really lovely gifts can be made from odds and ends of fabric and a few tins of dye. An old bed sheet could be made to produce dozens of delightful soft toys or some animal day-bed cushions. Simple garments can be personalized with names or mottoes and make very acceptable gifts.

Fabric painted gifts

162

Materials

For each colour,
    1 tin of Dylon cold water dye
    1 packet of Paintex and cold dye fix
    (these are sold together)
Hot water
Fabric, either white or coloured
Paint brushes
Polythene sheeting

Most natural fabrics, cotton, silk and linen, take fabric painting very well. It is worth noting that after dye-painting, neither bleaches nor biological detergents should be used in washing. Dye-painted items will, however, stand up to boiling.
Wash and iron the fabric. Lay it on a piece of polythene sheeting and draw in the design with a soft pencil. If a ready-made garment is being painted, slip a piece of polythene sheeting inside the garment so that the colour does not seep through to the back. Mix the dye-paints according to the manufacturer's instructions. Paint in the design and leave to dry for up to six hours. The longer the paint is left on the fabric, the deeper the colour will be. When the fabric and paint is quite dry, wash off the excess dye in cold water, then wash in hot suds and rinse until the water is clear. The painted design is now absolutely permanent.

Soft toys

illustrated on page 163

All the toys illustrated were made from an old bed sheet. The lion, dog and kangaroo were made using a commercial paper pattern. The sheep was traced from a child's picture book and ¼ inch turnings were allowed all round for seams.
The frog was also made from sheeting. The fabric for the frog was dyed Nasturtium. Coloured fabrics could, of course, be used if you prefer.

To make the toys Cut out the pattern pieces from the sheeting and lay them on polythene. Draw out the designs in soft pencil and paint them in. Finish the dye process and the laundering process as instructed. Sew up the pattern pieces and stuff the toys with sponge chips or with cut-up nylon tights. This ensures that the toys are washable.
Cold water dyes are non-toxic and safe for toys which babies and small children might chew!

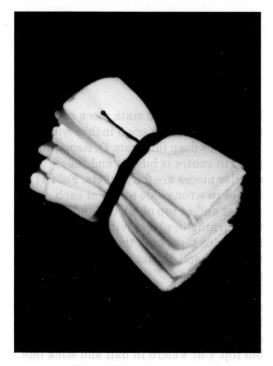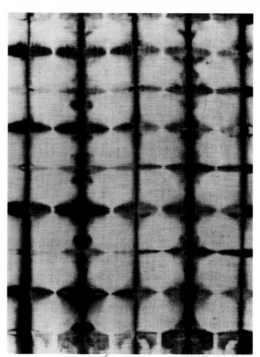

Stripes: Cloth folded in six, pleated and line bound.

Stripes: Cloth folded in half, pleated and open bound with rubber bands.

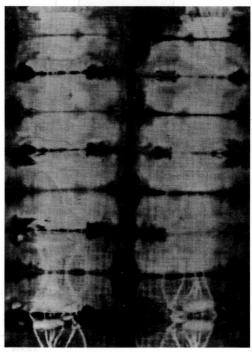

Fabric craft

Practical aprons

illustrated opposite

Father's apron:

Materials

1 plain piece PVC about 35 inches long
by 29 inches wide
2 waist strips 35 inches long by 3 inches
wide
2 shoulder strips 24 inches long by 3
inches wide
1 reel strong white thread
4½ yards white binding
4½ inches Velcro fastener
Strong glue

From the top of the main piece cut away,
from each side, a piece 9 inches wide and
10½ inches deep (diagram 1). Remaining
piece in centre is bib top and these
smaller pieces are for pockets. Fold 1¼
inches to wrong side at top of each
pocket and at top of bib top and machine
this turning in place. With white bias
binding or tape, bind the remainder of
the apron and pockets. Machine the
pockets in place.
Fold narrow turnings to wrong side on
all strips and machine in place. Attach
long strips at either side of waist, and
one end of shorter strips to outer edge of
bib top. Cut Velcro in half and stick one

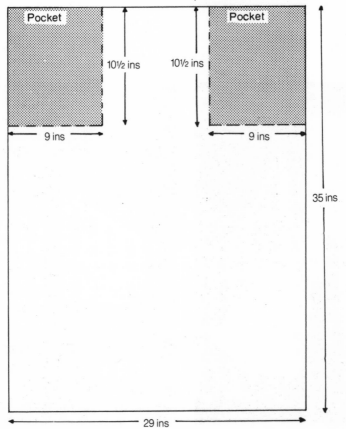

Practical aprons, appliqué table set

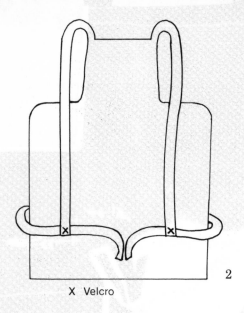

X Velcro

side to wrong side of one end of each short strip, try on apron and stick the other side of Velcro to right side of waist ties so that the shoulder strips, when fastened, fit well (diagram 2).

Mother's apron:

Materials
1 piece PVC 44 inches long by 27 inches wide
2 ties 27 inches long by 3 inches wide
9 inch white bias binding for pocket top
Thread to match PVC and binding

2   Round off the two lower corners of main piece, using plates to guide the curves.

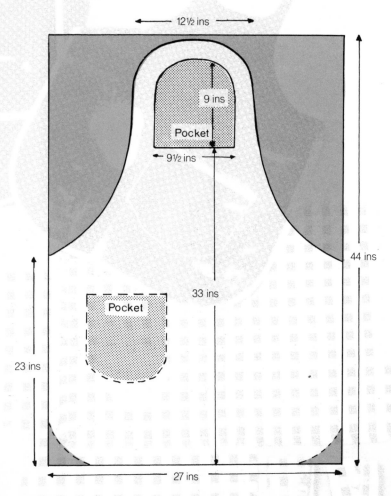

168

Mark 23 inches up from lower edge, at each side, for armholes, then cut away a big curve, using mixing-bowl as guide, from each side in turn, reducing width of bib top to 12½ inches (diagram 3).
At 33 inches up from lower edge, slit the centre 9¼ inches, leaving 1½ inches at either side: it is better to mark this first on wrong side of work, as it takes pencil marks easily. Mark a spot about 9 inches up from centre of slit. Using mixing bowl as guide, mark a wide curve from this centre spot to either end of the slit, the first few inches from slit ends going almost straight up. This is for the strap which goes round the back of the neck; the cut-away piece becomes the pocket. Now mark on the wrong side the outer edge of the neck strap, 1½ inches away from the inner edge all round and cut, so that there is a continuous neck strap to slip over the head, and pocket.
Turn in and machine a very narrow hem all round apron, lower and side edges of pocket, and waist ties except for one short end of each. Bind pocket-top with white binding and machine stitch pocket to apron front; attach ties firmly to either side by unhemmed ends.

Child's apron:

Materials
1 piece PVC about 34½ inches long by 15¾ inches wide
2 waist strips 17 inches long by 1½ inches wide
5 yards bias binding
1 reel matching machine thread
1 scrap contrast PVC
Strong glue
2½ inches Velcro fastener

Round off the two lower corners. 12¼ inches up from lower edge, cut away a wide scoop to reduce bib top to 6 inches width, then continue straight up for

outer edges of shoulder straps to end of material. At 17 inches up from lower edge, scoop out a centre curve to leave 1½ inches free at each end; continue this line parallel to outer edge of shoulder straps to end of material. From spare material cut pocket 5 inches by 6 inches. Round off lower edges of pocket. Bind all round apron including shoulder straps; bind top edge of pocket. Turn in tiny hem round remainder of pocket, and round waist ties except for one short end.

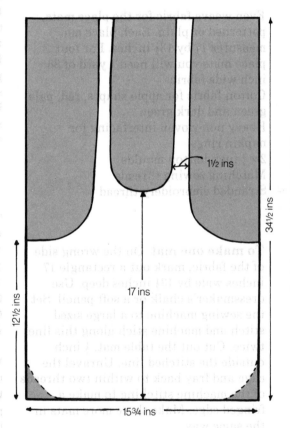

Machine pocket in place; firmly attach waist ties to each side in turn by the unhemmed short end.
From contrast PVC cut appliqué motif of choice, and stick in place. Halve the Velcro and stick in place on shoulder straps and waist ties, as Father's apron.

169

Appliqué table set

illustrated on page 167

Appliqué is the art of applying one material to another using sewing techniques. It is a wonderful way of using up scraps of dressmaking and furnishing fabrics to good effect and is a most satisfying handicraft. With the technique described here you can work appliqué on many other handmade gifts.

Materials

Even weave fabric for the place mats, patterned or plain. Each place mat measures 17 by 13½ inches. For four place mats you will need 1 yard of 36 inch wide fabric
Cotton fabric for apple shapes, red, pale green and dark green
Heavy non-woven interfacing for napkin rings
2 × ¾-inch button moulds
Matching sewing threads
Stranded embroidery thread

Place mats

To make one mat On the wrong side of the fabric, mark out a rectangle 17 inches wide by 13½ inches deep. Use dressmaker's chalk or a soft pencil. Set the sewing machine to a large sized stitch and machine stich along this line twice. Cut out the table mat, ½ inch outside the stitched line. Unravel the edge and fray back to within two threads of the machine stitching to make a fringed edge. Make three more mats in the same way.

Preparing for appliqué Trace the apple shape and the leaf given on page 173. Draw the apple shape down on to the wrong side of the apple fabric. If you have a swing needle machine, the appliqué can be worked using the zigzag stitch as follows: Set the machine to a narrow zigzag stitch and stitch along the outline on the wrong side of the fabric. Cut out the shape close to the stitching line. Pin and then baste the apple on to the place mat. Set the machine to a wider zigzag stitch and to the smallest stitch length on the machine. Stitch all round the edge of the apple, using a matching thread. Work the apple leaf in the same way and embroider the stem, by hand, in satin stitch.

If you are working the appliqué by hand, draw the apple shape on to the wrong side of the fabric adding ¼ inch turnings. Cut out the shape and press the turnings to the wrong side. Baste the turnings and then baste the shape to the background fabric. Stitch the apple shape to the place mat round the edge using either slip stitch or with a closely worked buttonhole stitch. Work the leaf in the same way and embroider the stem in satin stitch.

Napkin rings

To make 1 ring Cut 3 pieces of the table place mat fabric as follows:
1 piece 7 by 3 inches – A
1 piece 6¼ by 2¼ inches – B
1 piece 3 by 1¼ inches – C (button fastener)
Cut 1 piece from interfacing 6¼ by 2¼ inches – D

Working on piece A, fold and press to the wrong side ¼ inch turnings, mitreing the corners neatly. Slip the interfacing piece D under the turnings and baste both materials together.
Working on piece B, turn under and press ¼ inch turnings all round, mitreing the corners. Baste and then top stitch ⅛th inch from the edge.
Working on piece C, fold the fabric along the length and right sides facing. Machine stitch ½ inch from the edge. Turn the fabric inside out and press the 'tube' flat to make loop rouleau.

'His' and 'Hers' tidy bags

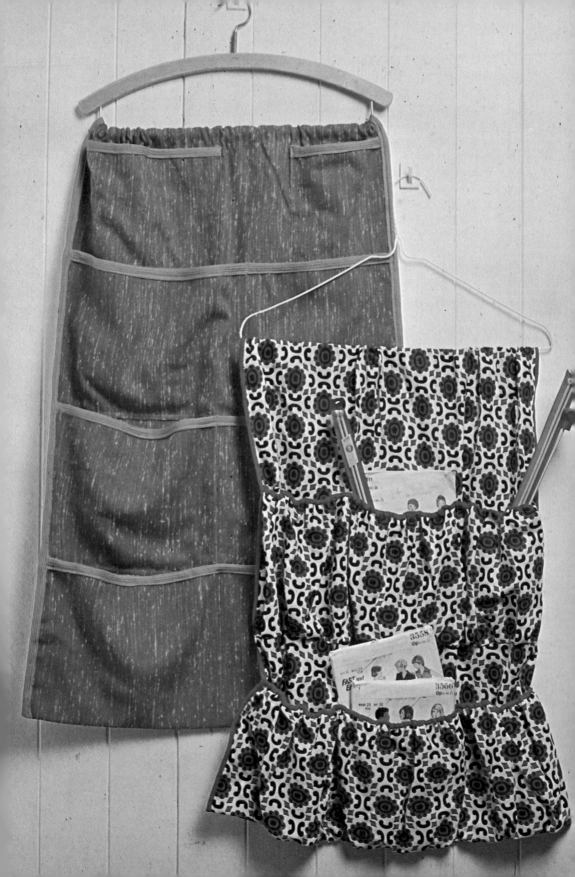

Pin the loop on one short end on the wrong side of the interfaced band with ¾ inch of the loop overlapping the edge. Baste and then top stitch the interfaced band, working ⅛th inch from the edge and catching in the loop.

Place the prepared piece B on the back of the interfaced piece A, wrong sides facing. Baste and then stitch together using small slip stitches and making sure that the stitches do not show through to the right side. Cover a button mould in fabric to match the apple motif. Stitch in position ½ inch from the edge opposite the loop.

'Her' tidy bag

illustrated on page 171

Materials
46 inches of 48 inch furnishing fabric

3½–4 yards braid
Matching thread
Wooden coat hanger

Cut the main strip 20 × 40 inches, two pockets 20 × 8 inches, one 6 inch square and one further piece 6 × 10 inches. Bind one long top edge of each of these pockets; bind one short end of the long main strip. Fold up this last bound edge to form lowest 8 inch pocket and pin in place; pin the other two pockets immediately above, the lower edge of each coinciding with top edge of pocket below; then pin in place the narrow and the square pockets immediately above third long pocket.

This should leave just sufficient material to fold over the bar of a wooden coat hanger. Machine the lower edges of all

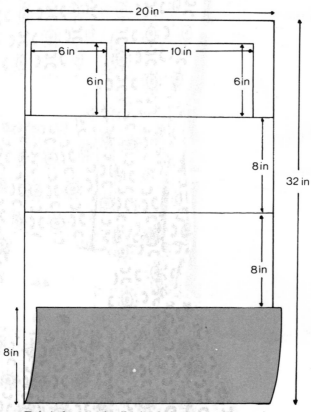

Fabric lay-out for 'his' tidy bag

Appliqué patterns for place mats

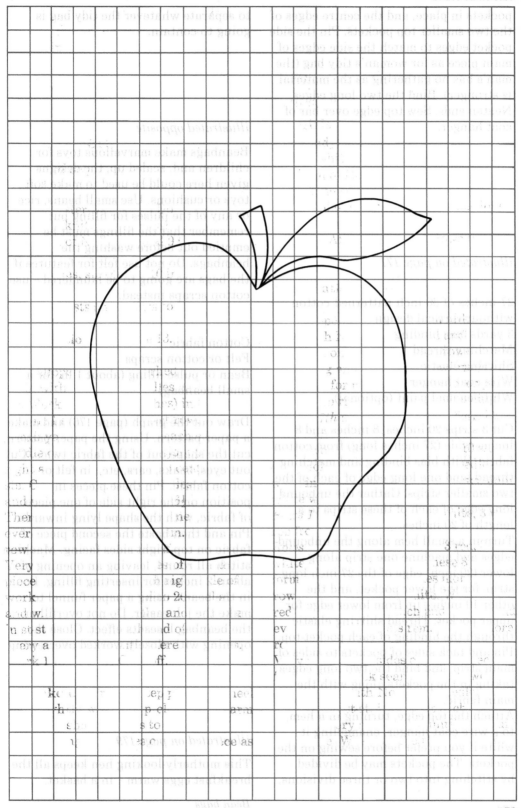

pockets in place, and the centre edges of the two smaller top pockets. Pin the side pocket edges to match the side edges of main piece as for woman's tidy bag (the man's has no gathering as the material is stronger). Bind the two long edges. Neaten ends. Sew top edge over bar of coat hanger.

'His' tidy bag

illustrated on page 171

Materials
27 inches of 36 inch patterned cotton without vertical design
3 yards bias binding
Matching thread
Shirring elastic
Wire coat hanger
White enamel paint (optional)

Cut 3 strips 20 inches, 8 inches and 8 inches wide (27 inches long) from cotton fabric. With bias binding and matching thread bind one long edge of each of the two smaller strips. Gather the unbound long edge of each of these strips to a length of 20 inches.

Turn in a small hem along the unbound edges and machine one strip along lower (20 inch) edge of the 27 inch long strip, for the lower pocket, and the other 10 inches up from lower edge for upper pocket. Thread shirring elastic through the binding of each pocket-top. Pin and tack sides of pockets to sides of main strip, and bind the two long edges taking in the pockets along with the main fabric.

Attach the top edge, turning in a hem, to a wire coat hanger, enamelling it white if you prefer before sewing on the pockets. The pockets may be divided by stitching into two or three divisions,

to separate whatever the tidy bag is going to contain.

Beanbags

illustrated opposite

Beanbags make marvellous toys for children and, scaled up, the designs given here could be used to make soft toys or cushions. Use small beans, rice or any of the pulses for filling but remember that the fillings must be emptied out before washing the beanbags. Do not use felt for features if the bags are going to be laundered – use cotton scraps instead.

Materials
Cotton fabric
Felt or cotton scraps
Bean or pulse filling (about 1 lb. for a small beanbag)

Draw out the graph (page 176) and make a paper pattern. Using the paper pattern, cut the shape out of the fabric twice. Cut out eyes, beaks, ears, etc., in felt or cotton fabric. Pin these pieces in position on the right side of one piece of fabric, with the shape lying inwards. Pin and then baste the second piece of fabric on top, right sides facing. Machine stitch all round, leaving an opening of about 2 inches for inserting filling. Pour in the beans, using a paper funnel to make the job easier. Do not overfill or the beanbag loses its effect. Close the opening with closely worked oversewing.

Egg-basket hen

illustrated on page 179

This motherly-looking hen keeps all the breakfast eggs warm – in a basket.

Bean bags

2 squares = 1 inch

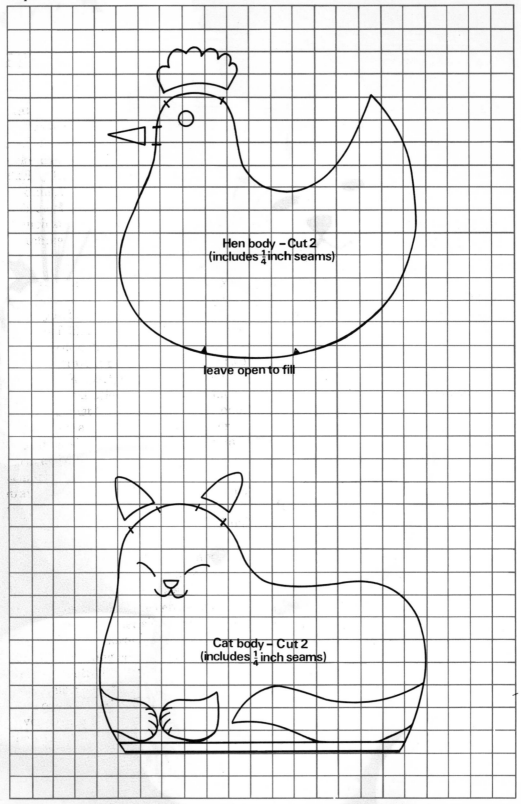

Hen body – Cut 2
(includes $\frac{1}{4}$ inch seams)

leave open to fill

Cat body – Cut 2
(includes $\frac{1}{4}$ inch seams)

Materials

½ yard patterned cotton fabric
½ yard matching cotton fabric in plain colour
½ yard heavyweight non-woven interfacing (or use a piece cut from an old blanket)
Red felt or red fabric for comb and wattle
Yellow felt or cotton fabric for beak
Black felt or cotton fabric for eyes
Matching sewing thread
Kapok stuffing
Matching bias binding
Press stud

(*Follow graph pattern on page 178*).

Cut the hen's body out of the patterned fabric twice, from the lining twice, and from the interlining twice. Cut out the comb, wattle and beak pieces. (If cotton fabric is being used, cut two pieces and seam on the wrong side.) Place two beak pieces together, stitch with stab stitches and stuff.

Lay the comb, wattle and beak on the right side of one head-body piece. Baste in position and place second head-body piece on top, right sides facing. Baste. Stitch along top from point A to B. Turn to right side and stuff hen's head.

Cut linings and interlinings off at the dotted line in pattern, D–E (to give final shape A–D–E–A).

Put one piece of interlining on flat surface. Place one lining on it right side up. Place second lining piece *wrong* side up. Place second interlining piece on top. Baste and seam from A–D–E. Pin lining and interlining into hen, pinning through top fabric as well from A–C–B. Baste. Top stitch for wings on dotted lines of pattern.

Apply bias binding all round hen's body from B–C–A, thus holding lining, interlining and top fabric together. Catch hen's tail together at C with press stud sewn on inside.

Lining a basket Line the basket with top fabric interlined with a piece of warm blanket.

Trace the base of the basket on to paper. Add ½ inch turnings all round. Measure the circumference of the basket. Double the measurement. Measure the depth from rim to base. Add 2½ inches. Cut a length of top fabric to this measurement. Cut the base shape. Join short ends of the strip on the wrong side. Gather one long edge and pin, baste and stitch to the base piece, pulling up gathers to fit.

Make a ½ inch casing on the other long, raw edge. Insert narrow elastic to fit over the edge of the basket. From the blanket fabric, cut a strip to exactly the circumference of the basket by the depth plus ½ inch. Cut the base shape out with ½ inch turnings. Seam the short ends of the strip. Join the resulting circle to the base piece, pleating to fit. Catch the top fabric to the interlining round the base piece.

Baby stockings

illustrated on page 183

Materials

Mushroom or fruit basket, approx 9½ × 6 × 4 inches deep
1 yard of 36 inch wide quilted fabric, nylon, cotton or plastic
1 yard of 36 inch wide cotton fabric for lining
1 yard of 11 inch wide white nylon or Terylene fabric
6 yards frilled nylon edging
6 yards of 1 inch wide insert lace
1½ yards of 4 inch wide lace fabric
3 yards narrow blue ribbon
3 yards narrow pink ribbon
Adhesive

Make a paper pattern for the base of the basket (A), one long side (B) and one short side (C). Cut a strip of quilted fabric, 32 inches long by 5 inches deep,

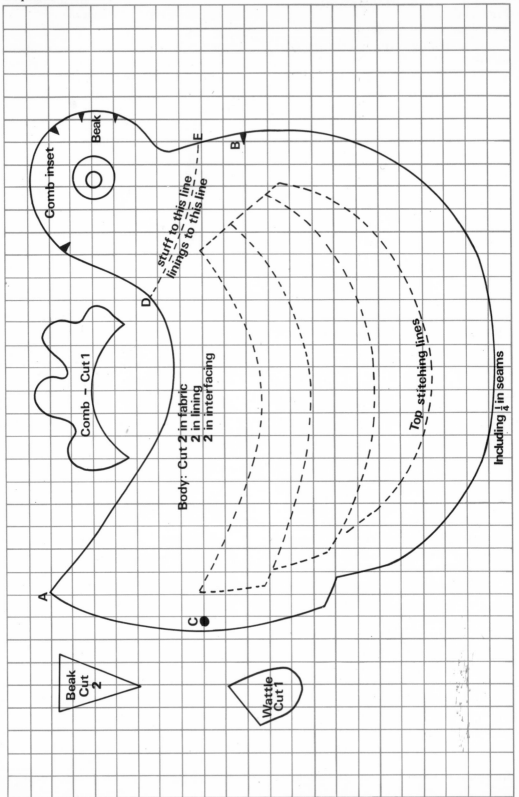

Comb inset

Beak

Comb – Cut 1

stuff to this line

linings to this line

Body: Cut 2 in fabric
2 in lining
2 in interfacing

Top stitching lines

Including ¼ in seams

E

B

D

A

C

Beak
Cut
2

Wattle
Cut 1

Egg-basket hen

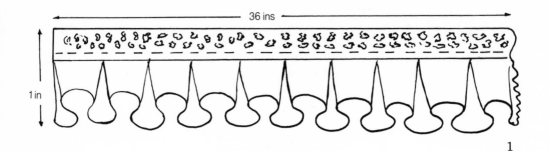

36 ins

1 in

1

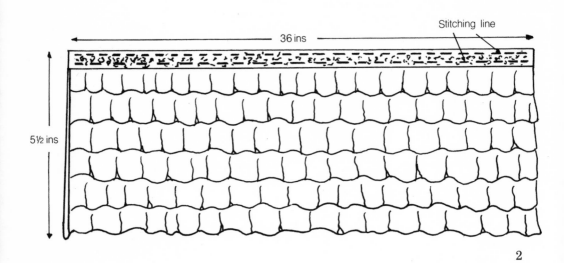

Stitching line

36 ins

5½ ins

2

180

to line the inner sides of the basket. Stick the quilting to the inside, folding the ends into one corner.

Using pattern A, cut a piece of quilting for the base of the basket, allowing $\frac{1}{2}$ inch turnings all round. Fold in the turnings and glue the lining to the base of the basket.

Pad the outer sides and base of the basket in the same way. Turn and stitch the padded linings at the top edge to neaten.

Next, make a cotton lining for the inside of the basket. Using the paper patterns, cut pieces of the cotton fabric, allowing $\frac{1}{2}$ inch seam allowances all around, as follows: two from pattern B, two from pattern C and one from pattern A. Machine the pieces together to make up the lining, and slip into the basket. Pad the handle of the basket and line with cotton.

Line the outside of the basket in the same way as the inside, but allowing 1 inch seam allowances for the padded thickness of the basket. Pin together the outer cotton lining pieces and check the fit on the basket. Stitch the pieces together and slip this cover over the basket. Turn the raw edges in at the top and slip stitch to neaten.

The nylon cover is then made as follows. Fold the piece of white nylon or Terylene fabric in half lengthwise. Cut 6 lengths of frilled nylon fabric, each 36 inches long and 6 × 36 inch lengths of insert lace. Join each strip of frilled nylon to a strip of lace, along the long edges of each (diagram 1).

Pin, baste and then machine stitch each of these 6 trimming strips to the folded nylon fabric to make 6 overlapping rows (diagram 2).

Wrap this trimmed nylon cover around the basket to fit, then stitch the short ends together. Turn the seam to the inside and slip over the basket. Turn in and stitch the top edge to the basket to secure. Cut approx 12 inches of 4 inch wide lace fabric to cover the handle. Thread pink and blue ribbon through the lace and cover the handle, stitching the trimming to the underside.

Thread ribbons through the remaining lace and hand stitch this around the top of the basket. Use remaining ribbon to make bows at each of the four corners.

Rag doll

illustrated on page 187

Rag dolls are always loved by their owners and you will enjoy making this one for a little girl. She is different from most rag dolls in that her features are delicately embroidered giving her a pert and charming look.

Materials
For the doll, approx. 15 inches tall
$\frac{1}{2}$ yard poplin or Viyella fabric, pale pink or cream

Kapok filling
Anchor stranded embroidery thread, blue
0155, black 0403, deep pink 035, pale
pink 030, white 0402
1 skein Aran knitting yarn for hair
Scraps of pink felt

For the doll's clothes, dress and chemise
½ yard broderie Anglaise with a deep
edging
¾ yard of 1 inch wide broderie Anglaise
insert trimming
½ yard of ½ inch wide cotton lace edging
1½ yards narrow pink baby ribbon
1 press stud

Graph patterns, pages 186–189, include
¼ inch seam allowance

The doll
Draw a paper pattern from the graph
given for the doll's body. Cut out the
head and body piece twice in the pink
or cream fabric. Transfer the features to

head lightly.
Embroider the features, using two
strands of thread throughout. Work the
outer pupil in blue in long and short
stitch. Work the inner pupil in black in
long and short stitch and outline the eye
in stem stitch. Work the white of the eye
in long and short stitch. Outline the
mouth in stem stitch using pale pink.
Work the lower lip in deep pink in satin
stitch and the upper lip in pale pink in
satin stitch. After completing the
embroidery, remove the stuffing from
the head, turn to the wrong side and
press the embroidery lightly. Restuff the
head and neck.
Stitch up the arms and stuff them, firmly
at the hands and wrists, more lightly
near the top of the arms. Oversew the
openings and insert the arms in the
body. Oversew the body turnings on to
the arms. Complete stuffing the body.
Make up the legs and stuff them. Stuff

one piece. Cut out the arm pattern four
times and the leg pattern four times.
Seam the two head and body pieces
together, right sides facing, leaving the
seam open where indicated so that the
arms and legs can be inserted. Stuff the

more lightly at the tops. Oversew the
top openings and insert the legs into the
bottom of the body, keeping the leg
seams to the front. Oversew, using neat
small stitches.
To make up the hair, cut the skein of

Baby basket

yarn through to make one long length and cut a 9 inch length from the bunch for the fringe. Place the bunch on a 9 × ½ inch strip of pink felt so that 2½ inches overlaps the felt, spread the strands out and then machine stitch them to the

of felt across the top of the head. Loop the hair back on each side where the ears would be and divide the hair at the back to make side bunches but take care that most of the back of the head is covered.

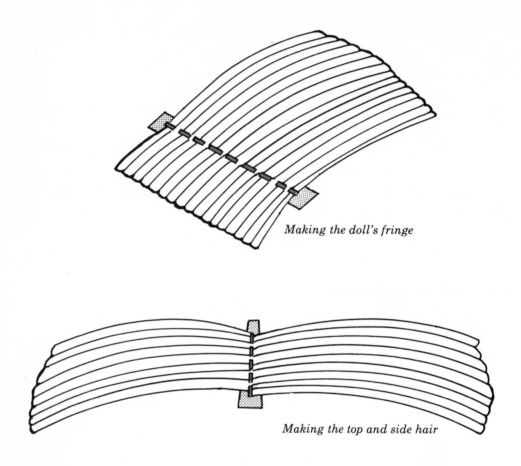

Making the doll's fringe

Making the top and side hair

felt. Pin the felt to the top of the head seam and stitch with small invisible stitches by hand. Trim the fringe if it is necessary just to clear the doll's eyes. Cut the remainder of the skein into two equal lengths and lay them side by side across a strip of felt 4 inches × ½ inch. Machine stitch along the centre, re-arranging the strands a little so that the felt is hidden along the 'parting'. Turn one short end of the felt under, out of sight, and place this just in front of the top of the head seamline. Stitch the strip

Doll's dress
Following the diagram for the dress pattern, draw out the shape on tracing paper for the measurements given. Cut the dress from the broderie Anglaise twice using the decorative edge for the hem of the dress. Join the shoulder seams first – these are approximately 1 inch wide.
Draw the sleeve pattern out. Cut two sleeves out of the broderie Anglaise and keep the patterned edge of the fabric for the wrist edge. Insert the sleeves into the

184

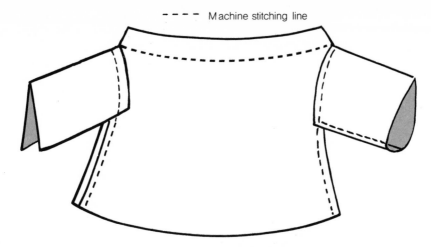

Machine stitching line

Setting in the sleeves and seaming

dress along the shoulder edges. Join the underarm seams of the sleeves. Join the dress side seams.

Make a narrow casing at the neck edge of the dress. Cut a small hole in the casing centre front. Neaten the edges of the hole with buttonhole stitches.

Insert a length of pink ribbon and draw the neckline up to fit the doll.

Doll's chemise
Some plain fabric will remain from the broderie Anglaise. From this, cut the chemise skirt pattern out twice and (*instructions continued on page 190*)

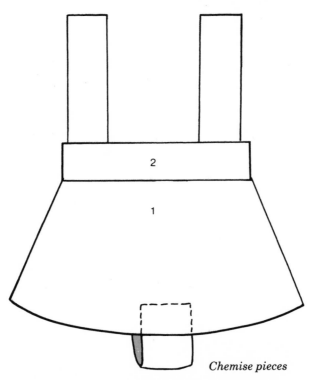

2

1

Chemise pieces

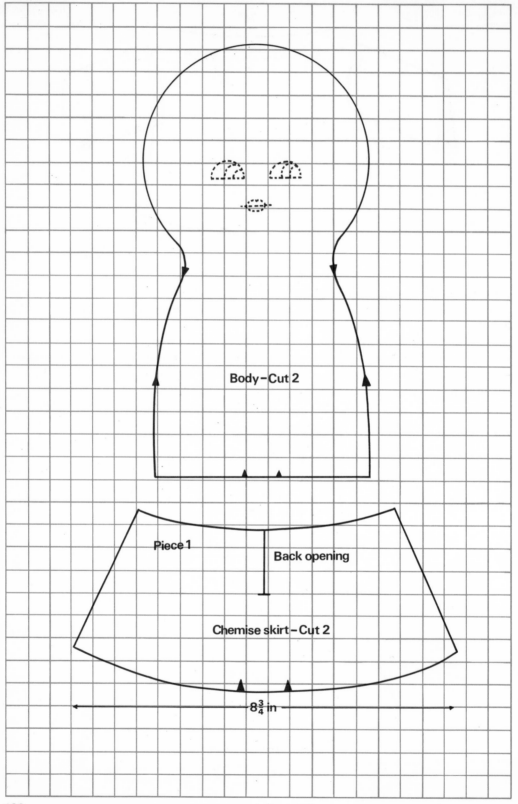

Body – Cut 2

Piece 1

Back opening

Chemise skirt – Cut 2

8¾ in

Rag doll

2 squares = 1 inch

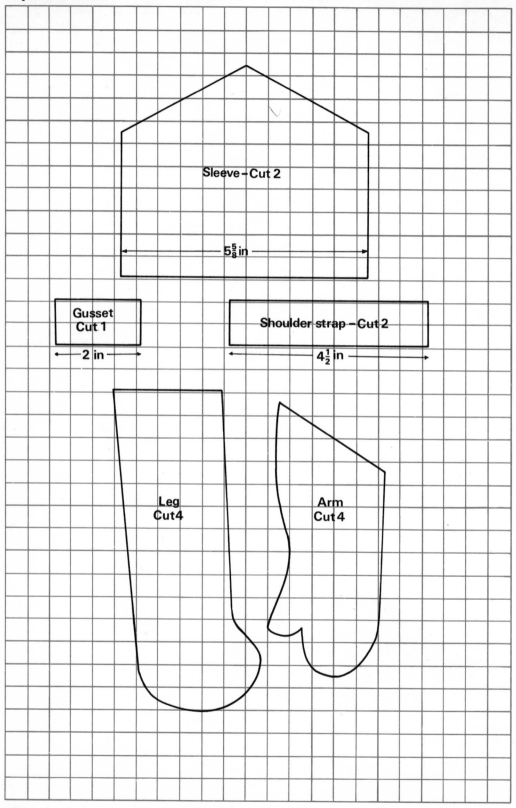

Sleeve – Cut 2

$5\frac{5}{8}$ in

Gusset
Cut 1

Shoulder strap – Cut 2

2 in

$4\frac{1}{2}$ in

Leg
Cut 4

Arm
Cut 4

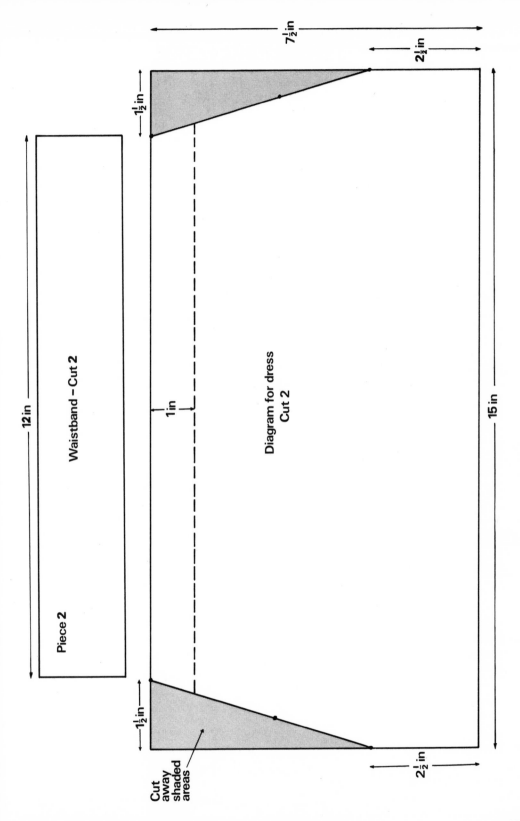

7½in

2½in

1½in

12in

Waistband – Cut 2

Piece 2

1in

Diagram for dress
Cut 2

15 in

1½in

2½in

Cut
away
shaded
areas

slash into one of the pieces for the back waist opening. Neaten this opening by making a narrow hem all round. Join the skirt side seams and trim the hem with the cotton lace edging.

raw edges under once. Finish the back waistband off by turning the raw ends under twice and hemstitching. Stitch a press stud to the back waistband to fasten.

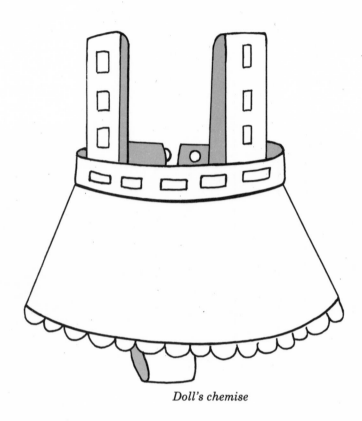

Doll's chemise

Cut shoulder straps, waistband and gusset from the broderie Anglaise insert trimming: the waistband is 12 inches long, the shoulder straps are 4½ inches long each and the gusset 2 inches long. Turn the ends under on the gusset piece and stitch to the wrong side of the back and front skirt hem, just above the lace. Stitch the waistband to the skirt waist, keeping the opening at the skirt back. Stitch the shoulder straps to the waistband at front and back, turning the

Ribbon tray holder

illustrated opposite

Here is a simple yet attractive gift to make for someone setting up a new home perhaps – it is low in cost but high in ingenuity!

Materials
Large sized curtain ring
2 yards wide ribbon or braid

Ribbon tray holder

Seam the two short ends of the braid and pass the loop through the ring so that the ends hang at equal length. Lay the braid and ring on a flat surface and move the ends of the loops apart about six inches. Place a pin through the braid just under the ring to hold the angle. Make a few invisible stitches across the four thicknesses, just under the ring to hold the angle. Hang the holder by the ring and one or more trays can be slipped into the loops. The weight of the trays holds them secure.

Cover the ring with thick cotton or string if you prefer.

Felt craft

Felt is a satisfying material to make gifts with because it is comparatively cheap, is available in a wonderful range of colours, requires only very simple sewing techniques and is suitable for embroidery decoration of different types. Felt can be used to make greeting cards, mounted on stiff card, for collage pictures, calendars, pot holders, note book covers and dozens and dozens of other small gifts. The ideas shown here are simple, quick to make and pretty.

Flower pencil tops

illustrated on page 195

Make a little felt flower head to fit on to the end of a pencil and plant six pencils in a flower pot, made from a plastic food pot, for a charming gift for a child or a bazaar.

Materials
Pencils
Felt scraps: yellow, pink, orange, black, lilac, green, white
Matching sewing threads
Small beads
Small plastic pot (e.g. yogurt or cream carton)
Brown felt, 9 inch square
Lump of green plasticine
All-purpose adhesive

Two basic flower shapes are given, one has five petals and the other is a daisy shape. The flower centres are cut from circular patterns in two sizes. The 'stem' pattern is used for both types of flowers.

Petalled flower
Cut out five petal shapes and stitch

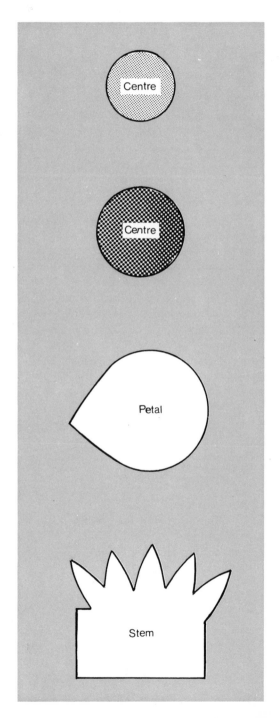

Daisy

them together at the points. Make a knot on the end of a piece of thread and bring it up through the centre of the flower so that the knot is underneath. Slip a centre circle on to the needle and push it down on to the petals. Slip a bead on to the needle and push it down on to the flower centre piece. Take the needle back through the felt flower centre and the joined petals and finish off the thread with two or three back stitches underneath the flower. Cut the 'stem' pattern out in green felt. Join the short straight edges and try the stem on the pencil to see that it has a close but not tight fit. Stitch the flower head to the 'stem' with matching green thread and small invisible stitches.

Daisy flowers

Cut out daisy flower heads and use both circular flower centres, one on top of the other. Finish off with a bead. Join to the stem as before.

Flower pot

Place the plastic pot on its side on the wrong side of the felt along one straight edge. Hold a piece of chalk against the rim of the pot and slowly roll the pot across the felt, following the rim with the piece of chalk. Put the pot back

where you started and roll it again, this time holding the chalk against the rim of the pot base. This will give you the shape for covering the pot with felt. An all-purpose adhesive is used to glue the felt to the pot. Apply the adhesive just below the rim of the pot and round the rim of the base. Press the felt on to it and join the two long edges with more adhesive. Push a lump of green plasticine into the bottom of the pot. Push the pencils into this at angles to look like growing flowers. You can add the child's name to the pot in cut-out felt letters or in embroidery.

Thimble holders

illustrated opposite

These thimble holders are made in the same way as fabric boxes – that is covering pieces of card with fabric on both sides and joining the covered pieces with an embroidery stitch. The two ends of the holder are pinched together to open the top. The animal designs shown here, a mouse, a rabbit and a fish design are obvious ones to make on the shape but equally pretty holders can be made simply using embroidered patterns or tiny beads and buttons. Work any embroidery or decoration on the fabric before cutting it out. A closely woven fabric should be used for these holders so that there is less likelihood of fraying Felt works extremely well.

Method

Work any surface embroidery or beadwork first. Trace the shape in the diagram overleaf and make a template in stiff card. Using this template cut out 3 shapes in fabric, adding $\frac{1}{4}$ inch turnings and 3 shapes, exactly to the size of the template, in non-woven interfacing for a lining. (Felt can be used for the lining if you prefer.) Using the same template, cut out three more shapes in light card. (The

Flower pencil tops, thimble holders, fruit brooches

card from which cereal boxes are made is about the right weight.) Smear fabric adhesive on one side of the card. Place this down on the fabric shape, centring it carefully. Leave to dry. When the adhesive is dry, fold the turnings over – you may need to press them with a cool iron to achieve a good, sharp edge and glue them down on to the card. Work

Thimble Holder Template

very slowly and use a sharpened matchstick to apply the adhesive. The smallest spot of adhesive spilt on the fabric will spoil the holder. Press the turnings down firmly with a thumb. Leave to dry. Smear adhesive on the wrong side of the lining and apply it to the card. Press it down firmly and leave to dry. When all three pieces of card have been covered and the adhesive is quite dry, join the three together using Cretan stitch, leaving the top seam open. Add ears, tail and eyes for animal designs.

Fruit brooches

illustrated on page 195

Gay fruit brooches made of brightly coloured and bead-worked felt are lovely gifts for teenagers – they wear them on hats, berets, tote bags; on their shoes and boots, or at the waistline – anywhere in fact where a spot of bright colour is needed.

Patterns for a strawberry, an apple, a pear, a grape and a carrot are given opposite and on page 198 but you will be able to design others for yourself quite easily once you know how.

Materials
Scraps of felt: scarlet, mauve, purple, lime green, yellow, dark green, orange
Beads for decoration
Anchor stranded embroidery cottons
Cottonwool or kapok for stuffing
Small safety pins

Cut out the pattern shape twice and leaf shapes once. Stitch two fruit shapes together using tiny stab stitches and a matching thread. Leave a gap in the seam for inserting filling. Push cotton wool in using a large darning needle. Close the seam and apply any bead or embroidery required for the character of the fruit or vegetable. Make up the leaves. Stitch to the fruit. Stitch the safety pin to the back of the brooch. The carrot has a green top which is gathered along the base before being attached.

The grapes are gathered into balls and stitched together on the leaf.

Book cover

illustrated on page 199

This is a simple and attractive idea for a gift. Choose a design for the cover which will make it a really personal present.

Materials
Enough felt to go round front, back and spine of chosen book with additional 5 inches on length (for flaps) and 1 inch on height (see diagram on page 200)
Felt scraps in different colours
Trimmings
Stranded embroidery thread

Fold the allowance for flaps (2½ inches at either end) back on to the wrong side.

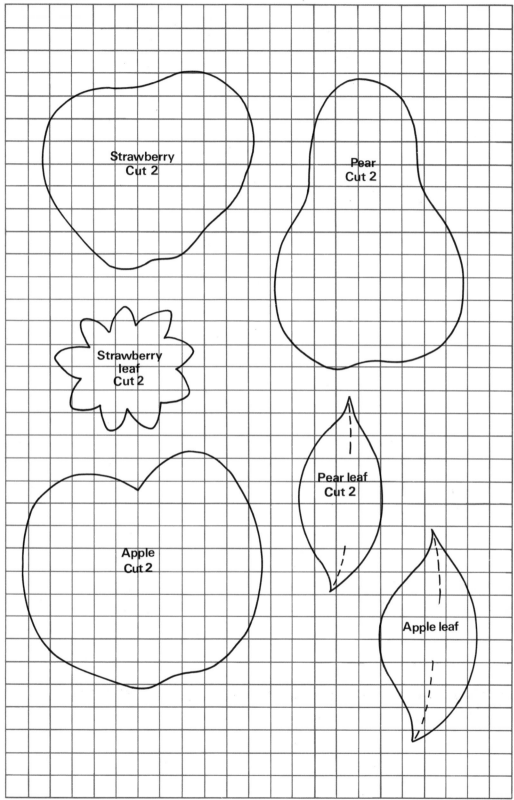

Strawberry
Cut 2

Pear
Cut 2

Strawberry
leaf
Cut 2

Pear leaf
Cut 2

Apple
Cut 2

Apple leaf

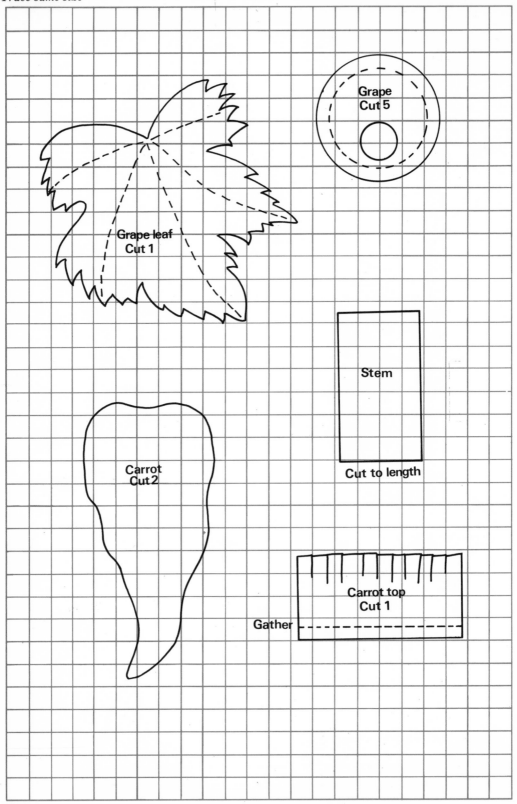

Grape
Cut 5

Grape leaf
Cut 1

Stem

Cut to length

Carrot
Cut 2

Carrot top
Cut 1

Gather

Book cover, picture

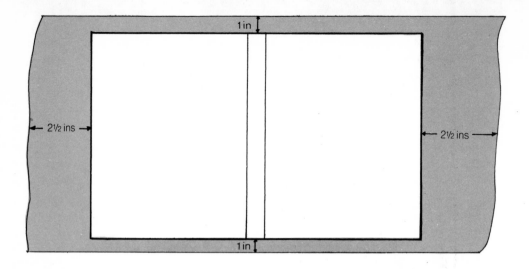

Trace the required design on to the front cover. Trace the design shapes on to the felt scraps. Cut out the felt shapes and position them on the front cover. Sew them very neatly into position, using 2 strands of embroidery thread.

On the book cover illustrated, the scissors and the end of string are embroidered, the scissors in stem stitch and the string in tiny back stitches. Work running stitches $\frac{1}{2}$ inch in from top and bottom edges of book cover, taking the stitches through both thicknesses at the flaps. Using a contrasting colour, whip the running stitches, sewing them always in the same direction.

Decorate the design with trimmings – metallic thread, lace or braid – as required.

Picture

illustrated on page 199

Materials
1 piece yellow linen or textured furnishing fabric, 10½ by 13 inches
1 piece of felt, 10½ by 4½ inches, for conifers
Scraps of felt in three shades, for red roofs and steeple
4 inch square of felt, for shingle
Five shades of larger squares of felt in blue, green and khaki, for mountains
Larger squares of turquoise and white felt, for lake and houses
Matching stranded embroidery thread (use 2 strands at a time)

Trace the design opposite on to the linen, then trace and cut the pieces comprising the design. Fit them together, stitching them very neatly in place. Embroider the windows with tiny straight stitches, those of the church in blue, those of the small left-hand cottage in deep red, and the others in green. Embroider the waterfall in white, filling the area with vertical stem-stitch to give the effect of water. If a piece is too small to cut successfully in felt, such as the eave of the lower centre house, embroider it instead.

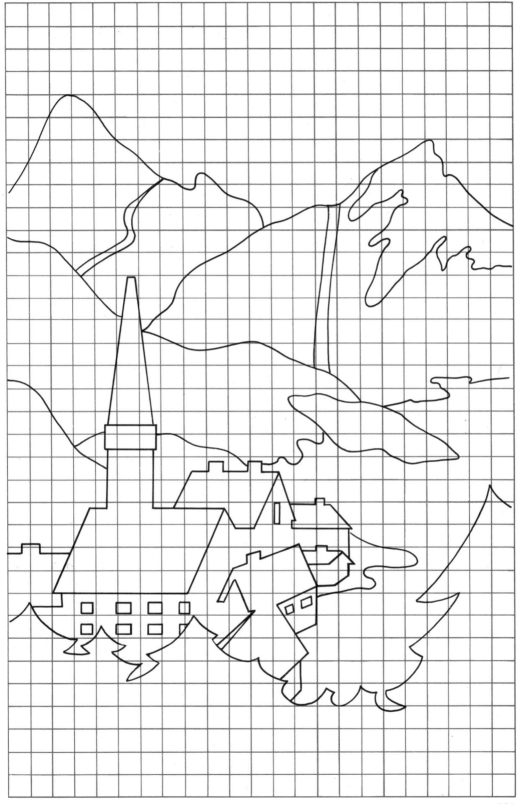

Knitting and Crochet

Baby stockings

illustrated opposite

Materials
Blue Stockings: 2 × 25 gram balls Lister
Baby-Bel Courtelle 4-ply (Fingering
3-ply)
Yellow stockings: 1 oz Patons Beehive
Baby Wool 4-ply (Fingering 3-ply).
¾ yard narrow ribbon
Pair each Nos. 11 (2) and 12 (1) knitting
needles
Note 3 needles would make foot
shaping easier.

Measurements Leg length, 6½ inches;
foot length, 4½ inches

Tension Over patt, unstretched, 7½ sts
and 10½ rows to 1 inch

Abbreviations See page 13.

Both socks are worked alike. With No.
12 (1) needles cast on 44 sts.
1st rib row: K3, *p2, k2; rep from * to
last 5 sts, p2, k3.
2nd rib row: K1, *p2, k2; rep from * to
last 3 sts, p2, k1. Rep these 2 rows 4
times more. Change to No. 11 (2) needles
and patt thus:
1st row: as 1st rib row.
2nd row: K1, p to last st, k1. These 2
rows form patt.

Shape knee Rib 24, ending with k3,
turn, k1, p2, k1, turn, k3, p2, k3, turn, k1,
p10, k1, turn; continue in this way,
working 4 sts more before turning on
every row and keeping in patt, until

'k1, p38, k1' has been worked, then turn
and work across all sts, in patt, until the
shorter side edge measures 5½ inches
from cast-on edge, ending after a 2nd
patt row.

Make Beading *Next row:* k1, *m1, k2
tog, m1, p2 tog, rep from * to last 3 sts,
m1, k2 tog, k1.
Next row: K1, p to last st, k1.

Shape Foot *Next row:* K17, (p2, k2,)
twice, k3, turn, k1, p10, k1, turn; work
in patt across these 12 sts for 12 more
rows for instep. Cut yarn and rejoin it,
right side of work facing, at point of
right needle after the 16 sts already
knitted at ankle; pick up and k10 sts
along nearer side of instep, k the 12 sts
from instep needle, pick up and k10
along other side of instep, then k across
last 16 ankle sts. 64 sts. K11 more rows,
using third needle if necessary, across
these sts.

Shape Heel and Toe *Next row:* K2,
k2 tog, k23, k2 tog, k6, k2 tog, k23, k2
tog, k2. K1 row.
Next row: K2, k2 tog, k22, k2 tog, k4,
k2 tog, k22, k2 tog, k2. K1 row.
Next row: K2, k2 tog, k21, k2 tog, k2,
k2 tog, k21, k2 tog, k2. K1 row. Cast off.

To make up Very neatly join long
centre-back and underfoot seam and
press it, using dry cloth and cool or
rayon-heat iron for Courtelle yarn and
damp cloth and warm iron for wool yarn.
Cut ribbon in half and thread through

*Baby stockings, baby waistcoat, child's
bonnet and scarf*

holes at ankle, tying in neat bow. Make the second stocking in exactly the same way, using the second half of the ribbon for threading through beading.

Knitted caps in pineapple stripes

illustrated on page 211

Instructions are given for the first size. Figures for the larger size, where they differ, are given in brackets.

Materials
2 × 25-gram balls of Sirdar Courtelle Double Knitting (knitting worsted)
Pair each of No. 11 (2) and 9 (4) knitting needles
1 Button (for the smaller size)
2 cardboard circles 1¼ inches in diameter for pompon (for smaller size)

Measurements Around head, 20 inches (22 inches), stretching to fit 22 inches (24 inches); depth from cast-on edge to top, 8½ inches (9¾ inches).

Tension, unstretched, 6 sts and 9 rows to 1 inch.

Abbreviations See page 13.

With No. 11 (2) needles cast on 120 (132) sts. Work 8 (10) rows in k1, p1 rib. Change to No. 9 (4) needles and work pineapple stripe patt thus:
1st row: K1, *p2, k6, p2*, k2, rep from * to *, k1.
2nd row: K3, *p6, k2, p2, k2; rep from * to last 9 sts, p6, k3. Rep these 2 rows once more.
5th row: K1, *p2, twist 3R, twist 3L, p2, k2; rep from * to end, ending with k1.
6th row: K3, *p1, k1, p1, k1, p2, k2, p2, k2; rep from * to last 9 sts, p1, k1, p1, k1, p2, k3.

7th row: K1, *p2, k1, p1, k1, p1, k2, p2, k2, rep from * to end, fin with k1.
8th row: As 6th row.
9th row: As 7th row.
10th row: As 6th row.
11th row: K1, *p2, twist 3L, twist 3R, p2, k2; rep from * ending k1.
12th row: As 2nd row.
These 12 rows form patt. Rep them until 46th (58th) patt row, in all, has been worked.

Shape Top, counting as from 1st row of shaping:
1st row: *K2 tog tbl, p1, twist 3L, twist 3R, p1, k2 tog, rep from * to end, 100 (110) sts.
2nd row: K2, *p6, k1, p2, k1; rep from * to last 8 sts, p6, k2.
3rd row: K1, p1, *k6, p1, k2, p1; rep from * to last 8 sts, k6, p1, k1.
4th row: As 2nd row.
5th row: *K2 tog tbl, k6, k2 tog; rep from * to end. 80 (88) sts.
6th row: K1, p to last st, k1.
7th row: K1, *twist 3R, twist 3L, k2, rep from * to end, ending k1.
8th row: K1, p1, *k2 tog, p2 tog, p4; rep from * ending k2 tog, p2 tog, p1, k1.
9th row: K2, *p1, k5; rep from * to last 4 sts, p1, k3.
10th row: K1, p1, *k1, p5; rep from * to last 4 sts, k1, p2, k1.
11th row: K1, *k2 tog tbl, k2 tog, k2, rep from * to end, ending k1.
12th row: As 6th row.
13th row: *K2 tog, k2 tog tbl; rep from * to end.
14th row: P2 tog across row. Cut yarn, thread through sts, pull tight and fasten off firmly.

To make up Very neatly join side edge for centre-back seam. Press over padded bowl, or wring out a cloth in cold water, lay over cap on bowl and leave until it dries. Sew button to top of larger cap,

204

as there is not enough yarn for a pompon. For the smaller, cut a ¾ inch hole in centre of each of the cardboard circles, lay them together, and wind wool over and over the double ring of card until the centre hole is completely filled. Slit along outer edge between the two card rings, tie very tightly between the card circles to bind the threads, then gently pull away the rings and fluff out the pompon; attach it to top of cap by the tie-strings.

Baby waistcoat

illustrated on page 203

This baby waistcoat is based on a French design, 'chauffe-coeur' or 'heart-warmer'. It is quick to make and provides just that fraction of extra warmth for a small baby.

Materials
2 × 25-gram balls of Lister Baby-Bel Courtelle 4-ply (Fingering 3-ply)
Pair each of Nos. 12 (1) and 10 (3) knitting needles
Small cable needle
4 small buttons

Measurements To fit chest size 18 inches; mid-shoulder length 8½ inches

Tension 7 sts and 9 rows to 1 inch

Abbreviations See page 13.

Back
With No. 12 (1) needles cast on 64 sts. Work 10 rows in k1, p1 rib. Change to No. 10 (3) needles.
1st row: Sl1 purlwise, k4, p2, k4, p2, k to last 13, p2, k4, p2, k5.
2nd row: Sl1 purlwise, k6, p4, k2, p to last 13, k2, p4, k7.
3rd row: Sl1 purlwise, k4, p2, c4R, p2, k to last 13, p2, c4L, p2, k5.

4th row: As 2nd row.
These 4 rows form back patt. Cont in patt inc on next and every foll 8th row, inside borders as follows: sl1 purlwise, k4, p2, k4, p2, pick 1k, k to last 13, pick 1k, p2, k4, p2, k5. Continue as indicated until 66th patt row has been completed. 80 sts.

Shape Shoulders Keeping borders as far as possible, cast off 5 sts at beg of next 2 rows, and 6 sts at beg of next 8 rows. Cast off rem 22 sts for back neck.

Left Front
With No. 12 (1) needles cast on 37 sts.
1st rib row: Work 32 sts in k1, p1 rib, k5 for button/buttonhole border.
2nd row: Sl1 purlwise, k5, p1, *k1, p1; rep from * to end. Rep these 2 rows 4 times more: but for a boy, make first buttonhole on next (3rd) row thus: Rib 32, k2, m1, k2 tog, k1.
When 10th welt row has been completed, change to No. 10 (3) needles and work first 4 rows of patt as given for back, with cable panel and borders at both ends. On next and every foll 8th row, 7 times more, work side inc only; making 3 more buttonholes for a boy in front border, on 5th, 17th and 29th rows:
5th row, for a boy, will read: sl1 purlwise, k4, p2, k4, p2, pick 1 k, k to last 13 sts, p2, k4, p2, k2, m1, k2 tog, k1. For 13th row omit buttonhole but work side inc. For 17th row work no side inc but make buttonhole. Do not work buttonholes for a girl. When the 32nd patt row has been completed, 41 sts are on needle.

Front Slope Continuing the side incs where required, begin to shape slope:
33rd row: Sl1 purlwise, k4, p2, k4, p2, k to last 15 sts, k2 tog tbl, p2, k4, p2, k5. Work 3 rows in patt.
37th row: Sl1 purlwise, k4, p2, k4, p2, pick 1 k, k to last 15, k2 tog tbl, p2, k4, p2, k5. Work 3 rows in patt. Rep last 8

rows 3 times more then work 2 more rows, dec. once more inside centre-front border on 65th row: 66 rows, 36 sts.

Shape Shoulder Keeping borders, and dec inside centre-front border once more, cast off thus:

67th row: Cast off 5, p1 more (2 on right needle), c4R, p2, k to last 13, p2, c4L, p2, k5.

68th row: Sl1 purlwise, k6, p4, k2, p to last 8sts, k2, p4, k2.

69th row: Cast off 6, p1 more (2 on needle), k to last 15 sts, k2 tog tbl, p2, k4, p2, k5.

70th row: Sl1 purlwise, k6, p4, k2, p9, k2.

71st row: Cast off 6, k until 5 sts are on right needle, p2, c4L, p2, k5. 18 sts.

72nd row: Sl1 purlwise, k6, p4, k2, p5.

73rd row: Cast off 6, (1 on right needle), k4, p2, k5. 12 sts.

74th row: Sl1 purlwise, k6, p3, p2 tog to stand for last front-slope dec.

75th row: Cast off 6, k to end. 5 sts. For back-neck border cont thus,

76th row: Sl1 purlwise, k4.

77th row: K5. Rep last 2 rows 6 times more, or until this strip, slightly stretched to prevent waviness, reaches halfway along back neck. Cast off.

Right Front
Work to match Left Front, reversing shaping and omitting buttonholes if garment is for a boy, but working buttonholes for a girl. The first row after casting-on will read, sl1 purlwise, k4, *k1, p1; rep from * to end.

2nd row: Rib 32, k5.

Next row, for a girl, will read k2, m1, k2 tog, k1, rib to end; for a boy it will read as 1st row. When 10th welt row has been completed, change to No. 10 (3) needles and work first 4 rows of patt, as given for Back. On 5th and every foll 8th row, patt to last 13 sts, pick 1k, p2, k4, p2, k5. For a girl, make buttonholes on 5th, 17th and 29th patt rows: K2, m1, k2 tog, k1, patt to end, inc before side

border on 5th, 13th, 21st and 29th rows. Complete 32nd patt row. While continuing to inc inside border, start neck slope.

33rd and every foll 4th row: Sl1 purlwise, k4, p2, k4, p2, k2 tog tbl, patt to end. When 67th patt row has been completed, cast off 5 sts once and 6 sts 4 times on next 5 wrong-side rows, while continuing to dec inside front border on 69th and 73rd rows.

77th row: Sl1, purlwise, k4.

78th row: K5. Rep last 2 rows until exactly same length as first neck border. Cast off.

To make up Pin out and press pieces, wrong side facing, with dry cloth and cool or rayon-heat iron for Courtelle. Join shoulder seams and ends of back-neck borders and press. Sew nearer edge of back-neck border very neatly in place and press seam. Join side seams from cast-on edge to end of welt ribbing only, at each side of work, but do not press. Sew on buttons to match buttonholes and darn in all loose ends.

12-section balls in knitting and crochet

illustrated opposite

Materials
Small balls of standard 4-ply yarn in as many colours as possible
Pair of No. 10 (3) knitting needles
No. 3.50 (D/3) crochet hook
Kapok for stuffing

Measurements Knitted ball, about 10 inch circumference; crochet ball, 13 inches

12-section balls, embroidered ball, ball bag

Abbreviations See page 13.

Knitted ball
For each section, with No. 10 (3) needles and working in st-st, cast on 9 sts; inc 1 st at each end of 3rd, 6th and 9th rows, then dec 1 st at each end of 12th row and on every row until 3 sts rem, k3 tog. Fasten off.

Crochet ball
For each section, with 3.50 (D/3) hook, make 9ch, turn.
1st row: Miss 1ch, 8dc(sc) in 8ch. Working in dc(sc), and always turning with 1ch, inc at each end of 2nd, 5th and 8th rows, then dec at each end of 11th row by missing 1dc(sc) at each end, then every row until 2dc(sc) rem. Fasten off.

To make up When 12 knitted or crocheted sections are worked, press them under damp cloth with warm iron. Choose one section as centre and sew one edge of other sections to each of the centre's 5 sides. Similarly treat the other 6 sections; then one cup shape will fit into the other. Join, leaving a space open for stuffing. Stuff with kapok and close last seam.

Embroidered ball

illustrated on page 207

Materials
1 oz each Emu Scotch Double Knitting (knitting worsted) in dark and light colours
Pair of No. 9 (4) knitting needles
Kapok or other stuffing

Measurements $13\frac{1}{2}$ inches circumference

Tension Unstretched, 6 sts and 8 rows to 1 inch

Abbreviations See page 13.

This ball is made in 6 similar sections, of which 3 begin with light colour, changing after 24th row to dark, the other 3 beginning with dark changing to light.
For each section, cast on 1 st.
1st row: K into back, front and back of this st. 3 sts.
2nd row: Inc1, p1, incl. Working in st-st, inc 1 st at each end of 3rd, 5th, 8th and 12th rows. 13 sts. Work 12 rows straight. Change colours. Work 12 more rows straight. 36 rows.
Dec 1 st at each end of 37th, 41st, 44th, 46th, 47th and 48th rows (the last row being p3 tog).

To make up Pin out pieces, wrong sides facing, and press lightly with warm iron and damp cloth. Embroider on each colour in contrasting shade, in Continental embroidery over 1 st and 2 rows. Insert embroidery needle, threaded with contrasting yarn, from wrong side of work, up at base of a st, insert it two rows up round the back of the st and back into the fabric at the same spot where it emerged, so that it gives the impression of being knitted-in. When the embroidery is completed, very neatly sew together the sections, alternating the colours and leaving a space for stuffing. Stuff. Close seam.

Ball bag

illustrated on page 207

Materials
2 × 25-gram balls of Wendy Invitation Crochet Cotton or any standard 8's cotton crepe

Small quantity of contrast cotton or cord
No. 2.50 (B/1) crochet hook

Measurements The bag will take a 26-inch circumference ball.

Make 7ch, join in ring with sl-st.
1st round: (7ch, 1dc(sc) into ring) 4 times. 4 loops. Always join with sl-st to top of first loop.
2nd round: (7ch, 1dc(sc)) twice into each loop. 8 loops.
3rd round: * (7ch, 1dc(sc)) twice into first loop, once into next loop; rep from * to end. 12 loops.
4th round: (7ch, 1dc(sc)) into every loop.
5th round: * (7ch, 1dc(sc)) twice into first loop, once into each of next 2 loops; rep from * to end. 16 loops.
6th round: As 4th round.
7th round: * (7hc, 1dc(sc)) twice into first loop, once each into next 3 loops; rep from * to end. 20 loops.
8th and 9th rounds: As 4th round.
10th round: * (7ch, 1dc(sc)) twice into first loop, once each into next 4 loops. 24 loops.
11th and 12th rounds: As 4th round.
13th round: * (7ch, 1dc(sc)) twice into first loop, once each into next 5 loops. 28 loops.
Rep 4th round until bag is deep enough to hold ball, allowing for gathering at top; on the last round, crochet 7dc(sc) into each loop to end for firm edge. Fasten off.
For a smaller bag, stop inc at 5th, 7th or 10th rounds and work straight thereafter. For a larger one, work a further inc round on 16th, or 16th and 20th rounds.
With contrast cotton or cord, make a chain long enough to go easily round ball and tie. Thread it through last row of loops then join ends of drawstring so that it cannot be pulled out.

Afghan in Tunisian crochet

illustrated on page 210

Materials
30 ozs Double Knitting (knitting worsted)
No. 5 (0·75 mm) tricot hook

Measurements Afghan is 9 patches wide × 11 patches long. (Enlarge by adding another row of patches to length or width.)

Note Two patches are made from 1 oz. 5 from 2 ozs.

For each patch. With No. 5 (0·75 mm) tricot hook – (a long straight hook with a knob at one end) make 21 ch, miss 1, *draw wool through next ch and retain loop on hook; rep from * to end. 21 loops on hook. Tunisian crochet is always worked on the right side and not turned.
Next row: Wool over hook, draw through first loop, * wool over hook, draw through next 2 loops; rep from * to end: 1 loop on hook.

Tunisian crochet

Next row: *Insert hook from right to left round back, between 1st and 2nd vertical stitch. (Not round the back, but round the single thread.) Draw wool through

page 210: Afghan in Tunisian crochet
page 211: Diagonal cushion

and retain loop on hook; rep with every vertical stitch to end. 21 loops on hook. Rep last 2 rows until 36 rows in all have been completed, or until work is square, finishing with 1 loop on hook.

To cast off Work as for single crochet, inserting hook in each case behind vertical thread, drawing loop through and through loop already on hook, to end of row. 'A row of chain stitches forms the foundation of all Tunisian crochet; a row of single stitches ends it.'

To make up When all patches are completed, pin out and press with a damp cloth and warm iron. Plan the distribution of the colours available, so that the rarer colours are reasonably dispersed and so that a pleasing arrangement results. In general put a dark colour next to a light one. Join the squares alternately side edge to cast-on or cast-off edge. This equalises the pull in wear. Sew all pieces together with matching yarn. Press when completed. Ease in the sides, which may be a fraction longer than top or bottom edge.

Edging
Work 2 rows of dc all round. On the 3rd row, on the longer sides only work *3ch, catch with sl-st into the same dc(sc) as last st, 1dc(sc) into each of next 3dc(sc), rep from * to end, working any left-over dc(sc) in dc(sc). From remaining yarns, cut 10 inch lengths for fringe. Taking 3 at a time, fold them double and knot into each of the 3 ch loops along both sides. Trim fringe.

Diagonal cushion

illustrated on page 211

This diagonally worked cushion is adaptable, in that although the original was worked in rainbow variegated wool,

it would be equally effective worked in stripes using up odd balls. The edging could be applied to other articles.

Materials
8 × 1-oz balls of Lister's Lochinvar Double Knitting (knitting worsted)
2 oz of plain contrast double knitting (knitting worsted) for edging
Pair of No. 8 (5) knitting needles
Cushion pad to fit

Measurements About 17½ inches square, without edging.

Tension 6 stitches and 8 rows to 1 inch.

Abbreviations See page 13.

Begin at one corner of main piece. With main wool cast on 1 st. K twice into this st.
Next row: P1, inc 1 in next st. 3 sts. Working in st-st, * Inc 1 st at each end of next 3 rows, then work 1 row straight. Rep from * until there are 145 sts on needle, ending with 1 row straight. **Dec 1 st at each end of next 3 rows, then work 1 row straight. Rep from **until 1 st rems. Fasten off. Work another main piece in same way.

Edging
With contrast wool, cast on 3 sts.
1st row: Sl1 purlwise, inc 1, k to end.
2nd row: K to last 2 sts, inc 1, k1. Rep these 2 rows 3 times more. 11 sts.
9th row: Sl1 purlwise, k2 tog, k to end.
10th row: K to last 3 sts, k2 tog, k1. Rep last 2 rows until 3 sts rem. Rep last 16 rows until straight edge measures 70 inches or 178 centimetres, or is long enough to fit around all 4 sides of cushion, ending after a 16th row. Leave these sts on holder for adjustment, either to add to or undo 16 rows as required.

To make up Pin out the two squares,

wrong side facing, and press lightly with warm iron and damp cloth. Join very neatly round 3 sides, insert cushion pad and close 4th side. Very neatly sew edging all round by straight edge, firm off the last sts when required.

Knitted tie

illustrated on page 215

Materials
1 × 50-gram ball of Patons Purple Heather 4-ply (Fingering 3-ply)
Pair of No. 11 (2) knitting needles

Measurements Width at broadest part, $2\frac{3}{4}$ inches; at narrowest, $1\frac{3}{8}$ inches; length, 51 inches.

Tension 7 stitches and 11 rows to 1 inch.

Abbreviations See page 13.

The tie is worked entirely in moss st and depends for its effect on the rainbow or random dye yarn.
Cast on 1 st.
1st row: (K1, p1, k1) into this st.
2nd row: K1, p1, k1.
3rd row: Inc in each of first 2 sts, k1. 5 sts.
4th row: K2, p1, k1, k1.
5th row: Inc in first st, k1, p1, inc in next st, k1. 7 sts.
6th row: K1, *p1, k1; rep from * to end.
7th row: Inc in first st, *p1, k1; rep from * to last 2 sts, inc in next st, k1, 9 sts.
8th row: K2, *p1, k1; rep from * to last st, k1.
9th row: Inc in first st, *k1, p1; rep from * to last 2 sts, inc in next st, k1. 9 sts.
10th row: As 6th row. Rep last 4 rows

until there are 19 sts or until tie measures required width.
Continue straight in moss st until tie measures 18 inches from point.
1st dec row: K2 tog tbl, *k1, p1; rep from * to last 3 sts, k1, k2 tog. 17 sts.
Next 17 rows: As 6th row.
2nd dec row: K2 tog tbl, p1, *k1, p1; rep from * to last 2 sts, k2 tog. 15 sts.
Next 17 rows: As 6th row. Rep last 36 rows, from 1st dec row, until 9 sts rem, then continue straight, always as 6th row, until tie measures 51 inches or required length. Cast off.

To make up Darn in any loose ends; press lightly with damp cloth and warm iron.

Crochet tie

illustrated on page 215

Materials
1 oz Wendy 4-ply Nylonized wool (Fingering 3-ply) in each of two colours
No. 3.00 (C/2) crochet hook

Measurements Width at widest part, 3 inches; at narrowest, $1\frac{5}{8}$ inches; length, $52\frac{1}{2}$ inches

Tension $6\frac{1}{2}$ stitches and 7 rows to 1 inch, measured on the straight.

Abbreviations See page 13.

Note The yarn must be darned in every 2 rows as it cannot be carried up along the side. When changing colours, leave only a short end to be darned, to avoid extra bulk.

With dark wool make 30 ch.
1st row: Turn, miss 1, 2dc(sc) into next

ch, 1dc(sc) into each of next 12ch, miss 1, 1dc(sc) in next ch, miss 1, 1dc(sc) into each of next 12 ch, 2dc(sc) into last ch.
2nd row: 1ch, 2dc(sc) into first dc(sc), 1dc(sc) into each of next 12dc(sc), miss 1, 1dc(sc), miss 1, 1dc(sc) into each of next 12dc(sc), 2dc(sc) into last dc(sc). This last row forms patt. Rep patt row, working 2 rows in light then 2 rows in dark, alternately, throughout.

When the 36th patt row (light) has been completed, begin shaping thus:
37th row: (dark), 1ch, 1dc(sc) into each of next 13dc(sc), miss 1, 1dc(sc), miss 1, 13dc(sc) (no incs at either end) (27dc(sc)).
38th and foll rows: 1ch, 2dc(sc) into first dc(sc), 11dc(sc), miss 1, 1dc(sc), miss 1, 11dc(sc), 2dc(sc) into last dc(sc).

When the 68th patt row has been completed from beginning,
69th row: (dark) 1ch, 12dc(sc), miss 1, 1dc(sc), miss 1, 12dc(sc). (25dc(sc)).
70th and foll rows: 1ch, 2dc(sc) in first dc(sc), 10dc(sc), miss 1, 1dc(sc), miss 1, 10dc(sc), 2dc(sc) in last dc(sc). When 80th patt row from start has been completed,
81st row: (dark) 1ch, 11dc(sc), miss 1, 1dc(sc), miss 1, 11dc(sc). (23dc(sc)).
82nd to 92nd rows: 1ch, 2dc(sc) in first dc(sc), 9dc(sc), miss 1, 1dc(sc), miss 1, 9dc(sc), 2dc(sc) into last dc(sc).
93rd row: (dark) 1ch, 10dc(sc), miss 1, 1dc(sc), miss 1, 10dc(sc). (21dc(sc)).
94th to 100th rows: 1ch, 2dc(sc) into first dc(sc), 8dc(sc), miss 1, 1dc(sc), miss 1, 8dc(sc), 2dc(sc) into last dc(sc).
101st row: (dark) 1ch, 9dc(sc), miss 1, 1dc(sc), miss 1, 9dc(sc). (19dc(sc)).
102nd to 108th rows: 1ch, 2dc(sc) into first dc(sc), 7dc(sc), miss 1, 1dc(sc), miss 1, 7dc(sc), 2dc(sc) into last dc(sc).
109th row: (dark) 1ch, 8dc(sc), miss 1, 1dc(sc), miss 1, 8dc(sc). (17dc(sc)).
110th to 116th rows: 1ch, 2dc(sc) into first dc(sc), 6dc(sc), miss 1, 1dc(sc), miss 1, 6dc(sc), 2dc(sc) into last dc(sc).
117th row: (dark) 1ch, 7dc(sc), miss 1, 1dc(sc), miss 1, 7dc(sc). (15dc(sc)).
118th to 124th rows: 1ch, 2dc(sc) into first dc(sc), 5dc(sc), miss 1, 1dc(sc), miss 1, 5dc(sc), 2dc(sc) into last dc(sc).
125th row: (dark) 1ch, 6dc(sc), miss 1, 1dc(sc), miss 1, 6dc(sc). (13dc(sc)).
126th to 132nd rows: 1ch, 2dc(sc) into first dc(sc), 4dc(sc), miss 1, 1dc(sc), miss 1, 4dc(sc), 2dc(sc) into last dc(sc).
133rd row: (dark) 1ch, 5dc(sc), miss 1, 1dc(sc), miss 1, 5dc(sc). (11dc(sc), 11 st). This completes tie shaping, until last few rows.
134th and foll rows: 1ch, 2dc(sc) into first dc(sc), 3dc(sc), miss 1, 1dc(sc), miss 1, 3dc(sc), 2dc(sc) into last dc(sc).
Cont thus, until 268th row has been completed, or until tie measures required length, ending after a 4th colour patt row.

Shape End Keeping colours correct.
Next row: 1ch, 4dc(sc), miss 1, 1dc(sc), miss 1, 4dc(sc).
Next row: 1ch, 3dc(sc), miss 1, 1dc(sc), miss 1, 3dc(sc).
Next row: 1ch, 2dc(sc), miss 1, 1dc(sc), miss 1, 2dc(sc).
Next row: 1ch, 1dc(sc), miss 1, 1dc(sc), miss 1, 1dc(sc). (3dc(sc)). Break wool and fasten off.

To make up Darn in all loose ends. Press lightly with damp cloth and warm iron.

Child's bonnet and scarf

illustrated on page 203

Materials
3 ozs of Wendy Nylonised 4-ply in yellow
Small ball of above wool in blue
Pair each of Nos 10 (3) and 11(2) knitting needles

Knitted and crochet ties

Measurements
Bonnet: round face edge: 16 inches
Scarf: 31½ inches long

Tension
About 7 sts and 9 rows to 1 inch over st-st

Abbreviations
See page 13.

Scarf
This is made in two similar pieces, joined at centre-back. For each piece, with No. 10 (3) needles and yellow cast on 41 sts.
1st row: K.
2nd row: Sl1, purlwise, k to end. Rep 2nd row 8 times more.
Begin patt: 1st row: As 2nd border row.
2nd row: Sl1 purlwise, k4, p to last 5 sts, k5. Rep these 2 rows once more.
5th row: Sl1 purlwise, k4, in yellow; join blue without cutting yellow and in blue (k3, put right needle into same st (that is last of 3k sts) *4 rows down* and pull loop through, put loop on point of left needle and k it tog tbl with next st – called k1 below – if you do not k the sts tog tbl, the contrast colour would be lost) rep to last 8 sts, k3; drop blue, join on another ball of yellow and k last 5 sts.
6th row: Yellow, Sl1 purlwise, k4, twist wools (lay one yarn over the other at back of work) and with blue p to last 5 sts, twist wools, k5 yellow.
7th row: With yellow, sl1 purlwise, k4, twist wools, k in blue to last 5 sts, twist wools, k5.
8th row: As 6th row.
9th row: Drop blue and second ball of yellow, and using first ball of yellow, slip 1 purlwise, k5; *k1 below, k3; rep from * ending k1 below, k6.
10th, 11th and 12th rows: As 2nd, 1st and 2nd rows.
The last 8 rows form patt. (4 rows alternately in blue and yellow, always with yellow border.) Rep patt until 36th

patt row has been completed. Discard blue and second ball of yellow for the meantime.

Begin shaping *37th row:* Slip 1 purlwise, k3, k2 tog, k to last 6 sts, k2 tog, k4.
38th, 39th and 40th rows: As 2nd, 1st and 2nd rows. Rep. last 4 rows until 21 sts rem. Work 3 rows after the last decs. Change to No. 11 [2] needles and k1, p1 rib, beg and ending alt rows either with k2, for neat knotted edge, or with p1 to keep rib right, until this half of scarf measures 15¾ inches long from cast-on edge, ending after a wrong-side row. Cast off in rib. Make another piece in exactly the same way.

Bonnet
With No. 10 (3) needles and yellow cast on 97 sts, and work exactly as for beg of scarf, for 28 patt rows in all, ending after a yellow stripe. Cut blue and second ball of yellow and reverse work, so that brim will fold over on to right side.
29th row: K1, p to last st, k1. Now working in st-st, cont without shaping until 6 inches of st-st have been worked, ending after a p row. Cast off 32 sts on each of next 2 rows. Work 4 rows without shaping on centre 33 sts, then dec 1 st at each end of next and every following 4th row, until 17 sts rem. Cont without shaping if necessary, until side edge of this part from the cast-off sets of 32 sts measures same length as cast-off 32. Cast off.

To make up Pin out pieces, with wrong side facing, to required measurements and press lightly with warm iron and damp cloth, avoiding the ribbing. Very neatly join the cast-off scarf ends and press seam lightly. Very neatly sew side extensions of bonnet to nearer set of cast-off sts, at each side of work, and press seams. Fold back brim on to right side of work and catch in place at sides. Sew the bonnet to the scarf, slightly gathering the lower edge of bonnet into the ribbed part and leaving about 24 rows of ribbing free at each end to tie. Press join.

Hut slippers

illustrated on page 219

Materials
3 ozs of Lister Lochinvar Double Knitting (knitting worsted)
Pair each of Nos 11 (2) and 9 (4) knitting needles
Pair of soles, size 5–6 or 10 inches long

Tension 6 sts and 8 rows to 1 inch

Abbreviations See page 13.

Both slipper-tops are worked alike. For each, with No. 11 (2) needles cast on 52 sts. Work 36 rows (4½ inches) in k1, p1 rib, inc 1 st in centre of last row. Break yarn. Sl 13 sts from each end of needle on to holders and rejoin yarn, right side of work facing, to centre 27 sts. Change to No. 9 (4) needles and st-st and work 52 rows straight. (6½ inches.) Then dec 1 st at each end of next and every alt row until 11 sts rem. Work 1 row after last decs. Cast off.
Very neatly join side edges of ribbed piece for back seam. With right side of work facing, rejoin wool to 26 heel sts and with No. 9 (4) needles and working in st-st, inc 1 st at each end of 1st and every alt row foll until there are 44 sts. Work 1 more row. Cast off.

To make up Press instep piece and heel piece lightly with damp cloth and warm iron. Sew shaped edges to heel piece neatly along side edges of instep piece as

far as they go without stretching. Press seams. Sew slipper-top to sole.

Junior hut slippers

illustrated on page 219

Materials
1 oz Wendy Nylonised 4-ply in each of red and white
Pair each of Nos. 12 (1) and 10 (3) knitting needles
Pair of soles, size 11–12 or 8 inches long

Tension About 7 sts and 9 rows to 1 inch

Abbreviations See page 13.

Both slipper-tops are worked alike. For each, with No. 12 (1) needles and red wool cast on 47 sts. Work 28 rows in k1, p1 rib, beg and ending alt rows with either k2, for neat knotted edge, or p1, to keep rib right, and making beading thus on *7th* and *21st rows:* K1, *m1, k2 tog; rep from * to end.
Break wool. Sl first 10, and last 10 sts on to holders. With No. 10 (3) needles work in st-st, on centre 27 sts, thus. Join white without breaking red.
Rows 1, 2, 3 and 4: 3 red, *3 white, 3 red; rep from * to end.
Rows 5, 6, 7 and 8: 3 white, *3 red, 3 white; rep from * to end. These 8 rows form patt. Rep them 4 times more then rows 1 to 4 once. Cut white. Working in red st-st, dec 1 st at each end of next and every row until 11 sts rem. Work 1 more row. Cast off.
Very neatly join sides of ribbed piece to form centre-back seam. Join red wool to 20 heel sts. With No. 10 (3) needles and working in st-st, inc 1 st at each end of 1st and every alt row foll until 40 sts are on needle. Work 1 more row. Cast off.

To make up Press instep piece and heel piece lightly with warm iron and damp cloth. Sew shaped edges of heel piece neatly along side edges of instep piece as far as they go without stretching. Press seams. Sew slipper top to sole. For ankle ties, use either cord, ribbon or crochet chain; fold ribbing in half to right side so that beadings coincide. Thread ties through holes.

Embroidery

Pillow cover

illustrated on page 223

Materials
1 piece black and red tweed or fairly
thick fabric, 18 by 16 inches
1 skein each black and red Patons
Turkey Rug wool
3 skeins, 2 in black and 1 in red stranded
embroidery thread
16 inch zip fastener
Matching thread

Trim the cut edges, making sure they
are perfectly straight. Fold the material
exactly in half, pin or tack along
halfway fold, then open out material and
draw the design on one half. With a
ruler or straight piece of wood draw two
lines, 1 inch apart, in the centre, and
other lines parallel to and about $\frac{1}{2}$ inch
apart. Against the outer lines place one
bowl or plate in centre with a smaller
one either side, at each side of work in
turn, and draw round them to form the
semi-circular scallop shapes, again
drawing other lines $\frac{1}{2}$ inch beyond round
the curves. This forms centre motif.
Similarly, either side of centre motif and
using same methods, draw single
parallel lines fully 1 inch apart and
about $8\frac{1}{2}$ inches away from the centre
lines at either side, and draw single
curves, the larger in the centre and
smaller ones at either side. Using three
strands of the embroidery thread at a
time, in matching colours, couch down
the four centre lines with black rug
wool: this means simply laying the wool
from one end to the other, and catching
it very neatly in place every $\frac{1}{4}$ inch with
the stranded cotton. Now couch a line

of red rug wool between each pair of
black centre lines. Couch red rug wool
round the centre pair of curves,
couching black wool as a sandwich
between them. For the outer motifs,
couch the two centre lines at each side
in red rug wool, and the curves in black
rug wool.
When the embroidery is completed, fold
the material right side in and machine
along the two long sides. Turn right side
out and sew in zip fastener, neatening
the ends.

Edging
To make the edging mark off, with pins,
along all four sides of the embroidered
half, every 2 inches. Starting at one
corner, couch down black wool all along
seams and fold, and at every pin mark,
loop the wool round your left forefinger,
catching this loop firmly in place: repeat
this all round.

Purse

illustrated on page 231

A pretty change purse makes a charming
gift and particularly when you have
embroidered it yourself. Purse frames
are obtainable from most large
department stores and needlework shops,
or you may find a beautiful antique
frame on a worn out purse in a junk
shop. Simply cut the worn purse away
and stitch a new purse to the old frame.

Materials
$2\frac{1}{4}$ inch wide purse frame

Pink evenweave fabric 14 by 8 inches
Matching lining fabric
Matching Drima thread
Non-woven interlining
Anchor stranded embroidery cotton,
Almond Green 0263; Muscat Green 0279;
Buttercup 0298; White 0402

Cut the fabric into two pieces, each
7 × 5 inches. Transfer the design
(diagram 1) on to one piece of the fabric

and work the design following the key
for colours and stitches.
When the embroidery is completed, press
the wrong side lightly. Make a pattern
following diagram overleaf and cut the
shape from the embroidered fabric and
from the piece of unembroidered fabric.
Cut the shape from the interlining twice.
Cut the shape from the lining fabric
twice. Place the interlinings on the
wrong sides of the two pieces of top

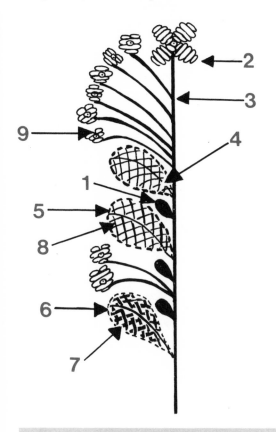

1

(including $\frac{1}{4}$ inch turnings)

Pillow cover, needlepoint pin cushion

fabric and making up as one, seam the two purse pieces together from ● to ●, right sides facing. Press the seam first flat and then open. Trim the seam and clip into the curves. Turn to the right side. The purse is attached to the frame as follows: pin and then baste the top of the purse to the frame. (You will find it easier to push pins through the holes in the frame to hold the fabric while you are basting.) Turn in ¼ inch of the fabric at the mouth of the purse and baste the fabric to the frame lightly, taking the basting stitches through the small holes in the purse frame. Make small oversewing stitches to secure the fabric to the frame, taking one stitch through every frame hole. Remove the basting stitches. Finish the edge with oversewing stitches in Muscat Green as illustrated. Make up the lining, right sides facing and trim the seam. Slip the lining into the purse and make a ¼ inch turning on the mouth of the purse lining. Slip stitch into position.

Florentine spectacles case

illustrated on page 227

This beautiful canvas work spectacles case is worked in a zigzag stitch called 'flame' and is one of the Florentine or Bargello patterns. For this kind of needlework the yarn colours must be chosen carefully to achieve the brilliant effect which is typical of Florentine embroidery. The colours should range from light to dark in a closely related scheme with one sharp or strongly contrasted colour. Florentine embroidery, which is amazingly quick to do, can be used to make a variety of acceptable accessory gifts, from belts and hairbands to handbags and smaller items.

Materials
12 by 12 inches single weave canvas, 16 threads to the inch.
1 skein Anchor tapisserie wool in each of the following colours: Cream 0366; Sand 0347; Amber 0427; Orange 0333; Brown 0379; Maroon 071
12 by 12 inches brown lining silk
1 skein Anchor stranded embroidery thread Cinnamon 0371
Tapestry needle
Embroidery needle

Draw out the shape of the case (opposite) and trace it on to the canvas, using either dark coloured water colour paint and a brush or a felt-tipped pen. Choose any of the colours for the foundation row and following the chart (diagram 1) work one row of the pattern right across the canvas from side to side of the case.

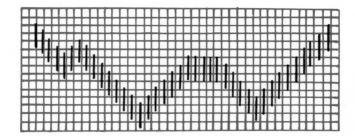

1

2 squares = 1 inch

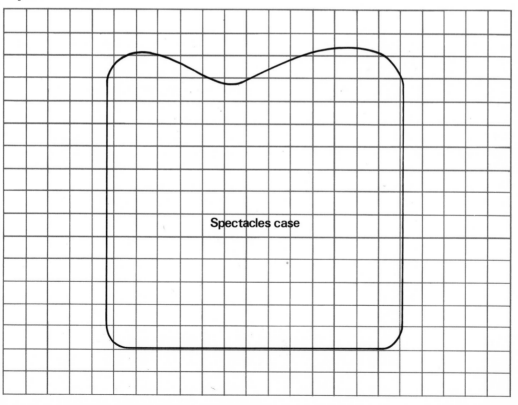

Spectacles case

You will find that you will work just over three repeats. Each stitch is worked over three threads of canvas. Once you have worked this foundation row it is a simple matter to work the rest of the pattern, changing to the next colour for each row. The flame pattern illustrated uses the yarn colours in the following order: cream, sand, amber, orange, brown and maroon.

When the embroidery reaches the edges of the outlined shape you will find that, to follow the curves, you may have to work over two or even a single thread. This is acceptable, as long as you keep to the order of the colours in the pattern.

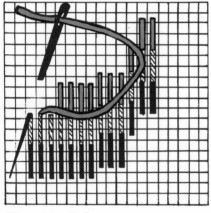

Florentine stitch

To make up When the embroidery is completed, stretch the canvas as follows: lay two or three thicknesses of blotting paper on a board and dampen the paper thoroughly. Place the embroidery face upwards on the dampened paper and using drawing pins, pin the work to the board, working from the centre of the top edge and outwards. Leave until the paper has dried out.

Unpin the canvas and trim the excess canvas away to within ½ inch of the embroidery. Fold the turnings to the wrong side and baste. It may be necessary to clip into the top edge curve to make the canvas fold more easily.

226

Make sure that no unworked canvas shows on the folded edge – if stitches have been missed out, this is the point at which they should be worked. Cut the lining fabric to match the trimmed canvas size and turn the ½ inch turnings to the wrong side. Press and then baste the lining to the wrong side of the canvas work, matching straight edges. Slip stitch all round.

Fold the spectacle case down the middle, matching the sides and oversew the long side and across the bottom with tiny, neat stitches.

Finish off these edges with Cretan stitch, worked in the stranded embroidery thread.

Needlepoint pin cushion

illustrated on page 223

Materials

Of double thread canvas, 10 threads to the inch:
    1 piece 5 inches square
    1 piece 13 by 2½ inches
Of Anchor stranded cotton:
    3 skeins in white
    2 skeins in each of black, poppy red, golden brown
4½ inches of 36 inch wide lining material
Matching thread for lining
4½ inch square of red felt
Matching red thread
Stuffing

Working from the chart, count 4 rows in from each edge, for turnings, before beginning the work. Tack a line down the centre of the canvas square, and work from the centre out. Use 6 strands of thread and work in simple cross-stitch, always keeping the upper stitch slanting in the same direction – upwards from right to left.

Florentine spectacles case

When the circle is completed, work the surrounding band. As the stitch repeat is only 2, the length can easily be adjusted. The original band was 120 threads long, and 17 threads deep.

/ = Black
X = Red
o = Gold

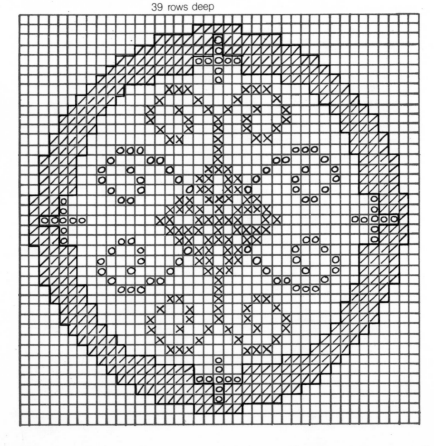

Chart for surrounding band

To make up When both pieces are finished, press them gently with a warm iron and a damp cloth. Trim round the circle leaving an unworked border about 4 threads deep for turnings. Cut 2 corresponding circles and one matching long strip from lining material. Form the long canvas work strip into a ring; fold the top turning to wrong side of work and buttonhole stitch in red along this top edge. Buttonhole stitch in black all round canvas work circle. Fit them in place and whip them together with the golden-brown thread. Make up the lining from the two circles (for top and

Pin cushion top: 39 stitches across
39 rows deep

base) and the encircling strip, leaving a small opening for inserting the stuffing. Insert stuffing and close the opening. Fit this pad inside the canvas work, keeping out the unworked canvas edges of the surrounding strip. Turn these back and lace them together, criss-cross, evenly over base of pad. Cut the red felt to match base circle and stitch very firmly in place.

Check cushion

illustrated on page 231

Checked material makes an interesting background for embroidery. The measurements given below are for the cushion illustrated but the instructions are easily adapted to suit any material. *See pages 229–233 for stitch diagrams.*

Materials
Piece of black and white needlecord 33 by 53 inches. (Cushion top will be 16½ by 26½ inches.)
Turquoise felt for circles
Matching turquoise thread
Anchor stranded thread in coral, black and white
Ric-rac or Vandyke braid to match felt
½ yard press stud tape

Cut out 12 circles from felt using a compass or drawing round base of a wine glass. Stitch one circle into each square of top of cushion, using matching thread. Using embroidery thread work a different pattern in each circle using coral, black and white. The circles in this cushion are filled as follows: Solid flystitch, two quarters in white and one quarter each in the other two colours; two curved segments, coral and white, in Roumanian stitch; two herringboned lines in right angles in black and coral with white star stitches between; stem stitch; wheatear stitch; back stitch; buttonhole-stitch and spider's web

filling. These circles can be filled to make a sample of stitches of your choice taken from a standard embroidery book.

To make up Fold the material in half. Seam each short end. Seam the remaining opening for 3½ inches at each end leaving central opening for inserting cushion. Turn in a small hem on each side of opening. Sew in press stud tape. Sew ric-rac braid all round top of cushion, ½ inch in from outer edge.

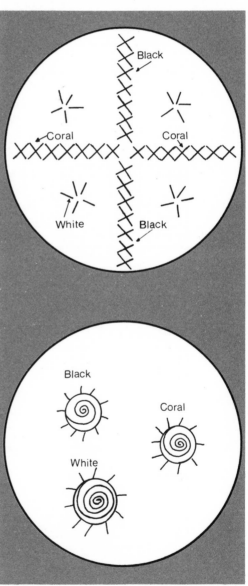

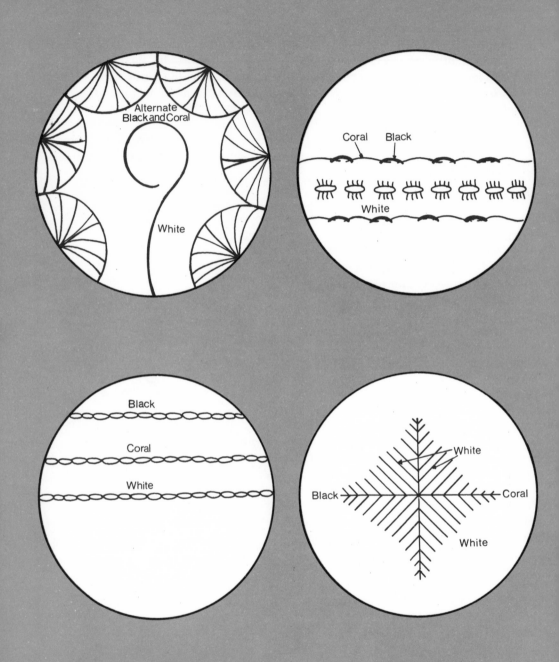

Alternate
Black and Coral

White

Coral   Black

White

Black

Coral

White

White

Black →   ← Coral

White

Purse, check cushion

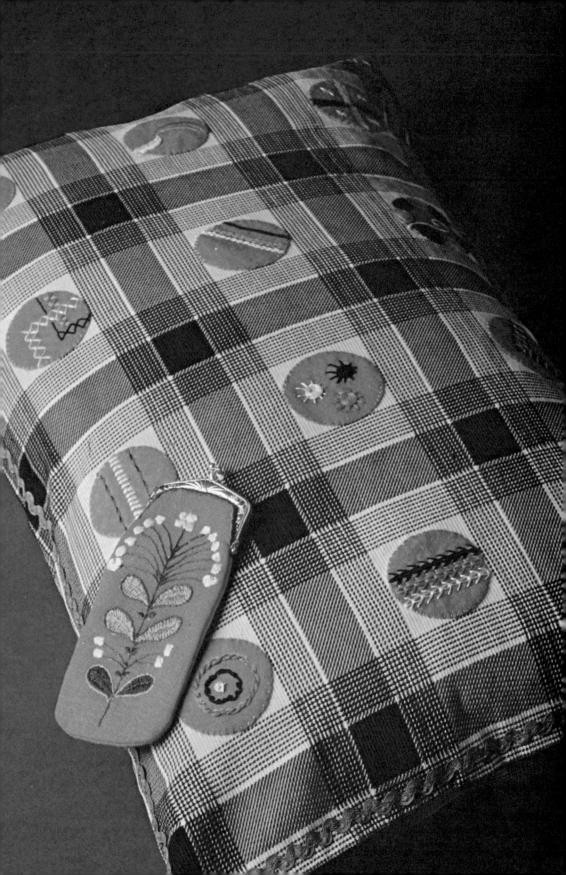

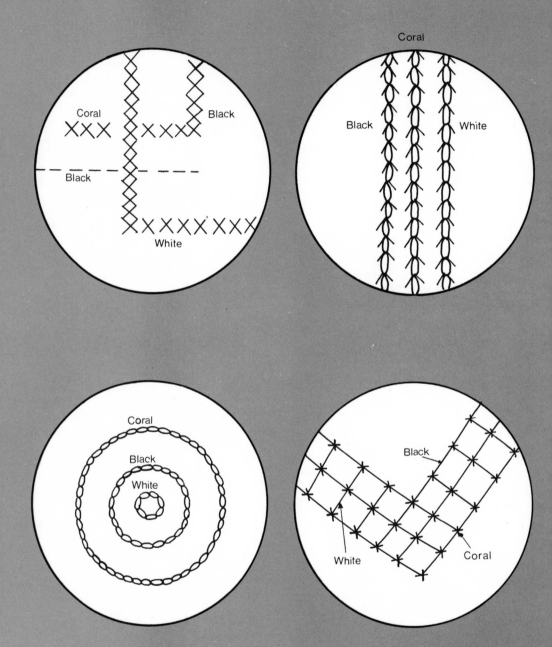

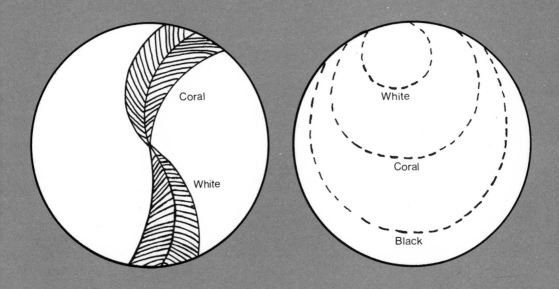

Coral

White

White

Coral

Black

Beadwork

Here are some lovely gifts to make using beads. Small embroidery beads have been used for some and wooden beads for others. The techniques are simple and you will have great fun making pretty and unusual jewellery for your friends. The woven bracelet illustrated was made on a bead loom but you can improvise a loom from a cardboard shoe box or make one from three pieces of wood. Two ways of improvising a loom are illustrated (diagrams 1 and 2).
The instructions for weaving are exactly the same whether you are working on a proper beadloom or a home-made loom.

one more warp thread than there are beads in the pattern and then, to give extra strength to the weaving, there should be one more thread on each side. The *two* outside threads are always used together.

Preparing the loom Cut the warp threads to the length of finished beading required plus 6 inches. (The bracelet has 10 beads across the width, so 13 threads were strung on the loom. The finished length of bracelet is 7 inches so 13 inches of thread would have been needed at least. In fact, beadweaving looms are

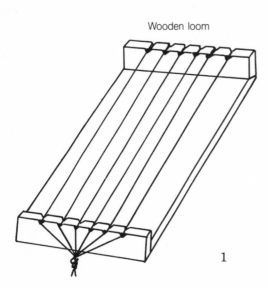

Wooden loom

1

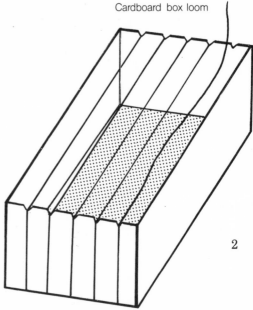

Cardboard box loom

2

The principle of bead weaving The lengthwise threads are called the warp threads and beads lie between them. Therefore the distance between the warp threads must be the same as the size of the bead you are using. Remember this point when cutting the notches on a home-made loom. There must always be

longer than this and it was necessary to cut the threads 20 inches long to allow for stringing up.)
Thread the needle with working thread. Tie the end to the double threads on the left of the loom. (Do not have too long a

Choker, woven bracelet, black and yellow necklace, white bead necklace

thread or it will become tangled, about 14 inches is long enough.) Weave four rows without beads to strengthen the weaving. Finish on the left. With the needle, pick up the beads needed for the first row of pattern. (If you are following a set pattern, start counting beads from the left.) Push the beads down on to the thread and place the thread with beads under the warp threads so that a bead lies between each of the warp threads. Press the beads up between the warp threads with a finger of the free hand (diagram 3). Pass the needle from right to left back through the hole in each bead, thus securing them between the warp threads (diagram 4). Pull the thread tight but not too tightly or the straight edge of the weaving will be distorted. Continue in the same way until you have the desired length of beading.

Finishing off Work two or three rows of weaving without beads. Take the working thread back through the last row but one of the weaving. Knot off and cut the thread. Lift the warp threads off the loom. Cut the warp threads to about 3 inches. Tie a loose knot in each thread, and take the thread back through the weaving. Move the knot up to the last row of beads with a pin. This is the method used if a fastening is not being attached to the weaving.

Designs in beadweaving You can work out your own designs for beadweaving on squared paper using coloured felt tipped pens. Simply decide the width of the finished work and the length. Count off the number of squares and colour them in, each square representing one bead. Remember, when following a pattern, the first bead picked up is the bead on the left of your drawn out pattern.

Woven bracelet

illustrated on page 235

Materials

Assorted embroidery beads, seven different tones of blue and green, plus white

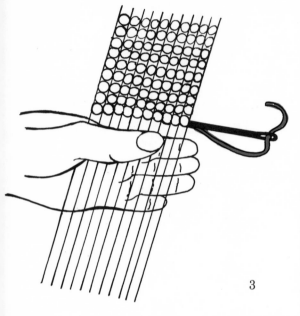

3

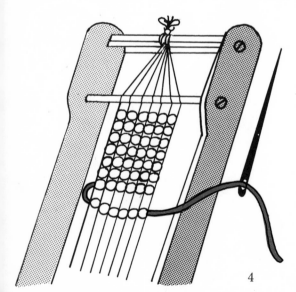

4

Linen beading thread
Beading needle
Bracelet clasp (jeweller's findings)

The bracelet is worked in a random
pattern as already described, with ten
beads across the width. It is finished off
as follows:
Work two rows of weaving without
beads. Thread warp threads 2 and 3 back
through the beads so that they lie
alongside the doubled outside threads.
Thread all four threads through five
more beads. Do the same with the
remaining beads, working in groups.

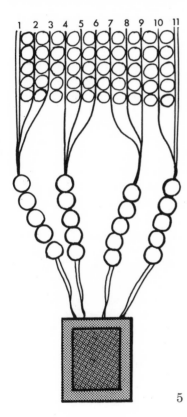

5

Thus, warp threads 1, 2, 3 have five
beads on them, 4, 5 and 6 have five
beads, 7, 8 and 9 have five beads and 10
and 11 have five beads. Knot the ends to
a bracelet fastening, (diagram 5). Work
the other end of the bracelet in the same
way.

Key ring mascot

illustrated on page 239

Amusing key ring mascots looking like
little character dolls can be made very
quickly and cheaply, using wooden or
plastic beads and wire. Choose beads in
colours to dress the doll and paint
features on the head bead.
The diagram gives the pattern for
threading up the mascot doll.
The mascot is fastened to a bought key
ring unit.

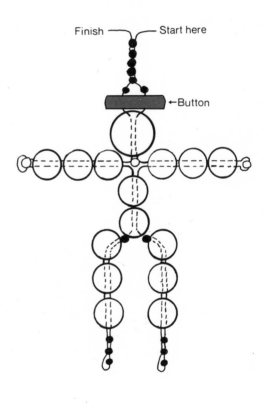

Bead butterfly

illustrated on page 239

The bead butterfly uses a different
beadwork technique, that of threading
beads on to wire. Silver jeweller's wire
is the best but 10 amp fuse wire works
just as well.

Materials

Silver wire or fuse wire
Pale blue and silver embroidery beads
Silver baguette beads
Large silver metal bead
Blue and green sequins
Brooch fastening (jeweller's findings)
Epoxy adhesive

Each wing is made in the same way and the wings are joined in forming the body and head.

Making a wing Cut 36 inches of wire and thread two silver beads on to it, centring them on the wire. This makes the first row. After this, *both* ends of the wire are threaded through each row of beads (diagram 1)

2nd row Thread 1 silver, 1 baguette, 1 silver bead.

3rd row 2 silver, 7 blue, 2 silver.

4th row 2 silver, 11 blue, 2 silver.

From this point, you will be able to follow diagram 2. Shape the wing as

shown in this diagram until the centre is reached. Do not cut the wires. Make the second wing in the same way.

The body is made up of two rows of

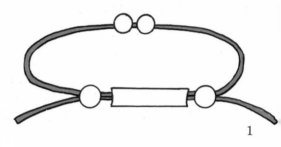

1

silver baguette beads, with a single silver bead between each. The tail consists of seven silver beads and the head is one large metal bead with a single silver bead on the end of the twisted wires for antennae.

Glue the brooch fastening to the back with epoxy adhesive. Attach sequins with epoxy adhesive.

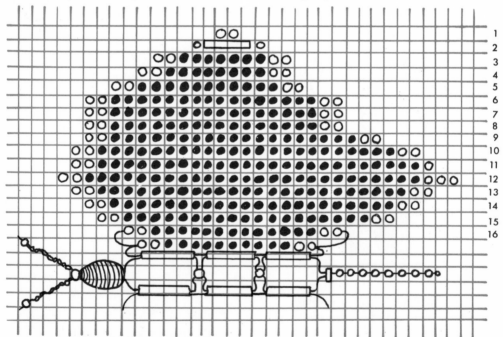

2. On the final, inside, row of the wing, the right-hand wire links the two body beads to the three baguette beads. It then goes through the head bead, makes the antennae and is twisted under the head bead to finish. The left-hand wire goes through the baguettes, into the tail and is twisted just above the tail to finish.

Wooden bead necklace, bead butterfly, key ring mascot

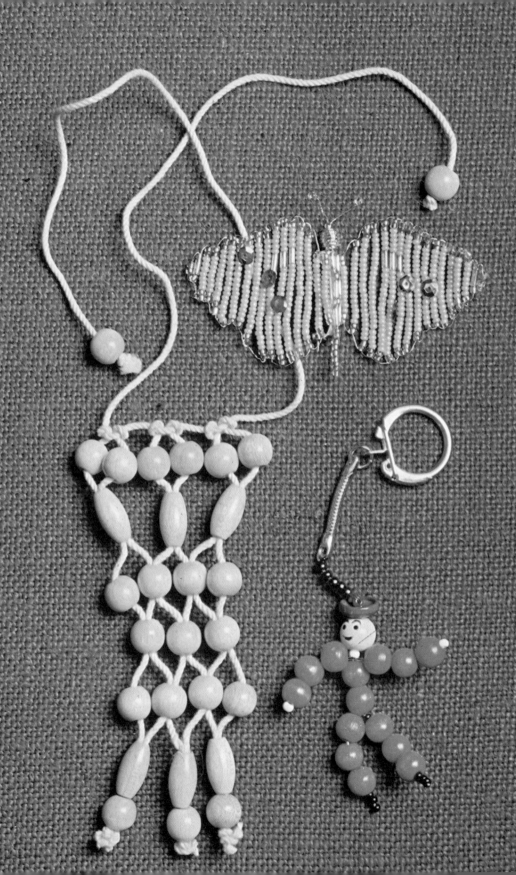

Wooden bead necklace

illustrated on page 239

This necklace uses a different technique: the cords on which the beads are strung are first knotted on to a leader cord. The pattern is achieved by passing the cords through adjacent beads. Soap the ends of the cords to make bead threading easier. Diagram 1 gives the pattern for the necklace illustrated.

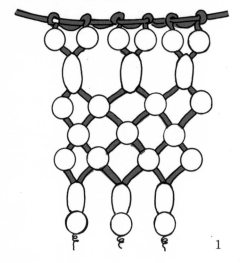

1

Materials
20 round wooden beads
6 long wooden beads
Macramé twine

Cut three lengths of twine, 16 inches long and one length 20 inches long. Double the three lengths and attach them to the long length of twine using the macramé knot (diagram 2).

2

String one round bead on each of the six ends. Pass both ends of each pair of cords through a single long bead. The third row has four round beads in

it; bead 1 goes on to cord one; bead 2 is strung on to cords 2 and 3; bead 3 goes on to cords 4 and 5 and the fourth bead goes on to cord 6.
Three round beads make up the next row: cords 1 and 2 go through the first bead; cords 3 and 4 go through the second bead and cords 5 and 6 go through the third bead.
The next row (5) has 4 round beads and the sixth row has the 6 cords passing through three long beads in pairs. One round bead is strung after each long bead and the ends knotted off.
Tie a single round bead on the necklace ends. Knot the ends to fasten the necklace.

White bead necklace

illustrated on page 235

Materials
2 packets small white embroidery beads
Linen beading thread
Necklace fastening (jeweller's findings)
2 beading needles

Cut a length of thread 90 inches long. Thread a needle on both ends.
Thread 12 beads on to the thread and centre the beads. Pass both needles

through one more bead. Thread 6 beads on to the left-hand needle and 6 beads on to the right, then pass both needles through one more bead. Continue threading the same way until the necklace is the desired length or until the thread has been covered. Make a loop of 18 beads on one end, taking one end of thread back through the fourth bead and knotting off the thread. Knot a large bead onto the other end of the necklace.

Black and Yellow necklace

illustrated on page 235

Materials
1 packet yellow beads
1 packet black beads
Linen beading thread or nylon thread
2 beading needles

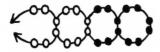

One whole pattern has 12 beads in it,
8 making a complete circle and four
making a half circle. Thread the first
6 beads on 90 inches of thread and pass
both ends through 2 more beads. Thread
2 more beads of the same colour onto
each end of the thread and then cross
the ends through 2 beads of the contrast
colour. Complete the circle in the second
colour with 6 beads, crossing the threads
through the last 2. Proceed in this way
until the necklace is the desired length.
Knot off the ends.

Choker

illustrated on page 235

Materials
1 packet of small beads in each of the
following colours:
scarlet, black, yellow, white
1 packet mixed small beads
4 beading needles
Linen or nylon thread
1 large bead

The choker is made separately from the
single strand attaching ends of the
necklace.
Cut two 90 inch lengths of thread and
put a needle on both ends of each length.
Thread one bead onto each length and
pin the beads to a pincushion or a
beading board.
Follow the diagram for the pattern

using the four ends as indicated. The
necklace illustrated has 3 repeats in
black, 8 in yellow, 3 in black, 8 in
scarlet, 3 in black, 8 in yellow, finishing
with 3 black. Fasten off the four ends by
crossing ends and threading back
through 3 patterns.

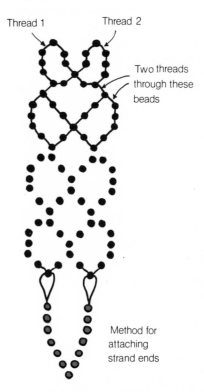

Thread 1   Thread 2

Two threads
through these
beads

Method for
attaching
strand ends

Make the ends
Make the looped end by cutting a 16 inch
length of thread and putting a needle on
each end. Thread 28 beads of mixed
colours on the thread passing both
needles through the last bead to make a
loop. Thread single beads onto both
threads until strand measures 5 inches.
Separate threads. Thread 8 beads onto
each, pass threads through the loops of
the last choker pattern (black) and back
through the 8 beads. Knot off. This
fastens the choker section to the strand
fastening.
Make the other strand fastening in the
same way but begin by threading on a
single large bead.

Candlemaking

Candlemaking is a craft which is open to everyone; hand-made candles are always very acceptable gifts and are sure sellers at fund-raising sales and bazaars.
The basic materials for candle making can be obtained in most large towns and cities and many of the suppliers will supply their goods by post. Moulds, wax, candle colours and wicks are all part of the candlemaker's basic equipment but if you want to make it an almost no-cost craft, old candles can be melted down and wax crayons used for colouring and decoration.

Materials
A large supply of newspaper
Large and small metal containers for melting down wax
Sugar thermometer
Spoons
Sharp knives
Wooden sticks
Paraffin wax
Stearin
Candle colourings
Candlewick
Moulds of different kinds

Paraffin wax Wax for candlemaking is supplied in solid blocks or in powdered form. Both are equally good but the powdered form is easier to use as the blocks have to be shaved down or broken up before melting.

Stearin Stearin is a type of wax which allows wax dyes to dissolve readily and with complete colour suspension. Stearin is not essential but it does produce a more opaque and intense colour and a more durable candle. It also acts as a mould release.

Candlewicks Authentic candlewicking, available from candlemakers' supply shops, is bleached linen thread, woven and graded to burn a certain area of wax without smoking or excessive melting. It is essential to use the right grade of wick in a candle: a wick designated as 1 inch will successfully burn a candle 1 inch in diameter. It will also burn a 1 inch hole in a thicker candle which will result in the wick being drowned in a pool of wax!
If candlewick really is impossible to obtain, you can make candlewicking at home, but it is not quite as satisfactory as the real thing. To make candlewick, use soft cotton string. Cut a length about 12 feet. Dissolve one tablespoon of salt and two tablespoons of borax in one cup of water. Put the string in the solution and let it soak for about 12 hours. Hang to dry out completely. When the string is dry, coat it by dipping in wax and use as directed.

Candle colours Candle wax dyes in powder form and in discs are available from craft shops. A small pinch of powder to a pint of liquid wax is usually enough to achieve a good colour. If the colour is too intense it can spoil the candle's glow.
Wax crayons can be used but experiment first before using them to make sure that you can achieve the effect you want.

Moulds Craft shops sell an exciting selection of ready-made moulds for candlemaking but improvised moulds work very well and produce fascinating shapes. Many kinds of household containers can be used as long as they

Twisted candle, sand candle, jewelled candle, moulded candle, layered candle

are leakproof and do not dissolve under heat of melted wax. Some plastics will do this and it is best to experiment with hot water first. Yoghurt and cream cartons, food cans, cardboard boxes and rubber balls are just a few of the things which can be used but remember that the candle has to be removed when set. The mould must therefore be able to be torn off the candle, or the neck must be large enough for the candle to slip out. Some cartons have a small mouth and a large base, and in this instance, the base can be cut off when the candle has set and the candle removed from this end. If cardboard moulds are used, oil the inside first so that the candle slips out more easily.

Measure out the powdered or broken up wax. Measure out the stearin – 1 part stearin to ten parts of wax. Melt the stearin gently in a saucepan and when dissolved, add the colouring agent. Melt the paraffin wax in a second saucepan and when this has melted, add the stearin colour mixture. Take care not to overheat wax and do not use water near it while it is hot or it will splutter and may cause burns.

The various temperatures for candlemaking are given with the specific instructions.

Moulded candles

Ready-made moulds, made of either latex or metal have no wick holes and these must be pierced with a needle. Dip the wick in wax to protect it then thread the wick through the hole and tie the other end to a wooden stick. Rest this across the top of the mould. Seal the hole and wick with mould seal or clay. (Plasticine will not do as it melts.) Support the mould by hanging it on a rack, which can easily be improvised by resting two long sticks across two or three bricks, books or flower pots. Heat the wax to 180°F and pour slowly into the mould. Tap the sides to release air bubbles. After a little while, a well will form round the wick as the cooling wax contracts. Prod the surface to break the skin and top up with wax, again heated to 180°F. Do this as often as the well forms. When the wax has completely hardened, peel back the surface of the mould with soapy hands. (The mould should be washed and dried carefully after use.) Trim the wick and polish the candle in the hands. If the mould is a decorative one, colour can be added by mixing a little water paint with soap. Paint the candle, rubbing some into the crevices of the design and then rub most of the colour off just before it dries. Use water colour sparingly as it does not burn and may clog the wick. An attractive zig zag candle can be made by first casting 5 yellow, 5 red and 4 turquoise wax discs in an egg poacher. When set, a wick hole is made in the centre of each disc. These are then dropped into a glass mould, one on top of the other so that the curved bases face alternately up and down. Very strongly dyed brown wax, heated to 240°F, is then poured in and the mould shaken to release any trapped air. The candle is then cooled rapidly and finally carved by hand and dipped into hot wax (230°F) to seal and gloss.

Improvised moulds If a simple container such as a soup can is being used as a mould, simply pour the melted wax into the can (180°F). Tie the wick to a stick and balance it across the top of the can. Leave to cool, topping up the well as before. Remove the hardened candle either by removing the bottom of the can and pushing the candle out or dip the can in hot water for a few moments.

For a different effect, make a 'jewelled' candle. Break up pieces of different coloured wax and stick them to the sides of the can with a little melted wax. Pour the wax in little by little, so that it sets round the pieces without melting them; or pieces of coloured wax can be added to a completed candle by dipping the pieces in melted wax and pressing them on the candle sides.

The 'jewelled' yellow and lilac candle (illustrated on page 243) is made by pouring yellow and lilac wax into round ice-cube moulds to half-fill these. When set, these half-spheres are fixed with wax glue to the sides of a white candle. The candle is then dipped into hot wax (230°F) to seal and gloss.

Carved candles

This type of candle involves a dipping technique, the oldest known method of making a candle. Fill a jug with wax heated to 180°F. The jug should be just deeper than the intended length of candle. Tie a short length of wick to a stick and dip it into the wax. Hold it in the air for about 30 seconds and the wax will harden. Dip again and again until the candle is thick enough. If a succession of different colours are used for dipping until each layer is about ¼ inch thick, the completed candle can be carved back in some areas to reveal the different colours.

For a simpler surface decoration, try impressing a finished candle with various sharp objects such as nails or screwheads, or small cookie cutters.

Twisted candles

These are made by flattening a dipped candle while still soft with a rolling pin. The flattened strip is held in both hands and gently twisted. The candle is then plunged into cold water to harden.

Layered candles

To make layered candles, have ready a large container of cold water. Pierce the can at the bottom and thread the wick through. Knot it underneath and then seal off with clay. Tie the other end to a stick and rest the stick across the can. Pour a little wax into the bottom of the can and stand it in the cold water, resting the can against the side of the container (diagram 1). As each layer sets, pour in different coloured waxes, layer by layer until the can is filled. (diagram 2)

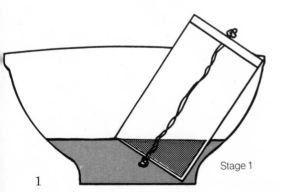

Stage 1

1

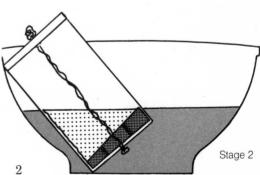

Stage 2

2

245

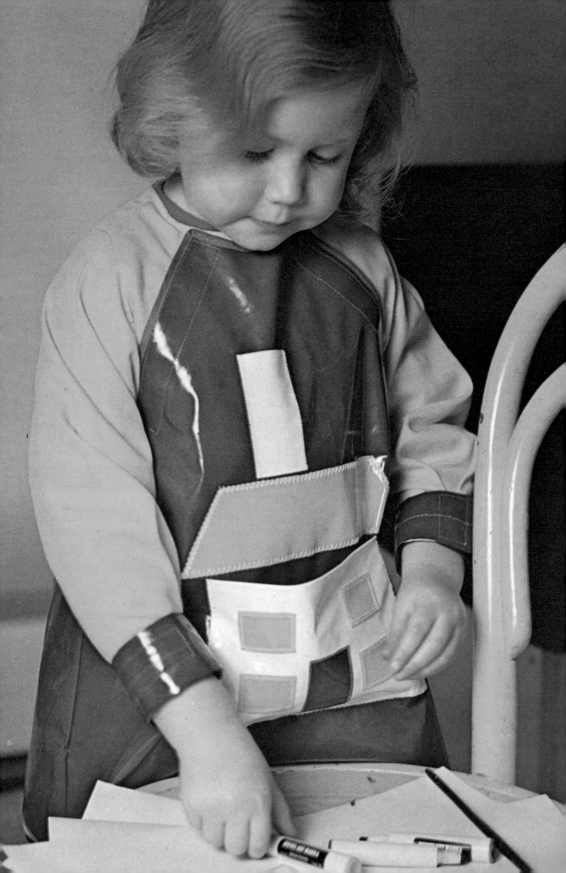

Making Things for Children

Adding Inspiration

Half the fun of making children's clothes lies in adding an individual touch to an often simple pattern. This chapter is designed to be helpful in several ways. There are smocking, crochet, embroidery and other ideas to make basic patterns more exciting. There is also an invaluable range of money-savers in the form of colourful knitting, sewing and crochet patterns. These are practical things that are usually expensive to buy. There are cheerful play clothes, beautiful party things and an excellent everyday range, as well as a comprehensive selection of baby clothes and nursery accessories.

Use the chapter as an "ideas-bank". You will be able to come back to it again and again, making up the patterns in other sizes and different colours, or adapting the ideas to your own particular style.

The sewing machine is a willing ally. Make it work for you. Use it to its full potential to help speed up sewing work. This will give you more time to spend on the decorative touches.

The many patterns illustrate a wide cross-section of different methods and crafts used for making children's things. As well as knitting, crochet, sewing and embroidery, there are instructions for patchwork, appliqué, collage, quilting, tie-dyeing and fabric painting. These are all original ideas, designed by a mother with young children for other mothers, grand-mothers and everyone who loves to make things at home.

Illustration on page 246:
Play apron (page 295)

Baby things

Knitted Matinee Set

This matinée set is ideal for a new baby girl. The dress has a decorative openwork stitch on the skirt and the coat, with an almost tweedy look, is a warm and practical idea. As an extra smart touch, the bonnet is decorated with a crochet flower motif. The set can be made up in a wide range of alternative colours, or the dress could be knitted in white and the coat and other accessories in navy blue and white or emerald green and white.

Materials

Lister Baby Bel 4-ply Courtelle or
Lee Target Lullaby 4-ply Courtelle,
(Fingering 3-ply)
25 gr balls:
Dress: 2 main colour, 2 contrast
Coat: 3 main colour, 2 contrast
Hat: 1 main colour, 1 small ball contrast
Bootees or mittens: 1 main colour
3 buttons for dress
4 buttons for coat
Ribbon for hat, mittens and bootees
Pairs of 10 (3) and 12 (1) knitting needles
No. 3·00 mm (D/3) crochet hook

Measurements To fit an 18 (20) inch chest.

Tension About 6 sts (1 complete patt) measures 1 inch.

Abbreviations, needle and size note
See pages 12 and 13.

Dress
Back

Using No. 10(3) needles and M, cast on 81(87) sts and work thus:

1st and 2nd rows K. Change to C.
3rd row K 1, sl 1 pw, * k 5, sl 1 pw. Rep from * to last st, k 1.
4th row P 1, sl 1 pw, * p 5, sl 1 pw. Rep from * to last st, p 1.
5th row K 1, sl 1 pw, * k 1, m 1, SK2tog.PO, m1, k 1, sl 1 pw. Rep from * to last st, k 1.
6th row As 4th row. Change to M.
7th and 8th rows K. Change to C.
9th row K 4, sl 1 pw, * k 5, sl 1 pw. Rep from * to last 4 sts, k 4.
10th row P 4, sl 1 pw, * p 5, sl 1 pw. Rep from * to last 4 sts, p 4.
11th row K 1, k 2 tog, m 1, sl 1 pw, * k 1, m 1, SK2tog.PO, m 1, k 1, sl 1 pw. Rep from * to last 4 sts, k 1, m 1, SKPO, k 1.
12th row As 10th row. Change to M.
These rows form patt. Cont straight in patt until work measures 7½(8) ins ending with a 2nd or 8th patt row. Break off C. Now use M. to complete the Back.
Next row (P 1, k 1) 1(4) times, (p 1, k 2 tog, p 1, k 1) 15(13) times, p 1, k 2 tog, p 1, (k 1, p 1) 0(5) times. 65(73) sts.
Next row * K 1, p 1. Rep from * to last st, k 1.
Cont in rib until work measures 8½(9) ins ending after a wrong side row.

Shape Armholes

Cast off 3(5) sts at beg of next 2 rows, then dec 1 st each end of every row until 49(53) sts rem. Cont in rib until work measures 10(11) ins ending after a wrong side row.

Divide for Back Opening

1st row (P 1, k 1) 13(14) times, p 1, leave rem 22(24) sts on a thread for other side. Work one row in rib.
Next row (buttonhole). Rib to last 3 sts, m 1, k 2 tog, p 1.

Cont in rib making a 2nd buttonhole 1¼ ins from base of first buttonhole and cont until work measures 12(13) ins ending at armhole edge.

Shape Shoulder

Cast off 6(7) sts at beg of next 2 armhole edge rows and leave rem 15 sts on a thread for neckband.
Return to other sts, rejoin yarn, cast on 5 sts for underflap and work to match other side, omitting buttonholes and reversing shoulder shaping.

Front

Work as for Back until armhole shapings are completed then cont in rib until work measures 11(12) ins ending after a wrong side row.

Shape Neck

1st row Rib 14(16) sts, k 2 tog, k 1, leave next 15 sts on spare needle for neckband and rem 17(19) sts on a st holder for other side.
2nd row P 2, rib to end.
3rd row Rib to last 3 sts, k 2 tog, k 1.
Rep 2nd and 3rd rows 3 times more, then 2nd row once more.

Shape Shoulder

Cast off 6(7) sts at beg of next row. Rib one row. Cast off rem sts.
Go back to other sts for other side.
1st row K 1, SKPO, rib to end.
2nd row Rib to last 2 sts, p 2.
Work to match other side, reversing shaping.

Sleeves

Using No. 12(1) needles cast on 49(55) sts, and work 6 rows in p 1, k 1 rib, thus beg and ending 1st row p 1, and 2nd row k 1.
Change to No. 10(3) needles and cont in rib until work measures 2 ins.

Shape Top

Cast off 3(5) sts at beg of next 2 rows, then dec 1 st at each end of next and every foll 4th row until 33 sts rem. Now dec 1 st each end of every row until 21 sts rem. Cast off 4 sts at beg of next 4 rows. Cast off rem sts.

Neckband

Join shoulders. Using No. 12(1) needles, rib across 15 sts of left side of Back, pick up and k 10 sts down left side of front, rib across 15 sts on spare needle, pick up and k 10 sts up right side of front, rib across 15 sts at right side of Back. (65 sts.) Work 5 rows in rib as set, working final buttonhole on 3rd row. Cast off in rib.

To make up

Press carefully, omitting ribbing. Join side and sleeve seams. Sew in sleeves. Sew under-flap in position at lower edge. Sew on buttons. Press seams.

Coat
Back

Using No. 10(3) needles and M, cast on 63(69) sts and work in patt as for Back of Dress until work measures 8(8½) ins ending after a wrong side row.

Shape Armholes

Cast off 3 sts at beg of next 2 rows, then dec 1 st at each end of every row until 51(57) sts rem. Cont in patt until work measures 12(13) ins.

Shape Shoulders

Cast off 6(7) sts at beg of next 4 rows. Leave rem 27(29) sts on spare needle for neckband.

Left front

1st size only Using No. 10(3) needles and M, cast on 30 sts and k 2 rows. Change to C.
3rd row K 1, sl 1 pw, * k 5, sl 1 pw. Rep from * to last 4 sts, k 4.
4th row P 4, sl 1 pw, * p 5, sl 1 pw. Rep from * to last st, p 1.
Cont in patt keeping row ends correct until work measures same as Back to armhole shaping.
2nd size only Using No. 10(3) needles and M, cast on 33 sts and work in patt as given for Back of Dress until work measures same as Back to armhole shaping.

Knitted matinée set

Both Sizes. Shape Armhole

Cast off 3 sts at beg of next row, then work one row in patt. Now dec 1 st at armhole edge on every row until 24(27) sts rem. Cont in patt until work measures 10 rows less than Back to shoulder shaping, ending at armhole edge.

Shape Neck

1st row Patt to last 10(11) sts, k 2 tog, k 1, leave rem 7(8) sts on thread for neckband.
2nd row P 2, patt to end.
3rd row Patt to last 3 sts, k 2 tog, k 1.
Rep 2nd and 3rd rows 3 times more, then 2nd row once more.

Shape Shoulder

Cast off 6(7) sts at beg of next row. Patt one row. Cast off rem sts.

Right front

1st size only Using No. 10(3) needles and M, cast on 30 sts and k 2 rows. Change to C.
3rd row K 4, sl 1 pw, * k 5, sl 1 pw.
Rep from * to last st, k 1.
4th row P 1, sl 1 pw, * p 5, sl 1 pw.
Rep from * to last 4 sts, p 4.
Cont in patt as set and complete to match Left Front reversing all shapings and working SKPO in place of k 2 tog at neck edge.
2nd size only Work as Left Front, reversing all shapings and working SKPO in place of k 2 tog at neck edge.

Sleeves

Using No. 12(1) needles and M, cast on 35(39) sts and work in k 1, p 1 rib. Change to No. 10(3) needles.
1st row K 4(3), * K21N, k 2. Rep from * to last 4(3) sts, K 21N, k 3(2). 45(51) sts.
2nd row K.
Cont in patt as given for Back, beg with a 3rd row, until work measures 6(7) ins.

Shape Top

Cast off 3 sts at beg of next 2 rows, then dec 1 st at each end of next and every foll 4th row until 33 sts rem. Dec 1 st at each end

of every alt row until 21 sts rem. Cast off 4 sts at beg of next 4 rows. Cast off rem sts.

Left front band

Using No. 12(1) needles and M, cast on 7 sts and work in k 1, p 1 rib until band is long enough, slightly stretched, to reach neck shaping. Leave sts on holder for neckband. Sew band neatly in position.

Right front band

First place pins on Left Front Band for buttonholes, the first pin one inch below neck shaping, with 2 more pins 1¼ ins below each other. Work as Left Front Band ending on same row as rib on Left Front Band, working buttonholes when positions are reached thus:
Buttonhole row Rib 3, m 1, k 2 tog, rib 2.
Leave sts on holder for neckband. Sew band neatly in place.

Neckband

Sew up shoulder seams. Now using No. 12(1) needles and M, rib across 7 sts of Right Front Band, k across 7(8) sts on thread, pick up and k 10 sts up right front, k across 27(29) sts at back neck, pick up and k 10 sts down left front, then k across 7(8) sts on thread, and finally rib across 7 sts of Left Front Band. 75(79) sts.
Work 5 rows in rib, working final buttonhole on 3rd row.

To make up

Join side and sleeve seams. Set in sleeves. Sew on buttons. Press seams.

Bootees

Using No. 10(3) needles cast on 39 sts.
** **1st row** * P 1, k 1. Rep from * to last st, p 1.
2nd row * K 1, p 1. Rep from * to last st, k 1.
Rep 1st and 2nd rows until work measures 2 ins.
Next row P 1, * m 1, k 2 tog. Rep from * to end. Work 3 more rows in rib **.

Shape Instep
1st row K 25, turn.
2nd row K 11, turn.
Work 16 rows in g st on these 11 sts. Break off yarn. Rejoin yarn to lower edge of instep, pick up and k 14 sts up instep, k across 11 sts on needle, pick up and k 14 sts down other side of instep, and k rem 14 sts. 67 sts in all. K 5 rows across all sts.

Shape Foot
1st row K 2 tog, k 25, SK2tog.PO, k 7, SK2tog.PO, k 25, k 2 tog.
2nd and alt rows K.
3rd row K 2 tog, k 23, SK2tog.PO, k 5, SK2tog.PO, k 23, k 2 tog.
5th row K 2 tog, k 21, SK2tog.PO, k 3, SK2tog.PO, k 21, k 2 tog.
7th row K 2 tog, k 19 SK2tog.PO, k 1, SK2tog.PO, k 19, k 2 tog.
Cast off rem sts knitwise.

To make up

Sew up foot and back seam. Thread ribbon through holes in rib. Press carefully.

Mittens

Using No. 10(3) needles, cast on 31 sts and work as given for Bootees from ** to **. Work 24 rows in g st.

Shape Top
1st row (K 2 tog, k 4) 5 times, k 1.
2nd and alt row K.
3rd row (K 2 tog, k 3) 5 times, k 1.
5th row (K 2 tog, k 2) 5 times, k 1.
7th row (K 2 tog, k 1) 5 times, k 1.
Break yarn, thread through rem sts, draw up and fasten off.
Sew side seam. Thread ribbon through holes in rib.

Bonnet
Side pieces (Two required)

Using No. 10(3) needles cast on 45 sts and k 4 rows.
Continue thus:
1st row K 21, SK2tog.PO, k 21.
2nd and every alt row P.
3rd row K 20, SK2tog.PO, k 20.
Cont in st st dec 2 sts in centre of every alt row until 21 sts rem. Still dec in centre of row as before, dec 1 st at each end of every alt row until 5 sts rem. Cast off.

Centre piece

Using No. 10(3) needles, cast on 20 sts and cont in g st until work measures 5 ins. Dec 1 st at each end of next and every 4th row until 8 sts rem. K 3 rows. Cast off.

Motif

Using No. 3·00 (D/3) hook, make 4 ch, and join into a circle with a sl st.
1st round Work 10 dc (sc) into circle, join with a sl st.
2nd round 2 tr (dc) in each dc (sc) working into front loop of dc (sc) only, join with a sl st.
3rd round 3 d tr (tr) in each dc (sc) of 1st round, working into back loop only.
4th round * 1 dc (sc) in 1st d tr (tr) 5 tr (dc) in next d tr (tr). Rep from * all round. Fasten off.

To make up

Sew side pieces to centre piece. Sew motif in position. Sew ribbon at each side to tie. Press carefully.

Stripey Crawlers

This shows how you can turn a simple idea into something exciting. These crawlers are easy to make in stocking stitch. The bright colours make them fun for a baby to wear and the protective suede knee pads and soles will help the garment live longer. To simplify the pattern, make it up in just one gay colour.

Materials

Mademoiselle Pingouin (Fingering 3-ply) 50 gr balls: 1 ball each in colours A, B, C and D (blue, yellow, green and red)
Pairs of No. 10(3) and 12(1) knitting needles
Set of 4 No. 12(1) knitting needles, pointed at each end
4 buttons
Scraps of suede for kneepads and soles (optional)

Measurements To fit a 16(18:20) inch chest.

Tension 7 sts and 9 rows to 1 inch using No. 10(3) needles.

Abbreviations, needle and size note
See pages 12 and 13.

Stripe Sequence This is worked in st st of 2 rows B, 2 rows C and 2 rows D.

Right leg

** Using No. 12(1) needles and B, cast on 58(66:74) sts and work thus:
1st row In B, K 28(32:36) place a different coloured thread into next st as a marker, k to end.
Work straight in st st in stripe sequence until 10(12:16) rows from beg have been worked, then change to No. 10(3) needles and work for 8(10:12) more rows. Now inc 1 st at each end of next row and every 4th row until there are 84(90:96) sts. Work straight for 6(6:6) rows then dec 1 st at each end of

next row and every alt row until 66(72:78) sts rem, then every 4th row until 42(46:50) sts rem. Work straight until leg measures 15½(16¼:17) ins from beg, ending with a p row in D. Change to No. 12(1) needles and work 8 rows. Change back to No. 10(3) needles **.

Shape Foot
Next 2 rows K 36(39:42), turn, p 12(14:16). Work 22 more rows on these 12(14:16) sts. Break yarn. Rejoin C to inside of the 24(25:26) sts already knitted, pick up and k 14 sts along side edge of foot, k across 12(14:16) sts of foot, pick up and k 14 sts along other side edge of foot, k across rem 6(7:8) sts.
Next row P across all sts including 24(25:26) sts at other side of foot.
Work straight for 6(6:8) rows.
Next row K 4(5:6), k 2 tog tbl, k 2 tog, k 31(33:35), k 2 tog tbl, k 2 tog, k 27(28:29).
Next row P.
Rep these 2 rows 2(2:3) times more, but allowing for dec sts by placing the decreasings above the previous ones. Cast off rem sts.

Left leg

Work as for Right Leg from ** to **.

Shape Foot
Next 2 rows K 18(21:24) turn, p 12(14:16). Work 22 more rows on these 12(14:16) sts. Break yarn. Rejoin C to inside of 6(7:8) sts already knitted, then pick up and k 14 sts along side edge of foot, k across 12(14:16) sts of foot, pick up and k 14 sts along other side of foot, k across rem 24(25:26) sts.
Next row P across all sts including 6(7:8) sts at other side of foot.
Work straight for 6(6:8) more rows.
Next row K 27(28:29), k 2 tog tbl, k 2 tog, k 31(33:35) k 2 tog tbl, k 2 tog, k 4(5:6).
Next row P.
Rep these 2 rows 2(2:3) times more allowing for dec sts by placing decreasings above previous ones. Cast off rem sts. Sew together leg and foot seams, then sew together front and back seams.

Back Bodice

Using No. 10(3) needles, A and with right side of work facing, pick up and k 57(65:73) sts across back, beg and ending with marker sts. Work in st st beg with a p row. Cast on 1 st at beg of first 2 rows, for side seams. Work straight for 17(17:21) more rows, thus ending with a p row. Break A. Change to the stripe sequence beg with B and work straight until 3 ins has been worked from picked up sts in A, ending after a p row **.

Shape Armholes

Next row Cast off 5 sts, work to last 5 sts, cast off 5. Break yarns.
Rejoin yarns and dec 1 st at each end of every row until 47(51:55) sts rem. Work straight until $4\frac{1}{2}(4\frac{1}{2}:4\frac{1}{2})$ ins have been worked from picked up sts in A.

Shape Neck

Next row Work 16(17:17) sts, cast off next 15(17:21) sts for neck, work to end. Now finish each side separately, dec 1 st at neck edge on next 10 rows. Cont straight until armhole measures $3\frac{1}{2}(4:4\frac{1}{2})$ ins from beg. Cast off.

Armhole and Neck Border

Using set of No. 12(1) needles, A, and with right side of work facing, pick up and k 38(40:42) sts round right armhole, 6(7:7) sts from shoulder, 67(73:81) sts round neck, 6(7:7) sts from shoulder and 38(40:42) sts round left armhole. Work in k 1, p 1 rib thus:
1st row Rib 38(40:42), inc 2 by working 3 times into next st, rib 4(5:5), inc 2 in next st, rib 67(73:81), inc 2 in next st, rib 4(5:5), inc 2 in next st, rib to end.
2nd and 3rd rows In rib.
4th row Rib 39(41:43), inc 2, rib 6(7:7) inc 2, rib 69(75:83), inc 2, rib 6 (7:7) inc 2, rib to end.
Cast off in rib.

Front Bodice

Work as for Back Bodice to **.

Shape Armholes and Neck

Next row Cast off 5, work 17(20:22) (including st on needle), cast off next 15(17:21) sts for neck, work to last 5 sts, cast off 5. Break yarns. Rejoin yarn and finish each side separately. Dec 1 st at neck edge on next 10 rows, *but at the same time*, dec 1 st at armhole edge on next 1(3:5) rows. Cont until armhole measures same as Back. Cast off.

Armhole and Neck Border

Using set of No. 12(1) needles, A and with right side of work facing, pick up and k 38 (40:42) sts round left armhole, 6(7:7) sts from shoulder, 83(89:97) sts round neck, 6(7:7) sts from shoulder, 38(40:42) sts round right armhole. Work in k 1, p 1 rib thus:
1st row Rib 38(40:42) inc. 2 as on Back, rib 4(5:5) inc 2, rib 83(89:97) inc 2, rib 4 (5:5) inc 2, rib to end.
2nd row Rib 38(40:42), cast off 2 for buttonhole, rib 6(7:7) cast off 2, rib 83(89:97) cast off 2, rib 6(7:7) cast off 2, rib to end.
3rd row In rib, casting on 2 sts over cast off sts of previous row.
4th row Rib 39(41:43), inc 2, rib 6(7:7) inc 2, rib 85(91:99) inc 2, rib 6(7:7) inc 2, rib to end.
Cast off in rib.

To make up

Do not press. Join side seams. Sew on buttons. Draw the outline of the baby's feet on scraps of suede to make soles for the crawlers. For knee pads cut $3\frac{1}{2}$ in long oval shapes from the suede. Sew the soles and knee pads on with a quick overcast stitch.

Quick-knit Jumper

This pattern is an invaluable one to learn. It is knitted in one piece from sleeve to sleeve, instead of the usual method from waist to neck. The garter stitch pattern makes it speedy to knit and the decorative embroidery on the front adds a delicate note. With buttons all the way up the back, the jumper is particularly easy to put on a tiny new baby. An older baby will not be able to undo the jumper and there is also no danger of him being able to suck the buttons.

Materials

Pingouin Superbebe, (Fingering 3-ply) 50 gr balls: 1(2:2)
Pairs of No. 10(3) and 12(1) knitting needles
5 small buttons
¾ yd narrow ribbon
Embroidery wool (yarn)

Measurements To fit a 16(18:20) inch chest.

Tension 7 sts and 13 rows to 1 inch over No. 10(3) needles.

Abbreviations, needle and size note
See pages 12 and 13.

Begin at Centre Back
With No. 10(3) needles cast on 39(45:51) sts for Left Back and work in g st for 22 rows.
Next row (neck edge) K 7, k twice into next st, k to end.
Next row K.
Rep last 2 rows until there are 51(59:67) sts, ending at neck edge. K 12(16:20) rows straight for shoulder.
** Cast on 23(25:27) sts for sleeve, k these 23(25:27) sts, then k across 23(25:27) more sts, sl and leave last 28(34:40) sts on a spare needle.
Work on the 46(50:54) sleeve sts for 50(54:58) rows, k 2 tog at each end of last row. 44(48:52) sts on needle.
Change to No. 12(1) needles and work in K 2,

P 2 rib for 10 rows. Cast off in rib.
Return to shoulder edge of 23(25:27) cast on sleeve sts, and with right side facing, pick up and k these 23(25:27) sts, then k across 28(34:40) sts on spare needle.
Next row K to last st, pick up end st from first g st ridge on shoulder and k it tbl tog with last st on needle.
Next row K.
Rep last 2 rows (to form shoulder) until 7(9:11) sts have been picked up and worked tog with previous st, and ending at neck edge.
Next row K 7, k 2 tog, k to end.
Next row K.
Rep last 2 rows until 39(45:51) sts rem and ending at neck edge **.
Cont thus:
1st and alt rows K.
2nd row K 29(35:41), p 8, k 2.
4th row K 27(33:39), p 8, k 4.
6th row K 25(31:37), p 8, k 6.
8th row K 23(29:35), p 8, k 8.
10th row As 6th row.
12th row As 4th row.
14th row As 2nd row.
K 2 rows.
Next row K 7, k twice into next st, k to end.
Next row K.
Rep last 2 rows until there are 51(59:67) sts ending at neck edge.
K 14(18:22) rows straight, then rep from ** to **.
K 18 rows straight.
Next row K 6, * yrn, k 2 tog (for buttonhole) k 7 (9:11). Rep from * twice more, yrn, k 2 tog, k to end.
K 3 rows. Cast off.

Neckband
Using No. 10(3) needles and with right side of work facing, pick up and k 82(90:98) sts round neck.
Next row * P 2, k 2. Rep from * to last 2 sts, p 2.
Next row * K 2, yrn, p 2 tog. Rep from * to last 2 sts, k 2.
Work 3 more rows in rib. Cast off in rib.

Welt

Using No. 10(3) needles and with right side of work facing, pick up and k 118(134:150) sts round lower edge.

Next row * P 2, k 2. Rep from * to last 2 sts, p 2.

Next row * K 2, p 2. Rep from * to last 2 sts, k 2.

Rep these 2 rows twice more, then 1st row again.

Next row K 2, p 2 tog, yrn (for buttonhole) rib to end.

Work 3 more rows in rib then cast off in rib.

To make up

Do not press. Join sleeve seams. Sew on buttons. Using embroidery wool work small flower motifs in Lazy Daisy stitch with French knots for centres, on the stocking stitch part at front of neck. Thread ribbon through holes at neck, draw up to required size and tie in a bow.

Quick-knit jumper

Crochet Sleeping Bag

This is the sort of practical idea that is not always easy to buy. The sleeping bag is made in an airy cellular stitch, and in a cotton yarn which absorbs moisture, so that it will be cool in the summer and warm in the winter. The bag has a flap at the foot for easy nappy changing. When the baby is bigger, the flap can be removed and the garment used as a dressing gown. It is an ideal choice for a baby who throws off his bedclothes, as it will keep him warm at night.

Materials

Twilley's Aquarius: 6(7) 50 gr balls

No. 3·50 mm (E/4) crochet hook
16 in zip fastener
¾ yd Velcro or 6 strong press studs (snaps)

Measurements From birth to 1 yr (1 yr–18 months)
Length: 25(27) ins
Sleeve seam: 5½(6¾) ins

Tension 3 complete 'V's measure about 2 ins

Abbreviations, hook and size note
See pages 12 and 13.

Back

Using No. 3·50 mm (E/4) crochet hook work 83(91) ch.
1st row 1 dc (sc) into 3rd ch from hook, miss 3 ch, 1 tr (dc) into next ch, * miss 1 ch, 1 tr (dc) into next ch, miss 1 ch, then into next ch work 1 tr (dc), 3 ch, 1 dc (sc) into 3rd ch from hook to form picot, 1 tr (dc) (1 'V' formed.) Rep from * to end. 20(22) complete Vs.
2nd row 4 ch, * miss 1 V, then into next single tr (dc) work 1 V, 1 ch. Rep from * working 1 tr (dc) into top of last st.
3rd row 6 ch, 1 dc (sc) into 3rd ch from hook, 1 tr (dc) into first sp, * 1 ch, 1 V into ch sp. Rep from * to end.

4th row 4 ch, into next sp work 1 V, * 1 ch, 1 V into next sp. Rep from *, ending 1 ch, 1 tr (dc) into top of last st.
Rows 3 and 4 form patt. Rep them until back measures 21(22½) ins ending with a 2nd patt row (row 4).
Next row 5 ch, 1 sl st into top of picot, * 2 ch, 1 sl st into top of next picot. Rep from * ending 2 ch, 1 tr (dc) into end st. Fasten off.

Flap

With right side of lower edge of Back facing, rejoin yarn at base of 2nd V from right hand end.
Next row 6 ch, 1 dc (sc) into 3rd ch from hook, 1 tr (dc) into base of same V, * 1 tr (dc) into next tr (dc) (into next V work 1 V).
Rep from * until 2nd last V from main part has been reached, turn.
2nd row As 2nd row of Back.
Now work in patt rep 3rd and 4th rows 3 times.
Next row 4 ch, 1 sl st into top of picot, * 1 ch, 1 tr (dc), between Vs, 1 ch, 1 sl st into top of· picot. Rep from * ending 1 ch, 1 tr (dc) in last st, turn.
Next row 1 ch, then work 1 dc (sc) into each ch sp, and 1 dc (sc) on each tr (dc) and each sl st, ending 1 dc (sc) on turning chain.
Work 3 rows of dc (sc), on dc (sc), but working into backs of loops and inc 1 st at each end of each row. Fasten off.

Side edging for flap
With right side of work facing, work 15 dc (sc) along one side of flap. Work 3 rows of dc (sc) into backs of loops inc 1 st on each row at lower end of flap to mitre corner. Work other side of flap in same way. Join shaped corners to top edge of flap.

Front

Using No. 3·50 mm (E/4) hook work 77(85) ch.
1st row 1 dc (sc) into 2nd ch from hook, * 1 dc (sc) into next ch. Rep from * to end, turn.

2nd row 1 ch, 1 dc (sc) into each dc (sc) working into back of loop only. Rep 2nd row twice more.

Next row 6 ch, 1 dc (sc) into 3 ch from hook, 1 tr (dc) in next dc (sc), then rep from * of 1st row of Back. 20(22) Vs.

Cont in patt from 2nd row as given for Back until work measures $3\frac{3}{4}(5\frac{1}{2})$ ins, ending with a 4th row.

Divide for Opening

1st row Work as for 3rd row working only 10(11) Vs including first V, turn.

Cont in patt on these sts only until front measures $18(19\frac{1}{2})$ ins from lower edge ending with a 4th row.

Next row As given for last row of Back. With right side of work facing, rejoin yarn to sp on left of centre picot. Complete as for first side.

Sleeves and yoke

Beg at left cuff. Using No. 3·50 mm (E/4) hook work 7(8) ch.

1st row Into 2nd ch from hook 1 dc (sc) * 1 dc (sc) into next ch. Rep from * to end, turn.

2nd row 1 ch, into back loop only work 1 dc (sc) into each dc (sc) to end, turn. Rep 2nd row 24(30) times more.

Next row Turn and work along one long side of ridged cuff, 1 ch, work 42(50) dc (sc) evenly along cuff. Cont thus:

1st row As given for 1st row of patt for front, turn. 11(13) Vs.

2nd row As given for 2nd row of Back.

Cont in patt until sleeve measures $6\frac{1}{2}(8)$ ins including cuff, ending with last patt row as given for flap before dc (sc) edging.

Work yoke

1st row 1 ch then working into back loop

only make 44(48) dc (sc) along row. Work dc (sc) on dc (sc) for 12(14) rows.

Shape Back

1st row 1 ch, into back loop only work 20(22) dc (sc), turn and complete Left Back on these sts.

Cont working in ridged dc (sc), dec 1 st at neck edge on next 2 rows. Work 7(9) rows more. Fasten off.

Left Front Yoke

Miss 6 dc (sc) at neck edge and rejoin yarn to next dc (sc).

1st row 1 ch, working into back loop only work 17(19) dc (sc), turn. Cont in ridged dc (sc), dec 1 st at neck edge on next 4 rows. Work 3(5) rows more. Fasten off.

Work other sleeve in same way, reversing Front and Back yokes only

To make up

Join edges of Back yokes together. Join sleeve seams to within $1(1\frac{1}{4})$ ins of top edge of patterned section. Join back skirt to back yoke between sleeve seams. Join fronts to front yokes between sleeves. Seam sides of back and front skirts. Fold up flap to right side and stitch on wrong side at sides to within 1 in of top flap edge. Sew Velcro to right side of front lower edge and under side of flap top edge.

Neck Edge and Opening

Work 1 row dc (sc) around front opening.

Neck Edging

Work 1 row dc (sc) around neck.

2nd row * 3 ch, 1 dc (sc) into 3rd ch from hook, miss 1 dc (sc), 1 dc (sc) into each of next 3 dc (sc). Rep from * ending dc (sc) in last dc (sc). Fasten off. Sew zip into front opening.

Crochet Pram Cover

The crochet motifs on this bright pram cover have an unusual raised effect. This is an ideal pattern for a beginner as it is simple and quick to make. It will look smart on a pram or cot and could be backed with a light wool or Courtelle fabric for extra warmth.

Materials

Madame Pinguoin:
1 50 gr ball in orange (A), 2 in yellow (B), 2 in gold (C)

No. 3·50 mm (E/4) crochet hook

Measurements 25 ins by 15½ ins

Tension Each motif measures about 4 ins

Abbreviations and hook note
See pages 12 and 13.

Using A make 6 ch and join into a ring with a sl st.
1st round 2 ch, 2 tr (dc) into ring, 1 ch, * 3 tr (dc) into ring, 1 ch. Rep from * 4 times more. Join with a sl st.
2nd round Turn work, (1 dc (sc) in 1 ch sp, 6 ch) 6 times, join with a sl st.
3rd round Do not turn. Join on C. [1 h tr (hdc), 2 tr (dc), 3 d tr (tr), 2 tr (dc), 1 h tr (hdc)] in each 6 ch loop, join with a sl st.
4th round Turn work. Join on B to 1st d tr (tr), * 3 h tr (hdc) on d trs (trs) 2 tr (dc) on 2 tr (dc), 2 d tr (tr) on last h tr (hdc) of group and 1st h tr (hdc) of next gr, 2 tr (dc) on 2 tr (dc). Rep from * all round, join with a sl st. Fasten off. One motif completed.

To make up

Do not press. Using B join motifs tog. alternating, 4 in one row, 3 in the next row, ending with 4 motifs in last row.

Edging

Working along a side long edge, join in B at a corner in the middle h tr (hdc) of motif. * Work 9 dc (sc) into next 9 sts, 2 ch, miss 2 sts, 1 tr (dc) in next tr (dc), 2 ch, miss 2 sts, 1 d tr (tr) in next tr (dc), 2 ch, miss 2 sts, 1 d tr (tr) in next h tr (hdc), 1 ch, 1 tr tr (d tr) on to join of 2 motifs, 1 ch, miss 2 sts, 1 d tr (tr) in next h tr (hdc), 2 ch, miss 2 sts, 1 d tr (tr) in next tr (dc), 2 ch, miss 2 sts, 1 d tr (tr) in next tr (dc), 2 ch, miss 2 sts, 1 d tr (tr) in next h tr (hdc), 1 ch, miss 2 sts, 1 tr tr (d tr) on to join, 1 ch, miss 2 sts, 1 d tr (tr) in next h tr (hdc), 2 ch, miss 2 sts, 1 d tr (tr) in next tr (dc), 2 ch, miss 2 sts, 1 tr (dc) in next tr (dc), 2 ch, miss 2 sts, 1 dc (sc). Rep from * twice more, work 25 dc (sc), [2 ch, miss 3 sts, 1 tr tr (d tr) onto join, 2 ch, miss 3 sts, 15 dc (sc)] three times, 1 dc (sc). Cont thus for other 2 sides of cover then join with a sl st.
Next round 1 dc (sc), * 4 ch, 1 dc (sc) in base of ch, miss 1 dc (sc), 3 dc (sc) in next 3 sts. Rep from * all round, join with a sl st. Fasten off. Press work very lightly.

Crochet Matinee Set

The loop stitch cape is simple to crochet and will keep a small baby warm on cold days. The smart jumper is long so will not come adrift at the waist. It also has an envelope neck that makes it simple to put on. Contrast colours and nautical motifs are the clever extras that make this little matinée set look so smart.

Materials

Robin Casino Crepe 4-ply (Nylon Sport Yarn), 25 gr balls:

Jumper: 4(5:6) balls white, 1 ball blue
Pants: 5(6:6) balls white, 1 ball blue
Mittens:1 ball white

Robin Vogue Double Double:
(Knitted Worsted or Bulky) 50 gr balls:
Cape: 8(9) balls blue, 1 ball white
8 buttons for cape
Elastic for pants
Crochet hooks in sizes 2·50 mm (B/1),
3·00 mm (D/3), 5·00 mm (H/8) and 6·00 mm (I/9).

Measurements
Jumper To fit a 16(18:20) inch chest.

Pants Length at side, 18(19:20) ins.

Cape To fit birth–3 months (4–9 months).

Mittens Width across palm, 2 ins.

Tension About 13 dc (sc) to 2 ins using No. 3·00 mm (D/3) hook and 4 ply wool.
3 sts measure 1 inch, using No. 6·00 mm (I/9) hook and double double.

Abbreviations, hook and size note
See pages 12 and 13.
Extra abbreviation: W, white; B, blue.

Jumper

The Back and Front Alike
Using No. 3·00 mm (D/3) hook and B 4 ply make 54(58:62) ch.

Next row 1 dc (sc) in 2nd ch from hook, 1 dc (sc) into each ch to end, 1 ch turn. 53(57:61) dc (sc).
Work 3 more rows dc (sc) turning each row with 1 ch. Break B, join in W and work in patt thus:
Foundation row (right side), 3 ch, 1 tr (dc) in first dc (sc) * miss 1 dc (sc), 1 dc (sc) in next dc (sc), miss 1 dc (sc), [1 tr (dc) 2 ch 1 tr (dc)]—known as tr (dc) gr—in next dc (sc). Rep from * to last 4 dc (sc), miss 1 dc (sc), 1 dc (sc) in next dc (sc), miss 1 dc (sc), 1 tr (dc) in last dc (sc), turn. 12(13:14) tr (dc) grs.
1st patt row 1 ch, 1 dc (sc) in tr (dc) * 1 tr (dc) gr in dc (sc), 1 dc (sc) in 2 ch sp of previous row. Rep from * ending 1 tr (dc) gr in last dc (sc), 1 dc (sc) in tr (dc), turn.
2nd patt row 3 ch, 1 tr (dc) in dc (sc) * 1 dc (sc) in 2 ch sp, 1 tr (dc) gr in dc (sc). Rep from * ending with 1 dc (sc) in last 2 ch sp, 1 tr (dc) in last dc (sc), turn.
Rep 1st and 2nd rows until work measures 9½(10¾:12) ins from beg ending on a wrong side row.

Shape Armholes
Next row Sl st over 2 complete patts, patt to last 2 patts, turn.
Work 3 rows in patt, then work 1 row dc (sc), working 37(41:45) dc (sc) evenly across row. Break W. Join in B and work straight on these dc (sc) until armhole measures 2¼(2½:3) ins.
Work across 11(12:13) dc (sc), turn.
Work 2 rows.
Next row Sl st across 3 sts, work to end. Now dec 1 st at neck edge on every row until 2 sts rem. Fasten off. Miss centre 15(17:19) dc (sc), join yarn in next dc (sc) and work to match first side. Work 3 rows dc (sc) round each neck piece and along 2 dc (sc) at top. Fasten off.

Sleeves

Using No. 3·00 mm (D/3) hook and B, make 25(31:39) ch and work 4 rows dc (sc).

24(30:38) dc (sc). Break B, join in W and inc 1 st at each end of the next and every 4th row until there are 32(40:48) dc (sc). Work straight until sleeve measures 7(7½:8) ins. Fasten off.

To make up

Press work on wrong side with a warm iron over a damp cloth. Join side and sleeve seams leaving about 1 inch open at top of sleeve to set into armhole. Overlap shoulders as illustrated. Sew in sleeves, joining sleeve extension to sts left at armhole. Press.

Motif

(4 B and 1 W required for set)
Using No. 2·50 mm (B/1) hook make 6 ch and join into a ring, with a sl st.
1st round 6 ch, [1 tr (dc) 3 ch] in ring, 5 times, sl st into 3rd of 6 ch.
2nd round [1 dc (sc), 1 htr (hdc), 3 tr (dc), 1 htr (hdc), 1 dc (sc)] in each 3 ch sp all round, join with a sl st. Fasten off.
Sew W motif to front of jumper.

Mitts (both alike)

Using No. 3·00 mm (D/3) hook and W, make 15 ch. Work 1 dc (sc) into 2nd ch from hook, then 1 dc (sc) into each ch to end. Working into *back* of each loop and turning with 1 ch work 28 rows dc (sc). Fasten off. Join short ends together. Join yarn to edge, 2 ch, work 32 dc (sc), join with a sl st, 2 ch. Work 4 rounds in dc (sc).
Next round 2 ch, work across 12 dc (sc), miss 8 dc (sc) (for thumb) and work across 12 dc (sc), sl st to join. Work on these 24 dc (sc) for 7 more rounds.

Shape Top

Next round 2 ch, * dec 1, work across 8 dc (sc), dec 1. Rep from *, sl st to join.
Next round 2 ch, * dec 1, work across 6 dc (sc), dec 1. Rep from *, join with sl st.
Cont working 2 sts less between dec until there are 2 dc (sc) between each dec, break yarn, join ends together.

The Thumb

Join yarn and work 7 rounds dc (sc).

Break yarn and draw sts tog and fasten off. Press as jumper. Sew on B motifs as illustrated.

Pants

2 pieces alike as work is reversible.
Begin at top of one leg. Using No. 3·00 mm (D/3) hook and B, make 54(58:62) ch.
Next row 1 dc (sc) into 2nd ch. from hook, 1 dc (sc) into each ch to end. 53(57:61) dc (sc).
Work 3 rows in dc (sc), turning each row of dc (sc) with 1 ch. Change to W and work 3 rows dc (sc).
Next 2 rows Work across 40 dc (sc), turn, sl st into next dc (sc), work to end.
Next 2 rows Work across 32 dc (sc), turn, sl st into next dc (sc), work to end.
Next 2 rows Work across next 24 dc (sc) turn, sl st into next 1 dc (sc), work to end.
Next row Work in dc (sc) working 1 dc (sc) into each sl st. 53(57:61) dc (sc).
Work straight until short edge measures 2½(3:3½) ins. Now inc 1 st at each end of next and every 4th row until there are 61(65:69) sts, then inc 1 st at each end of the next 2(4:6) rows. 65(73:81) sts. Work 3(3:5) rows straight.

Shape Inside Leg

Dec 1 st at *beg* of every row until 40 (48:54) sts rem. Now dec 1 st at each end of every row until 30(38:46) st rem. Work straight for 4(4½:5) ins or as required. Change to No. 2·50 mm (B/1) hook and work 3 rows dc (sc). Change back to No. 3·00 mm (D/3) hook.

Shape Foot

Work across 20(26:31) dc (sc), turn.
Work across 10(14:16) dc (sc) for instep and work on these dc (sc) for 2(2:2½) ins. Now dec 1 st each end of next row. Fasten off. Rejoin at lower right side of instep, work 10(10:12) dc (sc) up side of instep, then work across the instep sts, then work 10(10:12) dc (sc) down the other side, dc (sc) to end.
Work 3(3:4) rows straight, then work another 3 rows but dec 1 st each end of work and 2 sts in centre of instep sts on every row. Fasten off.

To make up

Press as jumper. Join leg, crutch and foot seams. Press. Sew on motifs. Join elastic into ring and sew inside waist using a herring-bone casing stitch.

Cape

With No. 6·00 mm (I/9) hook and B work 73(79) ch.
Foundation row (right side) 1 dc (sc) into 2nd ch from hook, 1 dc (sc) into each ch to end, turn. 72(78) dc (sc). Continue thus:
1st row 2 ch (counts as 1st st), miss 1st dc (sc), ML (see abbreviations) in each dc (sc) to ch at end, 1 dc (sc) in ch, turn.
2nd row 2 ch, miss 1st dc (sc), 1 dc (sc) into each st to end, working last dc (sc) in ch at end, turn.
These two rows form the patt. Work 11 more rows thus, ending on a loop row.
Dec row 2 ch, miss first st, 1 dc (sc) into each of next 15(16) sts, (dec 1) twice (see abbreviations), 1 dc (sc) in each of next 32(36) sts, (dec 1) twice, 1 dc (sc) in each st to end, working last dc (sc) in ch at end, turn. 68(74) dc (sc). Work 7(9) rows straight.
Dec row 2 ch, miss first st, 1 dc (sc) into each of next 14(15) sts, (dec 1) twice, 1 dc in each of next 30(34) sts, (dec 1) twice, 1 dc (sc) in each st to end, working last dc (sc) in ch at end, turn. 64(70) dc (sc). Work 7(9) rows straight.
Dec row 2 ch, miss first st, 1 dc (sc) into each of next 13(14) sts, (dec 1) twice, 1 dc (sc) in each of next 28(32) sts, (dec 1) twice, 1 dc (sc) in each st to end, working last dc (sc) in ch at end, turn. 60(66) dc (sc). Work 7(9) rows straight.
Dec row 2 ch, miss first st, *2nd size only*, 1 dc (sc) in next st. *Both sizes* (Dec 1, 1 dc (sc) in each of next 2 sts) 3 times, (dec 1) twice, 1 dc (sc) into each of next 2 sts, (dec 1, 1 dc (sc) into each of next 2 sts) 6(7) times, (dec 1) twice, (1 dc (sc) into each of next 2 sts, dec 1) 3 times, *2nd size only*, 1 dc (sc) in next st. *Both sizes*, 1 dc (sc) in ch at end, turn. 44(49) dc (sc).
Work 1 row straight.

Dec row 2 ch, miss first st (dec 1, 1 dc (sc) in next st) 2(3) times, (dec 1) 3(2) times, 1 dc (sc) in each of next 2 sts, (dec 1, 1 dc (sc) in next st) 4(5) times, dec 1, 1 dc (sc) in each of next 2 sts, (dec 1) 3(2) times, (1 dc (sc) in next st, (dec 1) 2(3) times, (1 dc (sc) in chain at end, turn. 29(33) dc (sc).
Work 1 row straight. Break yarn and fasten off.

Hood

Using No. 6·00 mm (I/9) hook and B, make 43(49) ch and work foundation as given. 42(48) dc (sc). Cont in patt and work for about $4\frac{3}{4}(5\frac{3}{4})$ ins from beg ending on a loop row. Break yarn and fasten off. Fold in half and join cast on ch edges together for back seam.

To make up

Press work lightly on wrong side using a warm iron over a damp cloth. Join short edges of hood to neck edge of cape, placing back seam of hood to centre back neck of cape and front edges of hood to centre front edges of cape. Press seam.

Edging

Using the 5·00 mm hook and W and with right side of work facing, begin at right lower edge and work 1 round dc (sc) around entire outer edge working 1 dc (sc) in each row and 1 dc (sc) to each st and 3 dc (sc) in each corner, join with a sl st. Place markers down right front for 8 buttonholes, 1 just below neck edge, 1 approx. $2\frac{1}{2}$ ($3\frac{1}{2}$) ins from lower edge and the others spaced evenly between.
Next round (buttonhole round) 2 ch, dc (sc) to first marker, 2 ch, miss 1 dc (sc), * dc (sc) to next marker, 2 ch, miss 1 dc (sc). Rep from * 6 times more then cont. in dc (sc) working 3 dc (sc) in each corner dc (sc), join with sl st.
Work one more round in dc (sc) working 1 dc (sc) into each 2 ch sp and 3 dc (sc) in each corner dc (sc), join with a sl st.
Break yarn and fasten off. Press as before. Sew on buttons.

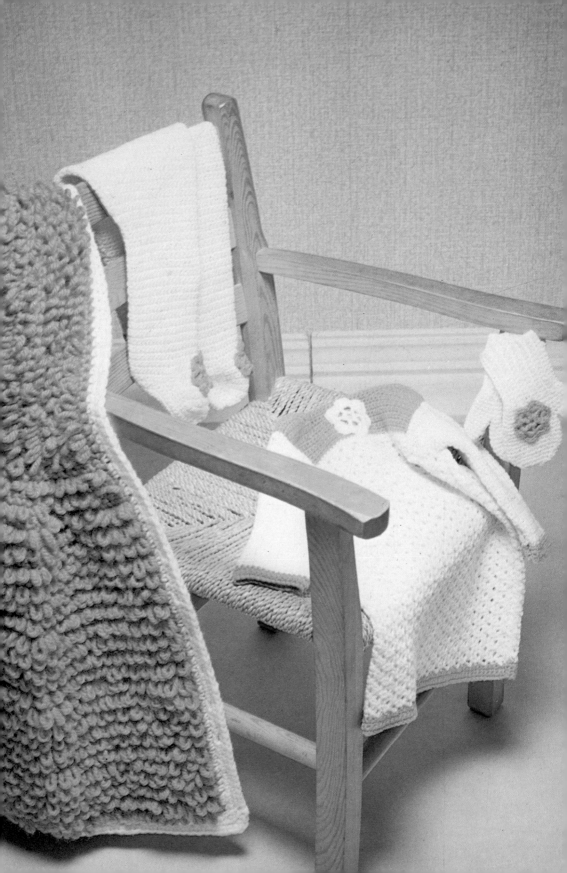

Dress and Pinafore

Baby dresses are fun to make, because they are so small and do not take long to sew. This one shows how decorative machine embroidery stitches can make a simple little pattern into something special. The set is made in a delicate lawn, the pale blue dress giving an attractive shadowed effect under the fresh white pinafore.

Materials

Dress 1½ yds fine cotton or lawn
Pinafore ¾ yd of same fabric in contrasting colour
¼ yd fine interfacing
Tracing paper
Bias binding
Thread and machine embroidery twist

Dress

1. After cutting out, overcast all seams, preferably using three-step zigzag on sewing machine. Gather along lines indicated on back and front of dress skirt.
2. Stitch centre back seam from dot to hem. Gather top of sleeve along lines indicated, using zigzag stitch over fine cord to give a controlled gather (see Good stitches to know, page 9).

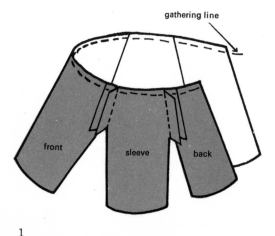

gathering line

front   sleeve   back

1

3. Stitch sleeves to front and back of dress, right sides together. Press seams towards bodice (diagram 1).
4. Baste or iron on fine interfacing to wrong side of yoke front and yoke backs. Stitch front yoke to back yokes at shoulder seams, then trim interfacing close to stitching. Pin yoke to dress, right sides together, adjusting gathers evenly along back, sleeve top and front (diagram 2). Insert zip in centre back seam. Press.

2

5. Stitch front lining to back lining at shoulder seams. Turn under small hem on back all round cut edges of lining. Then, placing right sides together, pin lining to neckline edge and stitch. Clip curve. Turn lining to inside and press. Slipstitch yoke lining into place, making sure it does not interfere with free running of zip.
6. Turn up hem as required. Baste tracing paper to underside of hem and use a machine embroidery stitch to decorate hem. The paper stops the fabric ruckling while it is being embroidered. Use a cam or disc for even stitches—shell stitch was used on the dress illustrated.
7. Stitch underarm seams of dress and sleeves. Turn narrow hem on bottom of sleeve, using either fine zigzag or overlock stitch on the

sewing machine. Stitch all round, cutting away surplus fabric afterwards. Run two rows of shirring elastic round cuff one inch from sleeve edge to form a shell (diagram 3).

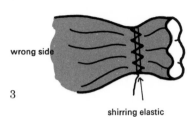

wrong side

3

shirring elastic

Pinafore

1. After cutting out, overcast all cut edges and continue as for step 1 of baby dress.
2. Attach interfacings as for yoke of dress. Stitch front yoke to back yoke at shoulder seams.
3. Neaten round armhole and along lower edge of yoke with bought bias binding.
4. Embroider decorative machine stitches to binding round edge of yoke, using the same stitch as on dress.
5. Pin skirt to yoke, adjusting gathers under binding evenly. Sink stitch gathers into place on line of join where binding meets yoke.
6. Join yoke linings at shoulder seams. Press and baste into position, wrong sides together.
7. Use the bias binding to attach yoke to yoke facing around neckline, leaving excess

binding to form ties at either end. Join side seams. Stitch more bias binding down back edges and round hem.
8. Fold in lower edge of yoke lining and slipstitch neatly on inside. (diagram 4).

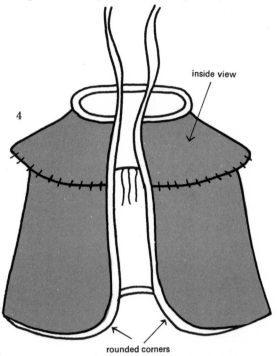

inside view

4

rounded corners

9. Use the machine embroidery stitch to decorate binding at neck, back and hem. Work the decorative daisy motifs on yoke and hem with an automatic Elna machine daisy disc, which is quick to sew. The shapes are sewn on at random.

5 squares represent 4 inches

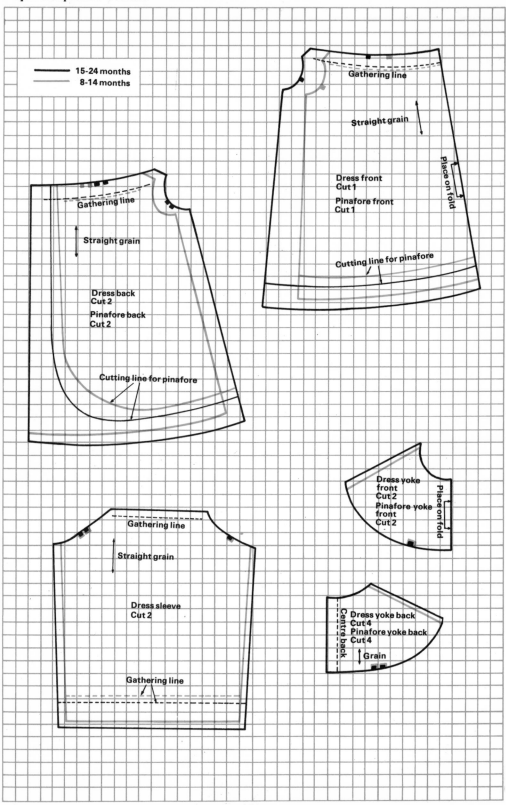

15-24 months
8-14 months

Gathering line

Straight grain

place on fold

Dress front
Cut 1

Pinafore front
Cut 1

Cutting line for pinafore

Gathering line

Straight grain

Dress back
Cut 2

Pinafore back
Cut 2

Cutting line for pinafore

Dress yoke
front
Cut 2
Pinafore yoke
front
Cut 2

Place on fold

Gathering line

Straight grain

Dress sleeve
Cut 2

Centre back

Dress yoke back
Cut 4
Pinafore yoke back
Cut 4

Grain

Gathering line

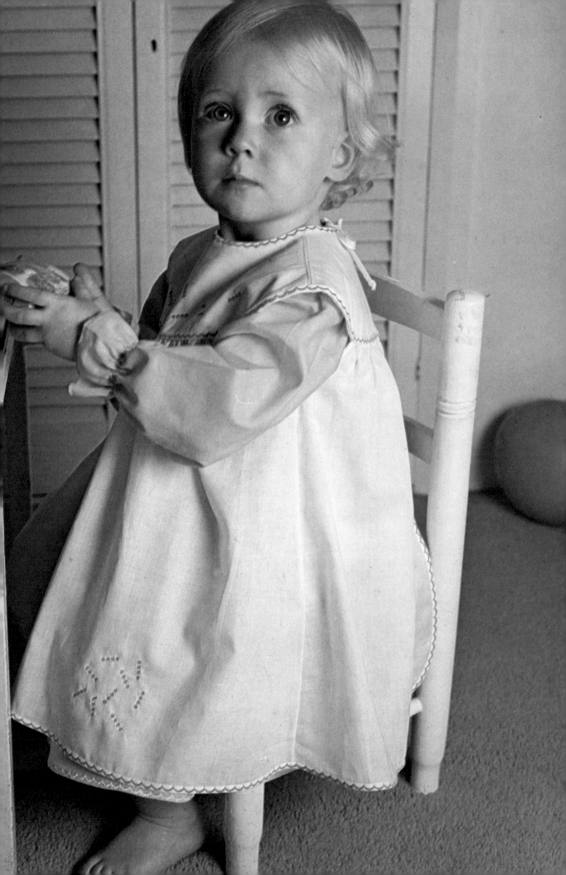

Lacy Wool Shawl

This beautiful shawl would make a perfect family heirloom. The centre pattern with its dainty flower motif is gossamer-fine, and the fringe helps to make it look graceful. Rather than use a pure wool yarn that may lose its freshness after frequent washing, the shawl has been made in a nylon yarn that is soft, yet wears well.

Materials

Patons Baby 2-ply, 100% Bri-Nylon (Fingering 3-ply) 20 gr balls: 13.
No. 2·50 mm (B/1) crochet hook.

Measurements Approx 36 ins by 36 ins square—excluding border and fringe.

Tension 4 patterns measure about 6½ ins.

Abbreviations and hook note
See pages 12 and 13.

Using No. 2·50 mm (B/1) hook, make 288 ch loosely, turn.
Foundation row 1 dc (sc) in 2nd ch from hook, * 1 dc (sc) in next ch, 4 ch, miss 3 ch, 1 tr (dc) in each of next 4 ch, 4 ch, miss 3 ch, 1 dc (sc) in each of next 2 ch. Rep from * to end.
1st row 1 ch, 1 dc (sc) in 1st dc (sc), * 4 ch, 2 tr (dc) in next 4 ch sp, 1 tr (dc) in next tr (dc), 8 ch, miss 2 tr (dc), 1 tr (dc) in next tr (dc), 2 tr (dc) in next 4 ch sp, 4 ch, miss 1 dc (sc), 1 dc (sc) in next dc (sc). Rep from * to end.
2nd row 6 ch, * 2 tr (dc) in next 4 ch sp, 1 tr (dc) in next tr (dc), 4 ch, 1 dc (sc) in next 8 ch sp, 4 ch, miss 2 tr (dc), 1 tr (dc) in next tr (dc), 2 tr (dc) in next 4 ch sp, 2 ch. Rep from * ending last rep 2 tr (dc) in last 4 ch sp, 1 ch, 1 d tr (tr) in last dc (sc).
3rd row 3 ch, 1 tr (dc) in 1 ch sp, * 1 tr (dc) in next tr (dc), 4 ch, 1 dc (sc) in next 4 ch sp, 1 dc (sc) in next dc (sc), 1 dc (sc) in next 4 ch sp, 4 ch, miss 2 tr (dc), 1 tr (dc) in next tr (dc),

2 tr (dc) in next 2 ch sp. Rep from * ending last rep 1 tr (dc) in last tr (dc), 1 tr (dc) in last ch sp, 1 tr (dc) in 5th of 6 ch.
4th row 9 ch, miss next tr (dc), * 1 tr (dc) in next tr (dc), 2 tr (dc) in next 4 ch sp, 4 ch, miss 1 dc (sc), 1 dc (sc) in next dc (sc), 4 ch, 2 tr (dc) in next 4 ch sp, 1 tr (dc) in next tr (dc), 8 ch, miss 2 tr (dc). Rep from * but at end of last rep omit 8 ch and work 4 ch instead then miss 2 tr (dc), 1 d tr (tr) into top of 3 ch.
5th row 1 ch, 1 dc (sc) in first d tr (tr), * 4 ch, miss 2 tr (dc), 1 tr (dc) in next tr (dc), 2 tr (dc) in next 4 ch sp, 2 ch, 2 tr (dc) in next 4 ch sp, 1 tr (dc) in next tr (dc), 4 ch, 1 dc (sc) in next 8 ch sp. Rep from * ending last rep 1 dc (sc) in 4th of 9 ch instead of into 8 ch.
6th row 1 ch, 1 dc (sc) in 1st dc (sc), * 1 dc (sc) in next 4 ch sp, 4 ch, miss 2 tr (dc), 1 tr (dc) in next tr (dc), 2 tr (dc) in next 2 ch sp, 1 tr (dc) in next tr (dc), 4 ch, 1 dc (sc) in next 4 ch sp, 1 dc (sc) in next dc (sc). Rep from * to end.
The last 6 rows form patt. Cont straight until work measures about 36 ins ending after a 3rd patt row, turn. Now work in rounds thus:
Next round 1 ch, 2 dc (sc) in 1st tr (dc) [place a marker in first of these 2 dc (sc)] * 1 dc (sc) in each of next 2 tr (dc), 3 dc (sc) in next 4 ch sp, 1 dc (sc) in each of next 3 dc (sc), 3 dc (sc) in next 4 ch sp, 1 dc (sc) in each of next 2 tr (dc). Rep from * ending last rep 4 dc (sc) in 4 ch sp, instead of 3, then 1 dc (sc) in each of next 2 tr (dc), 3 dc (sc) in top of 3 ch [place a marker in 2nd of last 3 dc (sc)], now work in dc (sc) down 1st side edge making sure that the number of dc (sc) along this edge, including last marked st, is a multiple of 5, plus an extra 4 sts, now work 3 dc (sc) in first ch of original ch [place a marker in 2nd of last 3 dc (sc)], work 287 dc (sc) evenly along lower edge [thus working 1 dc (sc) into each ch of foundation], and working 3 dc (sc) in the last ch [place a marker in 2nd of last 3 dc (sc)], now work in dc (sc) up 2nd side edge to match corresponding edge, then work 1 dc (sc) in the first st worked into, sl st in first marked st [note that there should be a multiple of 5, plus

4 extra sts in between each set of marked sts].
Work border thus:

1st round 1 ch, [1 dc (sc), 7 ch, 1 dc (sc)] in first marked dc (sc), [* 7 ch, miss 4 dc (sc), 1 dc (sc) in next dc (sc). Rep from * to next corner, thus ending with 1 dc (sc) in next marked dc (sc), 7 ch, 1 dc (sc) in same marked dc (sc)] 3 times, ** 7 ch, miss 4 dc (sc), 1 dc (sc) in next dc (sc). Rep from ** ending last rep, 3 ch, 1 d tr (tr) in first dc (sc).

2nd round 1 ch, 1 dc (sc) in top of d tr (tr), * 7 ch, 1 dc (sc) in next 7 ch sp. Rep from * ending last rep 3 ch, 1 d tr (tr) in first dc (sc).

3rd round As 2nd round.

4th round As 2nd round, but working [1 dc (sc), 7 ch, 1 dc (sc)] into each of the 4 corner 7 ch sp.

Rep last 3 rounds once more, then 2nd and 3rd rounds again.

Fasten off.

Block shawl out with pins and press lightly using a *cool* iron and *dry* cloth. Cut remaining yarn into 9 inch lengths and taking 5 strands together each time, knot all round edge in each 7 ch sp to form a fringe. Trim fringe.

Playtime and Partytime

Smocked Dresses

One of the most effective ways of decorating children's clothes is with colourful smocking. These dresses show two different and unusual ways of using it. The waist smocking goes all the way round and gives a flattering line to the garment. The elasticity of the smocking makes the dress extremely practical since the waistline will expand as the child grows. Add a generous hem and the dress can be used for a two- or even three-year period. The smaller dress shows how a block of smocking can be cut to shape over the shoulders, neck and round the armholes. It is worth trying this method, particularly on a small dress, as the smocking makes the dress fit so beautifully. Again the elasticity of the stitching means the dress can be worn over a longer growing period. Smocking is fairly slow, yet very simple to do. There are no short cuts for a perfect finish. It is an old craft but well worth learning. Page 10 shows how to sew a variety of smocking stitches used in the dresses illustrated.

Materials

Dress with smocked waist
Length of fabric for smocking should be three times the measurement of area to be smocked. For an 18 in waist, you need a 54 in length of fabric. The side measurement (for smocked waist and the skirt) should be from 2 ins above waist to 5 ins below knee, allowing generous hem for growth. Add on $\frac{1}{2}$ yd for bodice and sleeves.

Lacy wool shawl

Broderie anglaise frill to line frill on sleeve and broderie anglaise edging for collar and sleeves.

Dress with smocked yoke
The same fabric requirements apply for smocked area. Measure chest front. Multiply by three and add on 3 ins at either side to work out the amount of fabric needed.
A 10 inch chest front needs a 30 inch wide block for smocking plus 3 ins at either side for underarm shaping and seams. For length, measure from top of shoulder to knee and add extra for hem and top turnings. Add on $\frac{1}{2}$ yd for dress back, sleeves and lining. (The dress illustrated took $1\frac{1}{2}$ yds fabric.)
Buttons for covering
Broderie Anglaise edging
For the Smocking (both dresses)
Smocking dot transfers
Coats embroidery thread
Fabric note: When selecting fabric similar to that illustrated, check that the lines of spots are straight on fabric before buying. The dots can then be gathered up without aid of transfers. Otherwise use the special transfers for all types of fabric. Buy yellow dots to show up on dark materials and blue ones to show up on pale colours.

The Smocking

The smocking is done before making the dress up. It is basically a way of decorating gathers. Cut out block of fabric for smocking (see under Materials needed for correct measurements). Iron smocking dots on to wrong side of fabric. Join up dots with rows of gathering stitches, to ensure even smocking. Warning: don't be tempted to try smocking "freehand" because fabric tends to gather unevenly. To join dots, use double thread, firmly knotted at one end (diagram 1).

and baste a line of double thread $\frac{1}{2}$ in inside cutting edge, ensuring the pattern runs straight. Make two rows of machine stitching just inside cutting edge of yoke sides and top (diagram 2) (the bottom edge should not be

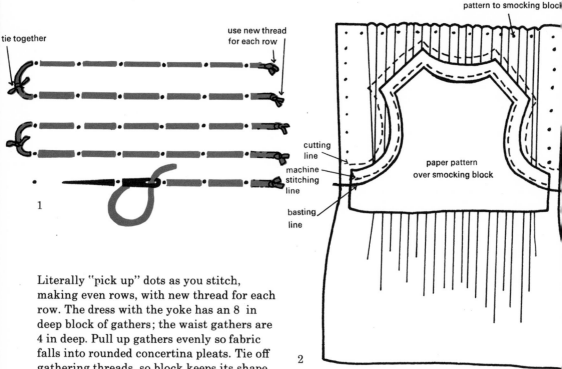

Literally "pick up" dots as you stitch, making even rows, with new thread for each row. The dress with the yoke has an 8 in deep block of gathers; the waist gathers are 4 in deep. Pull up gathers evenly so fabric falls into rounded concertina pleats. Tie off gathering threads, so block keeps its shape. Now start the smocking. Page 10 shows a selection of different stitches. Use three strands of embroidery thread at a time (two for a finer fabric like organza and four for a heavier fabric like wool). Keep smocking stitches even, using the same tension all the way. Do not pull stitches up too tightly, otherwise dress will have no elasticity. When smocking is complete, remove original rows of gathers. Neaten off loose threads. The dresses can now be made up.

Dress with smocked yoke

1. Cut out front bodice facing, sleeves and back pieces.
2. Spread out block of smocking over blanket on bed. Stab pins through fabric into mattress to keep smocking stretched out evenly.
3. Place yoke paper pattern over smocking

cut because this incorporates the skirt). Cut away surplus material outside stitching and overstitch raw edges with zigzag or overcasting by hand. Remove paper pattern and basting.
4. Join front yoke facing to newly shaped smocking. Pin round side and top edges and machine.
5. Join bodice back and front, right sides together, at shoulders, plus back facings (diagram 3). Press shoulder seam open so back facing hides join.
6. Gather back skirt and join to back yoke.
7. Join side seams.
8. Gather fullness on sleeve tops. Sew sleeve seam and set in sleeves at armholes. Hem base of sleeves and sew broderie anglaise edging round wrists. Thread elastic through hem. Bind or overcast seam edges round armholes inside.

9. Stitch back yoke and facing, right sides together, down both sides of back opening. Turn and press.

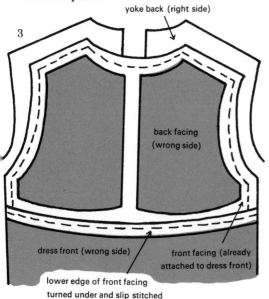

yoke back (right side)

3

back facing (wrong side)

dress front (wrong side)

front facing (already attached to dress front)

lower edge of front facing turned under and slip stitched

10. Cut a half inch wide bias strip, the same length as neck measurement plus one inch. Use this to neaten neckline, sewing it to right side first, then folding it over neck edge and slip stitching at inside.
11. Make buttonholes, cover buttons.
12. Cut 2 lengths 18 in by 3 in for sash. Fold in half lengthways and stitch (diagram 4). Turn right way out. Press flat. Neaten

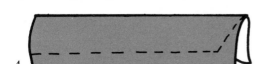

4

ends and stitch to dress over side seam just under arms.
13. Turn up hem and press.

Dress with smocked waistline

1. Cut out bodice, collar and sleeves.
2. Join bodice at shoulders and sides, with right sides facing.
3. Stretch out smocking and join skirt piece to bodice, right sides together, pinning, basting, then stitching. Make sure smocking is evenly distributed.
4. Join underarm sleeve seams. Cut out frills and broderie anglaise inner frills the same lengths. Join sides of frills and gather both together along upper edge. Attach to sleeve ends on wrong side, adjusting gathers to fit. Sew broderie anglaise edging to lower edge of outside frill.
5. Join collar pieces, right sides together. Stitch and turn right way out. Sew lower edge of collar to neckline, right sides facing. Turn in upper edge and sew it inside neckline.
6. Join bodice lining at shoulders (use silk or lightweight lawn for preference). Turn edge under and slipstitch into place inside bodice along neckline, round armholes, waist and back opening.
7. Make buttonholes. Cover buttons with matching fabric (optional) and sew to bodice opening.
8. Turn up hem. Press.

Note: When ironing smocking, press gently with a damp cloth under the iron.

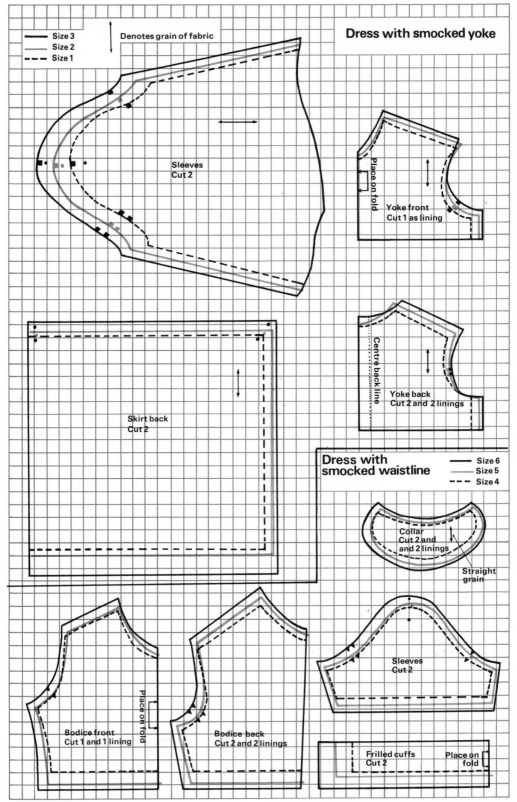

5 squares represent 4 inches

Size 3
Size 2
Size 1

↕ Denotes grain of fabric

Dress with smocked yoke

Sleeves
Cut 2

Place on fold

Yoke front
Cut 1 as lining

Skirt back
Cut 2

Centre back line

Yoke back
Cut 2 and 2 linings

Dress with smocked waistline

Size 6
Size 5
Size 4

Collar
Cut 2 and
and 2 linings

Straight
grain

Sleeves
Cut 2

Place on fold

Bodice front
Cut 1 and 1 lining

Bodice back
Cut 2 and 2 linings

Frilled cuffs
Cut 2

Place on
fold

278

Smocked dresses.

Beach Clothes

These bright beach clothes in cotton are cool to wear and straightforward to crochet. The co-ordinated patterns make them ideal for a brother and sister. The neat little sun top is useful for boys or girls.

Materials

Twilley's Stalite (Coats and Clark Knit Cro-Sheen *or* Bali) in 50 gr balls:

Boy's trunks and top: 4 balls of hot orange (A) and 1 ball of almond green (B)
Girl's swimsuit: 2 of hot orange (A), 2 of fiesta pink (C), 1 of almond green (B)
Nos. 4·50 mm (G/6) and 4·00 mm (F/5) crochet hooks

Waist length of elastic for boy's trunks
One buckle for either model

Measurements To fit a 23(24:25) inch chest.

Tension 4 h tr (hdc) to 1 inch using No. 4·50 mm (G/6) hook.

Abbreviations, hook and size note
See pages 12 and 13.

Sun Top
Front

** Using No. 4·50 mm (G/6) hook and A, work 49(51:53) ch.
1st row Into 2nd ch from hook work 1 h tr (hdc), then 1 h tr (hdc) into each ch to end, turn. 48(50:52) h tr (hdc).
2nd row 2 ch, * 1 h tr (hdc) into next h tr (hdc). Rep from * to end working last h tr (hdc) into 2nd of 2 ch.
This last row forms patt. Rep until work measures 8½(9:10) ins from beg.

Shape Armholes
1st row Sl st over next 8(9:9) h tr (hdc),

2 ch, 1 h tr (hdc) into each of next 31(31:33) h tr (hdc), turn **.
Work 1 row on these centre sts.

Work Left Shoulder
1st row 2 ch, 1 h tr (hdc) into each of next 6(7:7) h tr (hdc), turn.
Complete left shoulder on these sts, and work straight until armhole measures 4(4½:4½) ins ending at armhole edge.

Shape Shoulder
1st row Sl st over next 3 h tr (hdc), 1 h tr (hdc) into each h tr (hdc) to end. Fasten off. With right side of front facing, rejoin yarn to last 7(8:8) h tr (hdc) and work to correspond with other shoulder.

Back

Work as given for Front from ** to **. Work 7 more rows on these sts, then complete as for Front.

To make up

Join left shoulder seam. **Armhole Edging.** Using No. 4·00 mm (F/5) hook and B, work 1 row dc (sc) round armhole. Do not turn, but work 2nd row by working 1 row dc (sc) backwards along first row, omitting to work into corner sts of armholes. (This gives a firm edge.) Work neck edging in same way. Join right shoulder and work armhole to match first armhole. Join side seams.

Work Motifs
Apple Motif

Using No. 4·00 mm (F/5) hook and B, work 3 ch.
1st row 1 ch, then 2 dc (sc) into each of next 2 ch, turn. Working in dc (sc), inc 1 dc (sc) at each end of next 2 rows then on every alt row until there are 15 sts. Work

3 rows straight, then dec 1 st at each end of next 3 rows.
Next row 1 ch, 1 dc (sc) into next 2 dc (sc), sl st over 3 dc (sc) then 1 dc (sc) into each of last 3 dc (sc), turn.
Next row Sl st across all sts to last 2 dc (sc), 1 dc (sc) on each of last 2 dc (sc), turn.
Next row Sl st over 2 dc (sc), 1 ch, 1 dc (sc) into next st, turn.
Work 6 rows on 2 sts for stalk. Fasten off.

Leaf Motif

Using No. 4·00 mm (F/5) hook and B, make 8 ch.
1st row 1 ch, 1 dc (sc) into each of next 6 ch, 1 sl st into last ch, turn.
2nd row Sl st into next dc (sc), 1 dc (sc) into each dc (sc) to end, turn.
3rd row 1 ch, 1 dc (sc) into each of next 3 dc (sc), 1 sl st into next dc (sc), turn.
4th row As 2nd row. Fasten off.
Sew apple to front of top. Sew leaf to top of apple.
Press work lightly with a warm iron over a damp cloth.

Trunks
Right Leg

** Using No. 4·50 mm (G/6) hook and A work 59(61:63) ch.
1st row Into 2nd ch from hook, work 1 dc (sc), then 1 dc (sc) into each ch to end, turn. Turning each row with 1 ch, work 3 rows of dc (sc) on dc (sc) **.

Shape Body
1st row Sl st into 2nd dc (sc), 1 ch, 1 dc (sc) into each of next 53(55:57) dc (sc), turn.
*** Dec 1 st at each end of next row. Now dec 1 st at each end of next and every foll 8th row until 46(48:50) dc (sc) rem. Cont straight until work measures 6½(6¾:7) ins from beg of body shaping. Fasten off ***.

Left Leg

Work from ** to ** as given for Right Leg.

Shape Body
1st row Sl st into each of next 4 dc (sc),

1 ch, 1 dc (sc) into each of next 53(55:57) dc (sc), turn.
Complete as given for Right Leg from *** to ***.

Belt

Using No. 4·00 mm (F/5) hook and B, work 5 ch.
1st row Into 2nd ch from hook work 1 dc (sc) then 1 dc (sc) into rem ch, turn. Work in dc (sc) on dc (sc) until belt measures 26(27:28) ins, or required length. Fasten off.

Belt Tabs (4 required).
Using No. 4·00 mm (F/5) hook and B, work 8 ch.
1st row Into 2nd ch from hook work 1 dc (sc), 1 dc (sc) into each ch to end. Fasten off.

To make up

Join front and back seams. Work 2 rows dc (sc) round legs as given for Top armholes. Join leg seams. Sew 2 belt tabs to back and 2 to front. Sew buckle to belt end. Work a row of casing stitch around inside of waist edge and thread with elastic. Secure ends. Thread belt through tabs. Press very lightly.

Girl's one piece swimsuit
Right and Left Legs

Work as given for Boy's trunks.
Seam front and back seams together.

Top Front

Fold pants in half and mark sides (seams in centre).
Using No. 4·50 mm (G/6) hook and C, and with right side of pants front facing, join yarn to side.
1st row 2 ch, 1 h tr (hdc) in each dc (sc) across front to other side. 46(48:50) h tr (hdc) including first 2 ch, turn.
2nd row 2 ch. 1 h tr (hdc) into each h tr (hdc) to end. Cont in h tr (hdc) until top measures 6(6½:7) ins, inc 1 st at each end of 9th row.
Work as given for Boy's Top from armholes to completion.

Top Back

Using No. 4·50 mm (G/6) hook and C, and with right side of pants back facing, join yarn to side. Work as given for top front until 1 st has been inc at each end of 9th row. Work 1 row.

Divide for Back
1st row 2 ch, 1 h tr (hdc) into each of next 15(16:16) h tr (hdc), turn. Complete right back on these sts. Work until same length as front to armhole.

Shape armhole
1st row Sl st over next 8(9:9) h tr (hdc), 2 ch, 1 h tr (hdc) into each of next h tr (hdc) to end of row.
Cont on these sts, for Right Back until

armhole measures same length to shoulder as front, ending at armhole edge. Complete as for front shoulder. With right side of back facing, rejoin yarn to last 16(17:17) sts, and work left side to correspond with right side. Work Apple and leaf motifs, belt and tabs as given for Boy's Top and Trunks.

To make up

Work armhole and neck edgings in B as given for Boy's Top.

Leg Edgings
Work as for armholes only working dc (sc) into 2 out of every 3 sts along leg edge to draw leg opening in. Elastic may be threaded along this row if required. Seam legs. Sew on motifs and belt tabs. Sew buckle to belt and thread through tabs. Press lightly.

Games Set

Something in the colours of a favourite team is sure to please almost any small boy. This is a good basic pattern for a V-necked sweater plus scarf and balaclava. A clever pocket adds interest to the sweater front, so children can keep their hands warm on cool days. The strips of cable stitching are a decorative and simple design note.

Materials

Robin Vogue Double Knitting:
(Knitting Worsted), 25 gr balls
Sweater: 8(9 10) balls of white
Balaclava: 3(3:4) balls of white
Scarf: 6 balls of white
The coloured borders: 1 ball each of gold and emerald
Pairs of No. 8(5), 10(3) and 11(2) knitting needles
No. 3·00 mm (C/2) crochet hook.
Cable needle

Measurements

Sweater: To fit a 22(24:26) inch chest.
Scarf: Length, 36 ins (excluding fringes).
It can, of course, be made longer.
Balaclava: To fit average size head for chest sizes.

Tension 6 sts to 1 inch using No. 8(5) needles.

Abbreviations, needle and size note
See pages 12 and 13.
Extra abbreviations, W—white; G—gold; E—emerald.

Sweater
Back

Using No. 10(3) needles and W, cast on 79(85:91) sts and work in k 1, p 1 rib for 16 rows. Change to No. 8(5) needles and beg patt.
1st row K.
2nd row P 12(15:18), k 2, p 6, k 2, p 35, k 2, p 6, k 2, p 12(15:18).

3rd row K 14(17:20), C 6f, k 39, C 6b, k to end.
4th row As 2nd row.
5th, 6th, 7th and 8th rows Rep 1st and 2nd rows twice.
These 8 rows form patt. Rep them until work measures 8(9:10) ins from beg ending on a wrong side row.

Shape Armholes
Keeping continuity of patt, cast off 6 sts at beg of next 2 rows *. Now dec 1 st at each end of every row until 55(61:67) sts rem, then work straight until armhole measures 4½(5:5½) ins ending after a wrong side row.

Shape Shoulders
Cast off 7(7:8) sts at beg of next 2 rows and 6(7:8) sts at beg of next 2 rows. Leave rem sts on spare needle.

Front

Work as for back welt, then break yarn.
Slip first and last 27(30:33) sts onto spare needles. Rejoin yarn to centre 25 sts and with No. 8(5) needles work 24 rows st st, ending after a p row.
Break yarn and leave sts on spare needle and fold back on welt. Rejoin yarn to beg of first set of sts on spare needle and with No. 8(5) needles, k across first set of sts, with same needle pick up and k 25 sts from the first row of pocket at back, k across sts on other spare needle. 79(85:91) sts.
Now beg with a 2nd patt row work 23 rows of patt as for Back ending on a wrong side row.
Next row K 27(30:33), now with pocket at front k tog 1 st from pocket and 1 st from main part, then k 27(30:33). Cont in patt across all sts and work as Back to *.

Divide for Neck
Next row K 2 tog, patt 28(31:34) k 2 tog, k 1, turn and leave rem sts on a holder.
Now dec 1 st at side edge on next 5 rows, *but at the same time* shape neck edge as set on every right side row. Keeping armhole

edge straight, shape neck as before until 13(14:16) sts rem. Cont straight until work measures same as back to shoulder ending at side edge.

Shape Shoulder
Next row Cast off 7(7:8) sts, work to end. Work 1 row and cast off.
Leaving centre st on safety pin, rejoin yarn to inner edge of rem sts, k 1, SKPO, patt to last 2 sts, k 2 tog.
Now work to match first side.

Pocket edges

Using No. 10(3) needles and W, rejoin yarn and pick up and k 25 sts evenly from side of pocket and work 2 rows in rib. Cast off in rib. Work other side in same way. Sew edges of rib into place.

Sleeves

Using No. 10(3) needles and W, cast on 32(34:36) sts, and work 2 ins in k 1, p 1 rib. Change to No. 8(5) needles and patt.
1st row K.
2nd row P 3(4:5), k 2 (p 6, k 2) 3 times, p 3(4:5).
3rd row K 5(6:7), C 6f, k 10, C 6b, k 5(6:7).
4th row As 2nd row.
5th, 6th, 7th and 8th rows Rep 1st and 2nd rows twice. These 8 rows form patt. Cont in patt inc 1 st at each end of next and every foll 6th row until there are 36(44:52) sts, working extra sts into st st, then every 4th row until there are 52(56:60) sts. Work straight until sleeve measures 9(10½:12) ins from beg ending on a wrong side row.

Shape Top
Cast off 6 sts at beg of next 2 rows, then dec 1 st at each end of next 4(6:6) rows. Now dec 1 st at each end of every right side row until 24(24:26) sts rem then 1 st each end of every row until 12(12:14) sts rem. Cast off.

Neckband

Join right shoulder. Using No. 10(3) needles and W, and right side facing, rejoin yarn and pick up and k 35(39:41) sts from side of left neck, 1 st from safety pin (mark this st), 35(39:43) to shoulder seam, k across sts on spare needle, turn.
1st row With G, p to 2 sts before marker, p 2 tog tbl, p 1, p 2 tog, p to end.
2nd row Work in k 1, p 1 rib to 2 sts before marker, k 2 tog, k 1 SKPO, p 1, * k 1, p 1. Rep from * to end.
3rd row Rib to 2 sts before marker, p 2 tog tbl. p 1, p 2 tog, rib to end.
4th row With W, k to 2 sts before marker, k 2 tog, k 1, SKPO, k to end.
5th row As 3rd row.
6th row As 2nd row.
7th and 8th rows With E, rep 1st and 2nd rows. Cast off in rib dec as before.

To make up

Press work on wrong side using a warm iron over a damp cloth. Join left shoulder, neckband side and sleeve seams. Sew in sleeves. Press seams and edges.

Scarf

Using No. 8(5) needles and W, cast on 66 sts and work 16 rows in st st *. Change to G, and work 6 rows st st. Break G. Change to W and work 8 rows st st. Change to E and work 6 rows st st. Break E *. Change to W and work until scarf measures 10½ ins from beg ending after a p row. Rep. from * to * once more. Change to W and work until 23 ins are completed, ending after a p row. ** Change to E and work 6 rows st st. Break E. Change to W and work 8 rows st st. Change to G and work 6 rows st st. Break G. ** Change to W and work until scarf measures 31½ ins from beg, ending after a p row. Rep from ** to ** once more. Change to W and work 16 rows st st. Cast off. Press as sweater. Join side edges together with a flat seam. Turn scarf to right side and press with seam in centre. With W and No. 3·00 mm (C/2) hook work 1 row dc (sc) along edge working through both sets of sts, turn with 3 ch.
Next row * 1 dc (sc) in next dc (sc), 2 ch, miss 1 dc (sc). Rep from * to end, 1 dc (sc) in last dc (sc). Fasten off.
Work other edge in same way.
Cut yarn into 11 inch lengths in the 3 colours and knot through each chain sp alternating colours. Press and trim fringe.

Balaclava
Back

Using No. 10(3) needles and W, cast on 60(64:70) sts and k 4 rows.
Change to No. 8(5) needles. Work thus:
1st row K.
2nd row K 2, p to last 2 sts, k 2 *.
Rep these 2 rows until work measures 3(3:3½) ins from beg ending on a wrong side row.

Shape shoulders

Cast off 7 sts at beg of next 2 rows and 6(7:8) sts at beg of next 2 rows. Leave rem sts on spare needle.

Left front

Using No. 10(3) needles and W, cast on 30(32:35) sts and work as Back to *. Rep the last 2 rows 5(5:6) times more then the 1st row again to end at neck edge.

Shape neck

Next row Cast off 7 sts, work to end.
Next row Work to last 2 sts, k 2 tog.
Next row Cast off 2 sts, work to end.
Dec 1 st at neck edge on every row until 13(14:15) sts rem. Work straight for a few rows to same length as Back to shoulder ending at side edge.

Shape Shoulder

Next row Cast off 7 sts, work to end.
Work 1 row. Cast off.

Right front

Work as Left Front but working 12 rows before shaping neck.
Join shoulder seams.
With No. 10(3) needles and W and right side facing, pick up and k 89(95:101) sts evenly round neck edge.
Next row (wrong side) K 2, p 1, * k 1, p 1. Rep from * to last 2 sts, k 2.
Next row K 3, p 1, * k 1, p 1. Rep from * to last 3 sts, k 3.

Rep last 2 rows 3 times more, then first row again.
Next row Rib 15 as before, and leave these sts on safety pin. With No. 8(5) needles k to last 15 sts, turn leaving 15 sts on safety pin.
Next row P, *but 1st and 3rd sizes only* inc 1 st at centre. *2nd size only* dec 1 st at centre. 60(64:72) sts.
Work in st st until 3¾(4¼:4¾) ins from top of rib has been worked ending on a p row.

Shape Top

Next 2 rows K 44(47:53) k 2 tog, turn sl 1, p to last 16(17:19) p 2 tog, turn.
Next 2 rows Sl 1, k to last 15(16:18), k 2 tog, turn sl 1, p to last 15(16:18), p 2 tog, turn.
Cont dec in this way until all sts are on one needle. Cast off.
Place marker in centre of cast off edge.
With right side facing, leaving first 5 sts on safety pin, slip next 10 sts on to No. 10(3) needles, join in G, work thus:
1st row K.
2nd row K 2, p 6, k 2.
3rd row K 2, C 6b, k 2.
4th row As 2nd row.
5th, 6th, 7th and 8th rows Rep 1st and 2nd rows twice.
Rep these 8 rows until band fits to marker. Leave sts on safety pin. Slip first 10 sts of other side on to No. 10(3) needle leaving rem 5 sts on pin. Join in G and work to match other side but working cable C 6f instead of C 6b. Graft or cast off both sets of sts tog. Sew cable band into place.
With No. 10(3) needles and E, k across 5 sts on safety pin, then pick up and k 115(125:135) sts evenly from edge of cable, k across 5 sts on safety pin.
Next row K 2, p 1, * k 1, p 1. Rep from * to last 2 sts, k 2.
Next row K 3, p 1, * k 1, p 1. Rep from * to last 3 sts, k 3.
Rep last 2 rows once more. Cast off in rib.

To make up

Press as sweater. Join front edges together.

Games set

Tie-Dye Tunic

It is simple to use tie and dye work for making individual fabric patterns. This craft is an economical way of utilizing odd scraps of plain fabric like old sheets. These can be made into clothes like our play tunic and cheered up with colourful tie and dye design. The pattern is made by folding and binding the fabric, then dipping it in dye, so the colour reaches some parts of the fabric and not others, giving a beautiful shaded effect. For a two, or three-colour pattern, parts of the folding are protected by strips of polythene. This prevents the dye from penetrating into the covered sections of fabric while it is dipped and re-dipped. Surplus dye is removed after each dip by washing and rinsing fabric, which then becomes completely colour fast. When making clothes, the dyeing is done after cutting out and before making up. Similar effects can be gained by dyeing ready-made white garments such as inexpensive tee shirts.

Materials

Dylon Cold Dye: a tin each of Sahara Sun, Mandarin and Mexican Red
String, cord or tough elastic bands
Strips of polythene
1¼ yds white linen
5 in Velcro or 6 strong poppers (snaps)
Thread to match finished colour of dye

Measurements
Chest measurements 22, 23, 24 and 25 in.

1. Cut out fabric according to the pattern, preferably using pinking shears.
Alternatively finish off all raw edges with machine zigzag stitch before starting tie and dye work.
2. Mark centre of circle pattern on back, front and sleeves with a pin. Fold fabric back and furl it like an umbrella (diagram 1), then bind extra tightly in 3 places using rubber bands or string (diagram 2). Remove pins. Make the stripey pattern by folding

concertina pleats on the base of sleeves and hem on front and back pieces of tunic

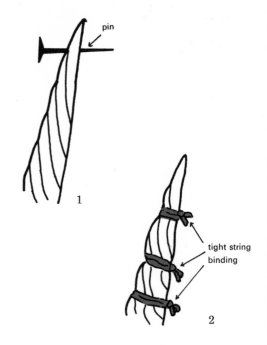

1

pin

tight string
binding

2

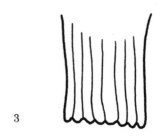

3

(diagram 3). Bind in 3 places and dye first in a pot of Sahara sun yellow. Wash and rinse the fabric pieces.

288

3. Cut one inch wide strips of polythene and bind these round each dyed portion of fabric, using string or elastic bands. Use two rows of polythene for each dyed portion and cover the "umbrella tips" with polythene too (diagram 4). Dye in a pot of Mandarin, then wash and rinse.

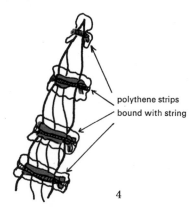

polythene strips
bound with string

4

4. Leave the polythene in place. Tie new string loosely above each binding and remove original bindings where fabric is still white underneath. Dye in a pot of Mexican Red, then wash and rinse, before pressing thoroughly.

5. Make neck fastenings by folding under the shoulder tops on the back and front pattern pieces, making a ¾ in turning. Overlap the shoulder tops by 1 in and attach Velcro or poppers to fasten. Do up the Velcro or poppers and stitch along armhole for 3 ins on top of shoulders to attach front of tunic to back (diagram 5). Sew up sides and arms

of sleeves. Attach sleeves to bodice. Neaten edge of sleeves. Turn up hem at the base of the tunic in the normal way or make a false hem.

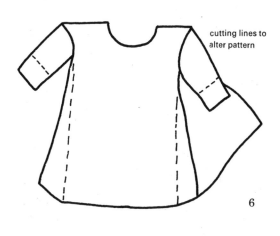

cutting lines to
alter pattern

6

7

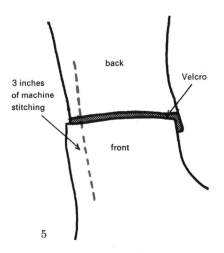

back

Velcro

3 inches
of machine
stitching

front

5

This pattern can be easily adapted for a boy by making the body less flared and the sleeves shorter (diagram 6), and by leaving a 4 in deep opening at the base of side seams for a casual look (diagram 7).

289

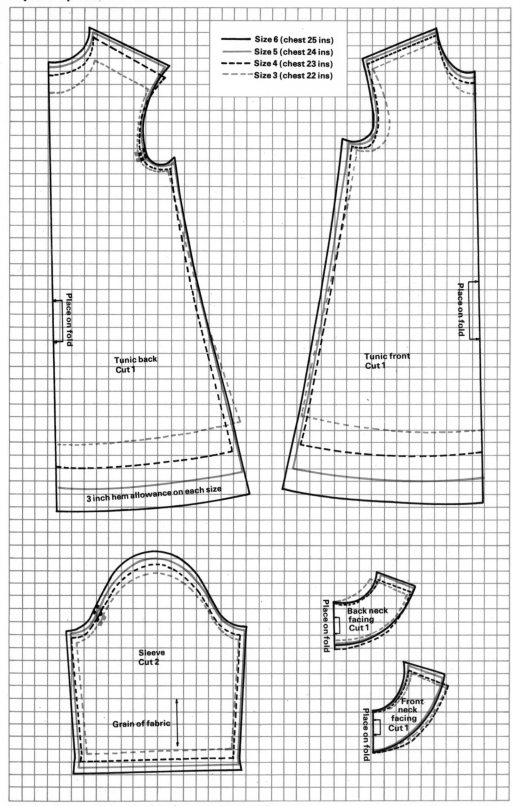

Size 6 (chest 25 ins)
Size 5 (chest 24 ins)
Size 4 (chest 23 ins)
Size 3 (chest 22 ins)

Place on fold

Place on fold

Tunic back
Cut 1

Tunic front
Cut 1

3 inch hem allowance on each size

Sleeve
Cut 2

Grain of fabric

Place on fold

Back neck
facing
Cut 1

Place on fold

Front
neck
facing
Cut 1

Party Cloak

This gorgeous party cloak is just what home sewing is all about. It should be almost impossible to buy a cloak like this ready-made, especially with the soft fluffy edging in crochet mohair. The cloak, with its matching lining, is easy to make and the crochet edging adds a smart touch of extravagance. Once you get into the swing of doing the looped crochet stitch, you will find it is the sort of straight-forward work you can do while watching television or chatting in the evenings.
This pattern can be adapted for other uses in several ways. For instance, make a winter cloak from warm tweed and make the crochet edging in double knitting wool for a "fun fur" effect. The crochet edging pattern can also be used for adding a decorative touch to cuffs, collars and hems of dresses and coats.

Materials

Velvet and lining:
2½ yds of 36 in fabric
1¼ yds of 54 in fabric
Crochet edging:
5 balls of Emu Filigree

A No. 6·00 mm (I/9) crochet hook
Large covered hook and eye for fastening

Cloak

1. Cut out cloak, making sure pile of velvet faces up to neck of garment.
2. Stitch darts in back, press towards centre. Stitch side seams, notching over shoulders. Then, placing right sides together, stitch hood, notching curves. Fold along lines to make pleats.
3. Make hood lining in the same way and attach to hood right sides together. Stitch hood to neckline, right sides together.

Stitch back neck facing to front facing, right sides together. Stitch facings to neckline all round, right sides together. Grade turnings and turn to right side.
4. Make the cloak lining in the same way as step 2 and stitch into place just inside edge of facing.
5. Turn up hem, being careful not to mark velvet on right side. Slipstitch lining into place along hemline. Attach fastening to front edges of neckline, making an edge-to-edge opening.
6. Slip-stitch crochet edging to cloak on right side using the same coloured sewing thread as the crochet and making sure the stitches do not go through the lining. Use a double thread and sew along centre of edging. It will be simple to remove, so garment and edging can be laundered separately.

Crochet Edging

Measurements 3½ yds long
Abbreviations see page 12
Work a chain 3½ yds long. If using a different yarn, the chain should be the same length as the required area to be edged. Instead of going all around the garment, it can be long enough to edge the hood alone, or to edge hood plus front.
1st row 1 dc (sc) in 2nd ch from hook, 1 dc (sc) in each ch to end, 1 ch, turn.
2nd row * Insert hook through next st, wind yarn twice round 2nd and 3rd fingers of left hand, clockwise. Now insert hook under top loops, yrh, pull through loops on fingers, yrh, draw through both loops on hook. Rep from * to end, 1 ch, turn.
3rd row 1 dc (sc) in each st of previous row, 1 ch turn.
4th row As 2nd row, but omitting 1 ch at end of row. Fasten off.

5 squares represent 4 inches

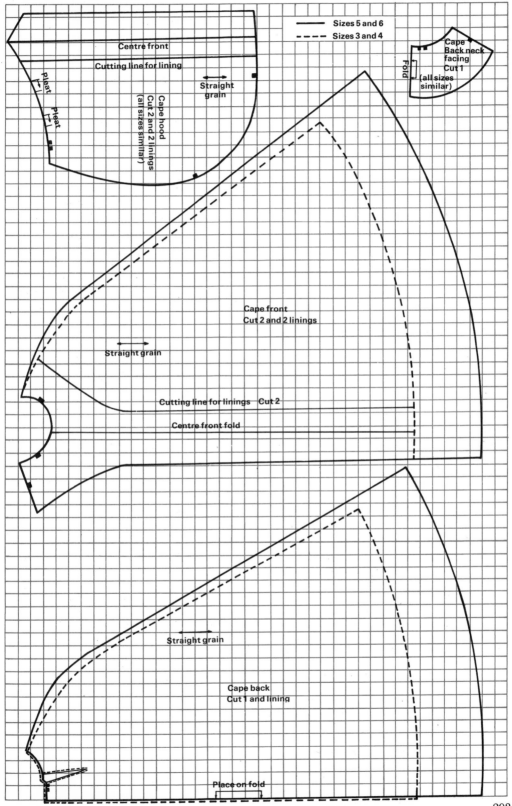

Sizes 5 and 6

Sizes 3 and 4

Centre front

Cutting line for lining

Straight grain

Pleat

Pleat

Cape hood
Cut 2 and 2 linings
(all sizes similar)

Cape
Back neck
facing
Cut 1

Fold

(all sizes
similar)

Cape front
Cut 2 and 2 linings

Straight grain

Cutting line for linings   Cut 2

Centre front fold

Straight grain

Cape back
Cut 1 and lining

Place on fold

293

Play Apron

This practical play apron is ideal for painting or mealtimes and has a cunning hidden bonus. The PVC overskirt and cuffs are attached with Velcro, so can be removed in a trice if paint or food has been spilt. It is a simple matter then to wipe away the mark and the whole garment will not need to be washed. Underneath the PVC is a tough and protective apron, made from sailcloth that is comfortable to wear for play-school or when helping Mum around the house. The velvet side of the Velcro strip looks decorative stitched to the apron front if the PVC overskirt is not in place, and the appliqué on the apron is also a pocket. This pattern is another good way of showing how a simple garment can be turned into something that is excitingly different as well as being ultra-practical

Materials

Sailcloth or tough cotton:
1⅛ yds of 45 in fabric
PVC:
¾ yd of green for overskirt
¼ yd each of yellow and white for trims
6 yds of bias binding
Tracing paper and sticky tape for sewing PVC
1. Cut out sailcloth and overcast all seam edges with three-step zigzag.
2. Stitch dart in head of sleeve and press. Join sleeves to front and backs. Stitch sleeves and side seams in one operation, right sides together, clipping on curves.
3. Neaten all edges round neck, back opening and hem by facing with bias binding. Leave extra bias binding at back neck opening to use as tie. Stop edges of tie fraying by knotting.
4. Turn up ½ in hem on bottom of sleeves and topstitch. Stitch Velcro on ends of sleeves so that an inverted pleat will be formed when closed. Also stitch a small oblong of Velcro on back section of sleeve close to seam at cuff edge (this is used to attach PVC cuff). Attach Velcro to bodice front, close to bodice/sleeve seam, also at centre back of both pieces (diagrams 1 and 2).

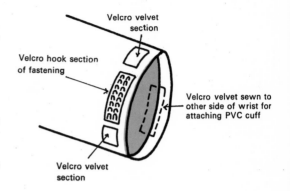

Velcro velvet section

Velcro hook section of fastening

Velcro velvet sewn to other side of wrist for attaching PVC cuff

Velcro velvet section

1

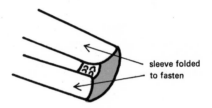

sleeve folded to fasten

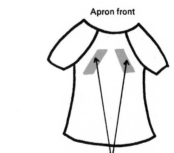

Apron front

2   sew Velcro velvet section here

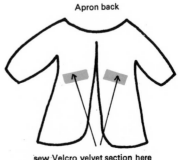

Apron back

sew Velcro velvet section here

5. Cut out PVC overskirt and join side seams.

6. Cut out the appliqué shapes and pieces of tracing paper the same size. The house is $7 \times 4\frac{1}{2}$ ins plus $\frac{1}{2}$ in top turning. Door: $2 \times 1\frac{1}{2}$. Windows: $1 \times 1\frac{1}{2}$. Roof: 2 ins deep, 6 ins along top and 8 ins along bottom. Chimney: 3 ins $\times 1\frac{1}{2}$.

7. Use sticky tape instead of pins to hold PVC in place. Place the cut paper over appliqué sections to prevent PVC from sticking in sewing machine. A special roller foot for the sewing machine also helps. Tape door and windows in place over house and stitch round edges, over paper. Turn under top $\frac{1}{2}$ in of white section and stitch. Attach this section, which will be a pocket for painting-things, to centre of apron front by stitching down sides and along bottom. Cut out roof and stitch to apron round all sides. Cut out white chimney, turning top under and stitching, before applying as a pocket for pencils. Trim back edges outside sewing lines and if required, overstitch with neat zigzag stitch, placing strips of tracing paper above sewing lines to facilitate sewing.

This appliqué method can be used for many different pocket ideas to decorate the apron front. The secret is to keep the shapes simple so the work does not become too fiddly.

8. Finish back edges and hem of overskirt with bias binding. Finish the top this way too, but leave enough bias at each end for ties. Apply the "hook" section of Velcro fastening inside top edge of overskirt. This will fasten up with the corresponding strip of Velcro on the yellow apron.

3

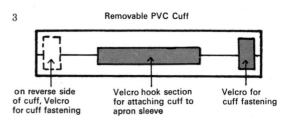

Removable PVC Cuff

on reverse side of cuff, Velcro for cuff fastening

Velcro hook section for attaching cuff to apron sleeve

Velcro for cuff fastening

9. Fold cuffs, right sides together, and stitch, leaving opening on one side to turn. Turn and stitch along centre to secure. Apply Velcro as cuff fastenings and add another 2 in strip to the inside of each cuff. This will correspond with the strips already applied to apron sleeves (diagram 3).

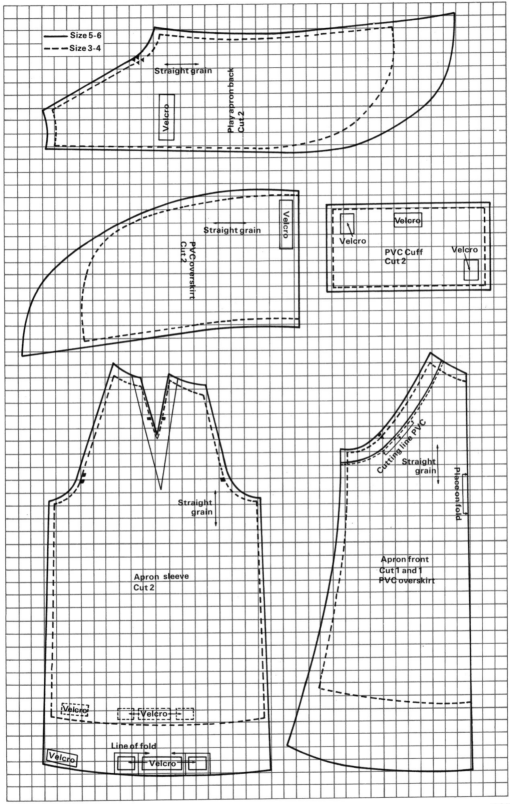

5 squares represent 4 inches

Size 5-6
Size 3-4

Straight grain

Play apron back
Cut 2

Velcro

Straight grain

Velcro

PVC overskirt
Cut 2

Velcro

Velcro

PVC Cuff
Cut 2

Velcro

Velcro

Straight
grain

Apron sleeve
Cut 2

Cutting line PVC

Straight
grain

Place on fold

Apron front
Cut 1 and 1
PVC overskirt

Velcro

Velcro

Line of fold

Velcro

Velcro

Hooded Play Jumper

Crochet borders, a gay fringe and smart cross stitch embroidery are the extra touches that make this warm play jumper unusual. The pattern is straightforward to knit in an extra thick yarn and an easy garter stitch. The cosy hood makes it an ideal garment for cool weather. It is loose fitting, allowing for plenty of movement and will be comfortable to wear over winter jumpers and trousers.

Materials

Robin Vogue Double Double
(Knitting Worsted or Bulky), 50 gr balls:
9(10:11) balls of red
1 ball each of blue and yellow
Pairs of No. 5(8) and 7(6) knitting needles
No. 4·50 mm (G/6) crochet hook
2 buttons

Measurements To fit a 22(24:26) inch chest.

Tension 4 sts to 1 inch over g st on No. 5(8) needles.

Abbreviations, needle and size note
See pages 12 and 13. Extra abbreviations:
R—Red; B—blue; Y—yellow.

Back

Using No. 5(8) needles and R, cast on 48(52:56) sts and work in g st until back measures 7(8½:9½) ins from beg.

Shape Armholes
Cast off 6(6:7) sts at beg of next 2 rows, 36(40:42) sts *. Cont straight until armhole measures 4½(5:5½) ins from beg.

Shape Shoulders
Cast off 5 sts at beg of next 2 rows and 4(5:5) sts on next 2 rows. Leave rem 18(20:22) sts on a holder.

Front

Work as Back to *, then work 2(4:4) rows straight.

Divide for Front Opening
Next row K 16(18:19), cast off 4, k to end. Work on last set of sts, ** work straight until armhole measures 3½(4:4½) ins ending at front edge.

Shape Neck
Cast off 3(4:4) sts at beg of next row and 3(3:4) sts on next alt row, then dec 1 st at same edge on next alt row 9(10:10) sts. Work straight until same length as back to beg of shoulder shaping ending at armhole edge.

Shape Shoulder
Cast off 5 sts at beg of next row, then work 1 row. Cast off rem sts.
Return to other sts, rejoin yarn at inner edge to rem sts and work to match first side working from ** to end.

Sleeves

Begin at shoulder.
Using No. 5(8) needles and B, cast on 36(40:44) sts and work in g st for 1¾(1¾:2) ins. Place marker at edge of last row. Work 4(6:8) rows more, then dec 1 st each end of next and every foll 8th row until 24(26:28) sts rem. Work straight until sleeve measures 7½(9:10½) ins from marker—or required length. Cast off.

Crochet Edgings
Join shoulder, side and sleeve seams. Using No. 4·50 mm (G/6) crochet hook, with wrong side facing and R, work thus round lower edges of back, front and sleeves.
1st round 1 dc (sc) into each st, join with a sl st.
2nd round In B as 1st round.
3rd round In Y as 1st round.
4th round As 2nd round.
5th round As 1st round. Fasten off.

Front Bands
Using No. 4·50 mm (G/6) crochet hook, R, and with wrong side facing, work 4 rows of

dc (sc) turning each time with 1 ch—along right front edge. Fasten off.

Work left front to match but making 2 buttonholes in 2nd row by working 1 ch instead of a dc (sc), 3 sts in from each edge. In 3rd row work a dc (sc) into the *1 ch sp*. Stitch down side edge at base, left overlapping right.

Hood

Using No. 7(6) needles and R and with right side facing and omitting frontbands, pick up and k 12(13:13) sts from right front neck, k 18(20:22) sts from back neck and 12(12:13) sts from left front neck. 42(45:48) sts. Work 4 rows g st. Change to No. 5(8) needles.
Next row K 1, inc in next st, * k 2, inc. in next st. Rep from * to last st, k 1. 56(60:64) sts.
Work straight in g st until work measures 7(8:8½) ins or length required. Cast off. Fold cast off edge in half and join on wrong side.

Hood Edging
With right side facing, and R, work crochet edging as before but work in rows, cutting each colour at end of row and beg all rows at same edge. Work last row across each side edge for a neat finish.

To make up

Press lightly on wrong side using a warm iron over a damp cloth. Set in sleeves, sewing the part above marker to cast off armhole sts. Cut 5 inch lengths of each colour and, alternating colours, knot a fringe all round lower edge, along join of hood and down centre of back hood to neck. Turn back hood edging and tack down at each side of neck edge.

Cross stitch embroidery
Work over 1 st in width and 1 g st ridge in depth. Mark centre 2 sts between front band and first row of crochet edging in B. Work 4 crosses at centre, i.e. 2 rows of 2 in B, then using Y and leaving 2 g st ridges above and below and 2 sts at each side, work '1 box' of cross sts around centre and another 'box' in B at same intervals as before, as shown in photograph. Sew on buttons.

Peasant Dress

Bold embroidery makes this colourful peasant-style dress into something unusual. The dress is in fresh-looking and inexpensive calico, and the embroidery is worked with tapisserie wool. The secret of making effective use of embroidery on children's clothes is to keep it simple. The chain stitch is quick to sew, and the thread is colour fast and easily washable. There are many variations on this theme; use the flowers in a small cluster to decorate a collar on a plain dress or shirt; in a panel down the front of a shift dress or in a deep border round the hem of a party dress. Pastel-coloured flowers would look effective against plain fabric in a deep colour.

Materials

Calico—1¾ yds 36 in wide fabric
Coats Anchor Tapisserie Wool:
2 skeins green, 1 red, 1 blue, 1 yellow
½ yd muslin for lining bodice (optional)
4 buttons to cover

1. Cut out calico, overcast all cut edges and make up dress. Sew bodice darts first, then join bodice at shoulders.
2. Gather sleeves and sew to bodice. Stitch underarm seam of sleeves and bodice side in one.
3. Measure round neck and armhole. Cut half inch wide strips of calico in the same measurements, adding one inch to each for turnings. These must be cut on the *bias*.
4. Neaten neckline with the bias strips. Gather in fullness at sleeve edge and neaten with bias strip.

5. Join skirt, leaving a 4 in opening below waist at back. Gather skirt top, pin, baste and stitch to bodice, adjusting gathers evenly before stitching.
6. Turn up hem to individual size.
7. Sketch embroidery pattern on to dress with a pencil. Work embroidery in chain stitch (see page 9), using one strand of wool, following colours on our pattern or choosing your own.
8. With green, embroider chain stitch in a neat row round neckline and armholes, sewing along the binding. Embroider more green just above the hem as in photograph. At each side make small curves the same as those on the bodice centre waist.
9. To make bow, twist four 6 ft long strands of thread together evenly. Pin ends firmly to upholstered chair or tie them round a door handle while you twist the other ends round and round with one hand. When twists become tight, hold middle of skein with spare hand and let threads twist up on themselves so they become half their original length. Knot each end, untie threads outside knot to make a tassel. Clip away spare thread ends.
10. Cut out circles of calico to cover buttons. Embroider small daisy shapes with 3 petals in centre of each circle, using one strand of tapisserie wool and assorted colours. Use the circles to cover buttons so that embroidery lies in centre of button. Make the button-holes.
11. Cut bodice back and front shape from muslin and use this as lining to neaten inside bodice. Join lining at shoulders and slip stitch by hand to wrong side of bodice, turning raw edges under.

5 squares represent 4 inches

Size 4 only

Dress front Cut 1 and 1 lining

Dress back Cut 2 and 2 linings

Sleeve
Cut 2

For skirt Cut a length measuring 16 ins × 56 ins

Peasant dress

Quilted Waistcoat

The quilted velvet and shining metal buttons transform this straightforward pattern into party wear, fit for the best occasions. With the aid of a special foot on the sewing machine, quilting is quick to do at home, although it can also be done by hand. This is the sort of special garment that is always good to make because it becomes something that is quite individual.

Materials

Velvet, lining and Courtelle wadding:
$1\frac{1}{2}$ yds of 36 in wide fabric or
$1\frac{1}{8}$ yds of 45 in wide fabric
Matching thread
6 metal buttons
18 ins silk cord for button fastening

1. Cut out the pattern pieces in the three fabrics, allowing an extra inch all round pattern. Make sure pile of velvet is going up towards neck.
2. Place wadding under velvet and tack together. Using quilting foot and guide on the sewing machine, quilt velvet on the bias into inch squares, making sure that lines match up the front. If your machine has no quilting foot, rule the sewing lines with pencil and sew with an ordinary straight stitch.
3. Complete quilting, then re-cut front and back of waistcoat to the right size. Stitch front to back at side seams. Clip curves.
4. Stitch the side seams of the lining. Press under $\frac{5}{8}$ in on shoulder edges. With right sides together, pin facing to vest, keeping raw edges even. Stitch all round except for shoulder edges and leave a 6 in. break in the stitching at the lower edge of back so the waistcoat can be turned the right way out. Trim all seams and corners. Clip curves. Turn and press. Either use a special velvet board, or lightly press using a Turkish towel as a base. Slipstitch back edge together along the 6 in break.
5. Sew shoulder seams of velvet with right

sides facing. Press seams open. Slipstitch shoulder edges of lining together.
6. Sew on buttons. Cut cord into 6 in lengths. Working one at a time, sew ends of

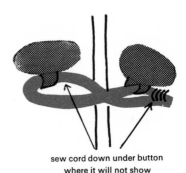

sew cord down under button
where it will not show

1

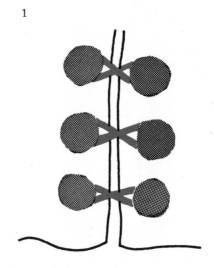

cord under buttons on right hand side, making three loops. These are then twisted once over the opening and looped round the left hand buttons for fastening (diagram 1).

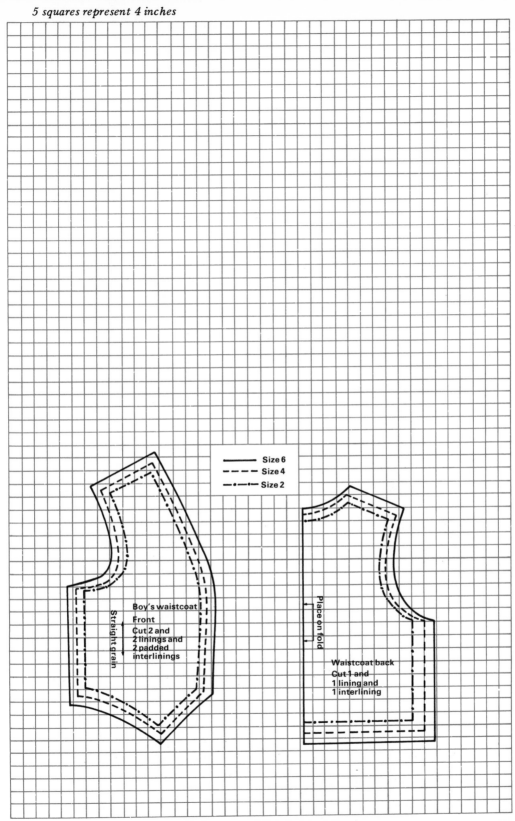

Size 6
Size 4
Size 2

Boy's waistcoat
Front
Cut 2 and
2 linings and
2 padded
interlinings

Straight grain

Place on fold

Waistcoat back
Cut 1 and
1 lining and
1 interlining

Simple Tabard

Beginners will find this crochet pattern an excellent one to try. It is quick, easy and practical. The tabard looks smart over play clothes, over matching tights and sweaters, or over long-sleeved blouses worn with trousers. There is a wide choice of alternative two-colour mixtures to think about, from scarlet with white to bright yellow with orange.

Materials

Pingouin Classique Crylor (Sport Yarn) 50 gr balls:

1(1:2:2) balls in dark shade (Dk), 1(1:1:1) balls in light shade (Lt)
No. 3·50 mm (E/4) crochet hook

Measurements To fit a 20(22:24:26) inch chest.
Length: about $11\frac{3}{4}(12\frac{3}{4}:15\frac{1}{2}:16\frac{1}{2})$ ins

Tension Motif measures $2\frac{3}{4}$ inches square
Note It is advisable to test tension before beginning garment and, if necessary, to change to a larger or smaller hook to obtain the correct tension.

Abbreviations, hook and size note
See pages 12 and 13.
Extra abbreviations, Dk—dark shade; Lt—light shade.

Motif

Using No. 3·50 mm (E/4) hook and Lt, make 6 ch and join into a ring with a sl st.
1st round Into ring work 2 ch [as 1st h tr (hdc)] 2 h tr (hdc), 3 ch, * 3 h tr (hdc), 3 ch. Rep from * twice, sl st to top of 2 ch.
2nd round Join on Dk, sl st to first sp, [2 ch, 2 h tr (hdc), 3 ch, 3 h tr (hdc)] into first 3 ch sp, * [1 ch, 3 h tr (hdc), 3 ch, 3 h tr (hdc)] into next 3 ch sp. Rep from * twice, 1 ch, join with a sl st.
3rd round In Lt, sl st to first sp, [2 ch,

2 h tr (hdc), 3 ch, 3 h tr (hdc)] into first 3 ch sp, * 1 ch, 3 h tr (hdc) into 1 ch sp, [1 ch, 3 h tr (hdc), 3 ch, 3 h tr (hdc)] into each corner sp. Rep from * ending 1 ch, 3 h tr (hdc) into 1 ch sp, 1 ch, sl st to join.
4th round In Dk, work 1 dc (sc) into each st all round, join with sl st and fasten off. This completes one motif. Work 24(24:40:40) motifs in all.

To make up

Do not press Form Back and Front of Tabard by joining 12(12:20:20) motifs tog for each side. Join 3(3:4:4) motifs in width and 4(4:5:5) motifs in length. With Dk, Work 2(4:3:5) rows in dc (sc) all round edges of Back and Front, working 1 extra dc (sc) in each corner on each row to keep work flat.
Work Shoulders (worked on one side of Tabard only)
1st and 2nd sizes only At one end of one side of Tabard, with Dk, work in dc (sc) to the centre of the first motif in row. Turn with 1 ch. Work 3(5) more rows in dc (sc) on this half motif, turning each row with 1 ch. Break yarn and fasten off. Rejoin yarn to centre of last motif in row and work in dc (sc) to end. Work to correspond with other shoulder.
3rd and 4th sizes only At one end of one side of Tabard, with Dk, work in dc (sc) across first motif in row. Turn with 1 ch. Work 7(9) more rows, turning each row with 1 ch. Break yarn and fasten off. Rejoin to beg of last motif in row and work in dc (sc) to end. Work to correspond with other shoulder. Join shoulders to other piece of Tabard.

Ties (4 required)

Using Dk, make a ch 12 ins in length and work 1 dc (sc) in each ch st. Break yarn and fasten off.
Now sew ties to sides of Tabard.

Everyday Clothes

Aran Sweater

This practical pattern, in the famous knitting style from the Aran islands, is useful to master. It can be used for both girls and boys. Especially warm and durable, it is a good money-saver when made at home as Aran-style clothes are expensive to buy.

Materials

Sweater 10(11:12:13) 25 gr balls of Lister Lavenda Double Knitting Wool (Knitting Worsted)

Pairs of No. 9(4) and No. 11(2) knitting needles

Measurements To fit a 24(26:28:30) in. chest

Tension 6 sts and 8 rows to 1 in using No. 9(4) needles

Abbreviations, needle and size note See pages 12 and 13.

Back

Using No. 11(2) needles cast on 80(84:92:96) sts, and work 10 rows in k 1, p 1 rib. Change to No. 9(4) needles and work in pattern thus:
1st row (K 1, p 1) 2(3:5:6) times, T2R, p 2 (k 4, p 4) twice, k 4, p 2, T2R, p 3, k 1, T2R, p 4, T2L, k1, p 3, T2L, p 2, (k 4, p 4) twice, k 4, p 2, T2L, (k 1, p 1) 2(3:5:6) times
2nd row (P 1, k 1) 2(3:5:6) times, p 2, k 2, (p 4, k 4) twice, p 4, k 2, p 2, k 3, p 3, k 4, p 3, k 3, p 2, k 2, (p 4, k 4) twice, p 4, k 2, p 2, (p 1, k 1) 2(3:5:6) times
3rd row M st 4(6:10:12), T2R, p 2, (C4F, p 4) twice, C4F, p 2, T2R, p 2, T2RP, T2R, p 4, T2L, T2LP, p 2, T2L, p 2, (C4B, p 4) twice, C4B, p 2, T2L, m st 4(6:10:12).
4th row M st 4(6:10:12), p 2, k 2, (p 4, k 4) twice, p 4, k 2, p 2, k 2, p 1, k 1, p 2, k 4, p 2,

k 1, p 1, k 2, p 2, k 2, (p 4, k 4) twice, p 4, k 2, p 2, m st 4(6:10:12).
5th row M st 4(6:10:12), T2R, p 2, (k 4, p 4) twice, k 4, p 2, T2R, p 1, T2RP, p 1, T2R, p 4, T2L, p 1, T2LP, p 1, T2L, p 2, (k 4, p 4) twice, k 4, p 2, T2L, m st to end.
6th row M st 4(6:10:12), p 2, k 2, (p 4, k 4) twice, p 4, k 2, p 2, k 1, p 1, k 2, p 2, k 4, p 2, k 2, p 1, k 1, p 2, k 2, (p 4, k 4) twice, p 4, k 2, p 2, m st to end.
7th row M st 4(6:10:12), T2R, p 2, (C4F, p 4) twice, C4F, p 2, T2R, T2RP, p 2, T2R, p 4, T2L, p 2, T2LP, T2L, p 2, (C4B, p 4) twice, C4B, p 2, T2L, m st to end.
8th row M st 4(6:10:12), p 2, k 2, (p 4, k 4) twice, p 4, k 2, p 3, k 3, p 2, k 4, p 2, k 3, p 3, k 2, (p 4, k 4) twice, p 4, k 2, p 2, m st to end.
9th row As 1st row.
10th row As 2nd row.
11th row M st 4(6:10:12), T2R, p 2, k 2, (C4FP, C4BP) twice, k 2, p 2, T2R, p 2, T2RP, T2R, p 4, T2L, T2LP, p 2, T2L, p 2, k 2, (C4FP, C4BP) twice, k 2, p 2, T2L, m st to end.
12th row M st 4(6:10:12), (p 2, k 2) twice, p 4, k 4, p 4, (k 2, p 2) twice, k 2, p 1, k 1, p 2, k 4, p 2, k 1, p 1, k 2, (p 2, k 2) twice, p 4, k 4, p 4, (k 2, p 2) twice, m st to end
13th row M st 4(6:10:12), T2R, p 2, k 2, p 2, k 4, p 4, k 4, p 2, k 2, p 2, T2R, p 1, T2RP, p 1, T2R, p 4, T2L, p 1, T2LP, p 1, T2L, p 2, k 2, p 2, k 4, p 4, k 4, p 2, k 2, p 2, T2L, m st to end.
14th row M st 4(6:10:12), (p 2, k 2) twice, p 4, k 4, p 4, (k 2, p 2) twice, k 1, p 1, k 2, p 2, k 4, p 2, k 2, p 1, k 1, (p 2, k 2) twice, p 4, k 4, p 4, (k 2, p 2) twice, m st to end.
15th row M st 4(6:10:12), T2R, p 2, k 2, p 2, C4F, p 4, C4F, p 2, k 2, p 2, T2R, T2RP, p 2, T2R, p 4, T2L, p 2, T2LP, T2L, p 2, k 2, p 2, C4B, p 4, C4B, p 2, k 2, p 2, T2L, m st to end.
16th row M st 4(6:10:12), (p 2, k 2) twice, p 4, k 4, p 4, k 2, p 2, k 2, p 3, k 3, p 2, k 4, p 2, k 3, p 3, k 2, p 2, k 2, p 4, k 4, p 4, (k 2, p 2) twice, m st to end.

17th row M st 4(6:10:12), T2R, p 2, k 2, p 2, k 4, p 4, k 4, p 2, k 2, p 2, T2R, p 3, k 1, T2R, p 4, T2L, k 1, p 3, T2L, p 2, k 2, p 2, k 4, p 4, k 4, p 2, k 2, p 2, T2L, m st to end.
18th row M st 4(6:10:12), (p 2, k 2) twice, p 4, k 4, p 4, (k 2, p 2) twice, k 3, p 3, k 4, p 3, k 3, (p 2, k 2) twice, p 4, k 4, p 4, (k 2, p 2) twice, m st to end.
19th row M st 4(6:10:12), T2R, p 2, k 2, p 2, C4F, p 4, C4F, p 2, k 2, p 2, T2R, p 2, T2RP, T2R, p 4, T2L, T2LP, p 2, T2L, p 2, k 2, p 2, C4B, p 4, C4B, p 2, k 2, p 2, T2L, m st to end.
20th row As 12th row.
21st row As 13th row.
22nd row As 14th row.
23rd row M st 4(6:10:12) T2R, p 2, k 2, (C4BP, C4FP) twice, k 2, p 2, T2R, T2RP, p 2, T2R, p 4, T2L, p 2, T2LP, T2L, p 2, k 2 (C4BP, C4FP) twice, k 2, p 2, T2L, m st to end.
24th row As 8th row
These 24 rows form patt. Cont in patt until work measures 9½(10:10½:11) ins ending after a wrong side row.

Shape Armholes
Keeping continuity of patt, cast off 5(4:5:4) sts at beg of next 2 rows.
3rd row K 2, SKPO, patt to last 4 sts, k 2 tog, k 2.
4th row K 1, p 2, patt to last 3 sts, p 2, k 1**.
Rep 3rd and 4th rows until 28(30:32:34) sts rem. Leave sts on spare needle for neckband.

Front

Work as for back to **, then rep 3rd and 4th rows until 42(46:50:54) sts rem.

Shape Neck
1st row (right side) K 2, SKPO, patt 10(12:14:16) sts, turn
2nd row P 2, patt to last 3 sts, p 2, k 1.
3rd row K 2, SKPO, patt to last 3 sts, k 2 tog, k 1.
4th row As 2nd row.
Rep last 2 rows until all sts worked off, working without edge sts as numbers decrease.
Return to other sts, sl next 14 sts on to a safety pin, rejoin yarn and patt to last 4 sts, k 2 tog, k 2

Next row K 1, p 2, patt to last 2 sts, p 2
Next row K 1, SKPO, patt to last 4 sts, k 2 tog, k 2.
Complete to match other side.

Sleeves

Using No. 11(2) needles, cast on 36(36:40:40) sts and work 14(14:18:18) rows in k 1, p 1, rib. Change to No. 9(4) needles.
1st row (K 1, p 1) 2(2:3:3) times, T2R, p 2, (k 4, p 4) twice, k 4, p 2, T2L, (k 1, p 1) 2(2:3:3) times.
2nd row (P 1, k 1) 2(2:3:3) times, p 2, k 2, (p 4, k 4) twice, p 4, k 2, p 2, (p 1, k 1) 2(2:3:3) times.
3rd row (K 1, p 1) 2(2:3:3) times, T2R, p 2, (C4F, p 4) twice, C4F, p 2, T2L, (k 1, p 1) 2(2:3:3) times.
4th row As 2nd row.
Cont in patt as now set, working cable patt as Back and inc 1 st each end of next and every foll 6th row working inc sts into m st, until there are 58(60:66:68) sts. Cont in patt until work measures 11(12:13:14) ins, or required length.

Shape Top
Work as Back armhole until 6 sts rem for each size. Leave sts on spare needle.

Neckband

Sew in sleeves, leaving Left Back armhole open. Now with right side of work facing and beg with left sleeve, rejoin yarn and using No. 11(2) needles, k across 6 sts at top of sleeve, pick up and k 14(16:18:20) sts down left front, k across 14 sts of front neck, pick up and k 14(16:18:20) sts up right front, k across 6 sts at top of sleeve and 28(30:32:34) sts at back neck. 82(88:94:100) sts.
Work 7 rows in k 1, p 1 rib. Cast off in rib.

To make up

Press work on wrong side with a warm iron over a damp cloth. Join left back armhole. Join side and sleeve seams. Press seams.

Fair Isle Pullover

Designs like this are always fashionable and always a pleasure to knit. A sleeveless pullover is excellent to make for either boys or girls.

Materials

Emu Machine Washable 4-ply wool: (Fingering 3-ply):

Pullover: 2(3:3) balls of natural, 1 ball each of new white, Spanish gold and maize. Pairs of No. 10(3) and 12(1) knitting needles

Measurements Measures 22(24:26) inches. Length: 14(14½: 15) inches.

Tension 7 sts to 1 inch over stocking stitch.

Abbreviations, needle and size note See pages 12 and 13. Extra abbreviations, G—Spanish Gold; W—White; M—Maize.

Back

** Using No. 12(1) needles and mc, cast on 77(85:93) sts and work thus:
1st row K 1, * p 1, k 1. Rep from * to end.
2nd row P 1, * k 1, p 1. Rep from * to end.
Rep last 2 rows 4 times more. Change to No. 10(3) needles and work in st st for 2 rows. Beg patt.
1st row Using G, k.
2nd row P 1 M(3 G, 2 M : 2 M) * 5 G, 2 M. Rep from * to last 6(3:0) sts, then 5 G, 1 M (3 G : 0).
3rd row K 2 M(2 G, 4 M : 3 M) * 3 G, 4 M. Rep from * to last 5(2:6) sts, 3 G, 2 M (2 G : 3 G, 3 M).
4th row P 3 M(0 : 4 M) * 1 G, 6 M. Rep from * to last 4(1:5) sts, 1 G, 3 M (0 : 4 M).
5th row As 3rd row.
6th row As 2nd row.
7th row Using G, k.
8th row Using mc, p.
9th row K * 1 mc, 3 W. Rep from * to last st, 1 mc.

10th row P * 2 mc, 1 W, 1 mc. Rep from * to last st, 1 mc.
11th row K * 1 W, 1 mc. Rep from * to last st, 1 W.
12th row P * 1 W, 3 mc. Rep from * to last st, 1 W.
13th row K * 2 W, 1 mc, 1 W. Rep from * to last st, 1 W.
14th row Using mc, p.
15th row K 2 M (2 M, 1 mc, 3 M : 2 M) * 4 M, 1 mc, 3 M. Rep from * to last 3(7:3) sts, 3 M(4 M, 1 mc, 2 M : 3 M).
16th row P. 0 (1 M, 1 mc, 1 M, 1 mc : 0) * 5 M, 1 mc, 1 M, 1 mc. Rep from * to last 5(9:5) sts, 5 M, then for 2nd size only, 1 mc, 1 M, 1 mc, 1 M.
17th row K * 1 mc, 3 M. Rep from * to last st, 1 mc.
18th row For 1st and 3rd sizes only, 1 M, 1 mc, 1 M, 1 mc. All sizes * 5 M, 1 mc, 1 M, 1 mc. Rep from * to last 1(5:1) sts, 1(5:1) M.
19th row K 2(6:2) M, * 1 mc, 7 M. Rep from * to last 3(7:3) sts, 1 mc, 2(6:2) M.
20th row Using mc, p.
21st row K 5(1:5) mc, * 3 G, 5 mc. Rep from * to last 0(4:0) sts, k 3 G, 1 mc for 2nd size only.
22nd row P * 2 G, 1 mc, 1 G. Rep from * to last st, 1 G.
23rd row As 21st row.
24th row Using mc, p.
25th row K 5(3:1) W, * 1 mc, 5 W. Rep from * to last 0(4:2) sts, then for 2nd and 3rd sizes only, 1 mc, 3(1) W.
26th row P 1 mc (2 W, 3 mc : 3 mc) * 3 W, 3 mc. Rep from * to last 4(2:0) sts, then for 1st and 2nd sizes only 3 W 1 mc, 1st size and 2 W 2nd size.
27th row K 2 mc, 1 W (1 W : 4 mc, 1 W), * 5 mc, 1 W. Rep from * to last 2(0:4) sts, 2(0:4) mc.
28th row As 26th row.
29th row As 25th row.
30th row Using mc, p.
These 30 rows form patt and are rep throughout. Cont in patt until work measures 8½(9:9½) ins from beg ending with a p row **.

Shape Armholes

Keeping continuity of patt, cast off 4(6:8) sts at beg of next 2 rows, then dec 1 st at each end of next and foll 3 alt rows. 61(65:69) sts. Work straight until armhole measures 5½(5½:6) ins ending with a p row.

Shape Shoulders

Cast off 6 sts at beg of next 4 rows, then 5(6:7) sts at beg of next 2 rows. Leave rem 27(29:31) sts on a spare needle.

Front

Work as for Back from ** to **.

Shape Armhole and Neck

Next row Cast off 4(6:8) sts, patt 34(36:38) (including st already on right hand needle from casting off) turn, and leave rem sts on spare needle. Now dec 1 st at armhole edge at beg of foll 4 alt rows, *at the same time* dec 1 st at neck edge on next and every 3rd row. Keeping armhole edge straight, cont dec at neck edge as before until 17(18:19) sts rem. Work straight until front measures same as Back to shoulder, ending with a p row.

Shape Shoulder

Cast off 6 sts at beg of next and foll alt row. Work 1 row and cast off rem 5(6:7) sts. Sl centre st onto a safety pin, rejoin yarn to other sts on spare needle and patt to end. Work to match other side, reversing shaping.

Neckband

Join right shoulder. With right side of work facing, using mc and No. 12(1) needles, pick up and k 50(50:54) sts down left side of neck, k st from safety pin (mark this st with coloured thread) pick up and k 50(50:54) sts up right side of neck and k across 27(29:31) sts of back neck.

1st row Work in k 1, p 1 rib to within 2 sts of marked st, p 2 tog, p 1, p 2 tog tbl, rib to end.

2nd row Rib to within 2 sts of marked st, p 2 tog, k 1, p 2 tog, rib to end. Rep these 2 rows twice more. Cast off in rib, dec on this row as before.

Armbands

Join left shoulder. With right side of work facing, using mc and No. 12(1) needles, pick up and k 96(96:104) sts from armhole and work 6 rows in k 1, p 1 rib. Cast off in rib.

To make up

Press work on wrong side with a warm iron over a damp cloth. Join side and armband seams, matching patt. Press seams.

Knitted Dress

The decorative stitch on the full skirt makes
this smart dress into something special. It is
simple to knit and the close-fitting yoke and
sleeves add a tailored touch. A simple variation
on the style would be to make the yoke and
sleeves in a contrasting colour to the skirt.
The dress is made in a practical Tricel/nylon
yarn that washes easily and holds its shape
well.

Materials

Patons Kingfisher Tricel/Nylon 4-ply crepe

50 gr balls: 4(4:5)
Pairs of No. 11(2), 10(3) and 3(10) knitting
needles
Cable needle
3 small buttons
3 press studs (snaps)

Measurements To fit a 22(24:26) inch chest.
Length from top of shoulders, (approx)
17(19:21) ins. Sleeve seam, 8½(10:11½) ins,
adjustable.

Tension 7 sts to 1 inch over st st using
No. 10(3) needles.

Abbreviations, needle and size note
See pages 12 and 13.

Front

** Using No. 10(3) needles cast on
141(147:153) sts. Change to No. 11(2) needles
and beg with a k row, work 4 rows st st.
Change to No. 10(3) needles.
Next row (picot row) K 1, * y fwd, k 2 tog.
Rep from * to end.
Beg with a p row, work 7 rows st st, dec 1 st
in centre on last row. 140(146:152) sts.
Now work in patt thus:
Change to No. 3(10) needles.
1st row K.
2nd row P.

3rd row K 1, * C 6f. Rep from * to last st, k 1.
Change to No. 10(3) needles.
4th–10th rows Beg with a p row, work 7 rows
st st.
These 10 rows form patt. Work 3(13:23) rows
more in patt.

Shape thus:
Next row (P 14, p 2 tog) 3 times, p to last
48 sts, (p 2 tog, p 14) 3 times.
Work 29 rows straight in patt.
Rep last 30 rows once more, then 1st of these
rows again. 122(128:134) sts. Cont straight in
patt until Front measures 12½(14:15½) ins
from picot row, ending after a wrong side row.

Shape armholes
Keeping continuity of patt, cast off 6 sts
at beg of next 2 rows then dec 1 st at each
end of next 3 rows, then on every alt row
until 98(104:110) sts rem.
Cont straight until Front measures about
14½(16:17¾) ins from picot, ending with a 7th
or 9th patt row. Cont in st st using No. 10(3)
needles *only* for remainder of Front, working
thus:
Next row P 10(11:12), (p 2 tog) 39(41:43)
times, p 10(11:12). 59(63:67) sts **.
Beg with a k row, work 10(12:14) rows st st.

Shape Neck
Next row K 22(23:24) turn and leave rem
sts on spare needle. Cont on rem sts for first
half thus:
*** Dec 1 st at neck edge on every row until
17(18:19) sts rem. Work straight until Front
measures 1½(1¾:1¾) ins from beg of neck
shaping, ending at armhole edge.
Shape Shoulder
Cast off 6 sts at beg of next 2 armhole edge
rows. Work 1 row straight then cast off rem
5(6:7) sts.
Return to other sts, sl centre 15(17:19) sts
on a spare needle, rejoin yarn to rem sts and
k to end.
Now work to match other half, working from
*** to end.

Knitted dress

Back

Work as Front from ** to **, then cont straight in st st until Back matches Front to shoulder edge, ending with a p row.

Shape Shoulders

Cast off 6 sts at beg of next 4 rows then 5(6:7) sts at beg of next 2 rows. Sl rem 25(27:29) sts on st holder.

Sleeves

Using No. 11(2) needles cast on 44(46:48) sts and work in k 1, p 1 rib for $1\frac{1}{2}$(2:2) ins. Change to No. 10(3) needles and cont in rib inc 1 st at each end of 1st and every foll 6th (6th:8th) row until there are 54 sts for each size, then each end of every 8th row until there are 60(64:68) sts, working inc sts into rib.
Cont straight until sleeve measures $8\frac{1}{2}$(10:$11\frac{1}{2}$) ins, or length required.

Shape Top

Cast off 6 sts at beg of next 2 rows, then dec 1 st each end of next and every alt row until 24(26:28) sts rem, then on every row until 18(20:22) sts rem. Cast off loosely in rib.

Neckband

First press yoke only on wrong side using a cool iron over a dry cloth. Join right shoulder. Using No. 11(2) needles and with right side facing pick up and k 16(17:19) sts along left front shoulder, 1 st from corner, 16(18:20) sts down left side of neck, k across centre front sts, dec 2 sts evenly across, pick up and k 16(18:20) sts up right side of neck, k across back sts, finally pick up and k 16(17:19) sts from left back shoulder. 103(113:125) sts.
Beg with a p row, work 3 rows st st, inc 1 st on every row at neck corner of left front shoulder. 106(116:128) sts.
Next row K 2, * y fwd, k 2 tog. Rep from * to end.
Beg with a p row, work 2 rows st st, dec 1 st in each row at neck corner. Cast off loosely.

To make up

Fold neck picot in half to wrong side and slip-stitch in position. Overlap front shoulder over back and tack together at armhole edge. Using a flat seam for ribbing and a fine back-stitch seam, join side and sleeve seams. Sew in sleeves. Fold picot at lower edge in half to wrong side and slip-stitch into position. Press picot borders and seams on wrong side. Sew press studs to shoulder picot, 1st to come $\frac{1}{2}$ inch from neck, remaining 2 spaced evenly. Sew buttons over press studs.

Everyday Dress

This handy little dress could not be easier to sew. It shows how to make exciting use of a bold fabric pattern. The fabric is also an ideal choice for a garment of this type as it is a tough and colourful furnishing cotton, which will wash and wear particularly well. A decorative pocket has been cleverly sewn to the dress front, so that it does not interfere with the pattern of the fabric. The zip is sewn on in a special way that is both decorative and quick to do.

Materials

Furnishing cotton: 1⅝ yds of 36 in fabric or 1¾ yds of 45 in fabric
3 yds of bias binding
Thread and machine embroidery twist
8 in square scrap of iron-on Vilene

1. After cutting out, overcast all edges. Stitch back shoulder darts and press.
2. Place zip down centre front line on right side of fabric and sew round edge with decorative embroidery stitch or satin stitch, using the sewing machine for speed.
3. Iron Vilene on to wrong side of pocket. Overcast top edge and fold over a ½ in flap. Using straight machine stitch, sew round edge of pocket, following outline of fabric pattern. Cut raw edges back outside stitching line. Pin pocket in place over dress front so fabric matches pattern exactly. Oversew round edges in decorative stitch to match zip. The house roof above the pocket on the dress illustrated is also outlined with machine embroidery stitch to give a more finished effect to the dress.
4. Stitch shoulder and side seams.
5. Turn dress to wrong side and cut away excess fabric under zip so it can be opened and closed.
6. Gather sleeve head between dots, using a small zigzag stitch over cord to help make even gathers. Stitch sleeve seams and attach sleeves to dress in the normal way. Adjust sleeve length to individual fit. Make a small casing at wrists by turning up a ½ in hem, then insert elastic as required.
7. Overcast hem and stitch into place by hand or machine.
8. Neaten neckline with bias binding, folded over the neck edge and stitched. Leave enough binding on each side of neck opening to make a decorative tie. Small knots tied in ends of binding prevent fraying.

Cutting out note

Before cutting out, arrange pattern so the bold design is used to best advantage. The pocket is the same shape as the house on the

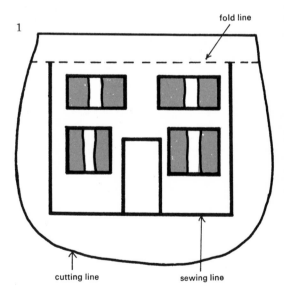

dress illustrated. To use this idea, which can be adapted for any bold fabric design, cut out a piece of fabric for the pocket which matches a section of the pattern on the dress front, allowing an extra ½ in on top and ¼ in round sides and bottom (diagram 1).

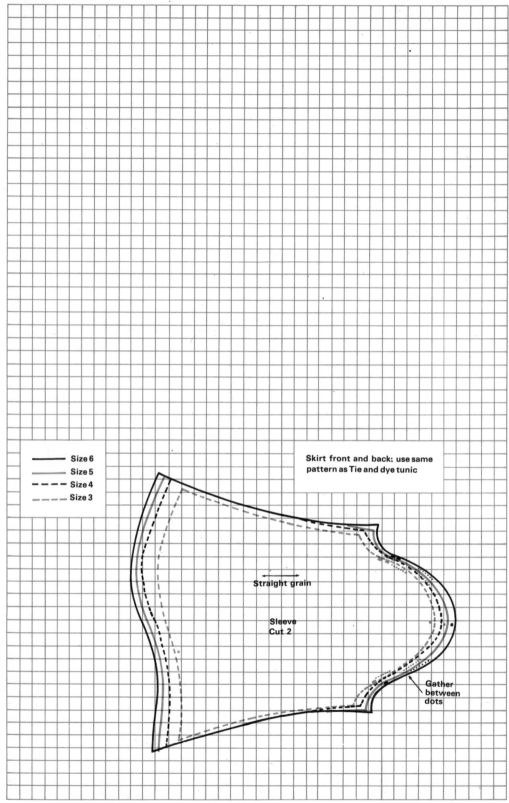

Size 6
Size 5
Size 4
Size 3

Skirt front and back: use same
pattern as Tie and dye tunic

Straight grain

Sleeve
Cut 2

Gather
between
dots

Tucked Dress

This little dress shows how to make unusually effective use of check or striped fabrics. The decorative tucks on the bodice emphasize the colours and add a smart tailored look to a basically simple flared dress pattern. This idea can be used for all sorts of different fabrics, but is especially good for boldly striped cottons and colourful ginghams.

Materials

2 yds striped or check fabric
Thread to match
Zip fastener

1. Cut out a square of fabric for the dress front, 36 × 32 ins (size 6); 36 × 28 ins (size 4) or 36 × 22 ins (size 2).
Fold, pin, then baste tucks to make a dense block of colour in the centre of what will become the bodice front. The tucks should be folded so one of the fabric colours will be emphasized (diagram 1). The size of the tucks

fabric before tucking

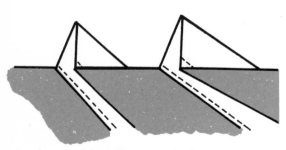

1   – – – – – – sewing line

will depend on the fabric pattern you choose. When folded, the block of tucks should measure 11 ins wide (size 6); 9 ins wide (size 4) or 7 ins wide (size 2), not including the spare fabric on either side. Machine the tucks

down for 12 ins (size 6); 10 ins (size 4) or 8 ins (size 2). On the wrong side, iron the tucks with the folds pressed outwards. Mark the centre front line with basting. Pin the tucks down at what will be hem level, making

2   tucks sewn down to waist level

cutting line

tucks pinned at hem level to facilitate cutting out pattern

a square block of fabric that is now ready to be cut to shape (diagram 2).
(On the larger sizes if tucks are very deep ones using up most of the width of the fabric, it may be necessary to add 6 in panels on either side. This will make the material the right width for cutting out the dress front.)
Place the dress front pattern over the prepared piece of fabric, making sure the centre fronts coincide. Now cut out the dress front, stay stitching tucks on the shoulder and neckline.
2. Cut out back and sleeves and overcast all cut edges with zigzag stitching.

3. Join the two back pieces, right sides together. Make a seam from waist level and insert a zip fastener from the waist to the neck.

4. Make gathering stitches along upper edge of sleeves between notch marks. Pin sleeves to armholes, right sides together, adjusting gathers to fit and making sure notches match. The large notch in the centre top must match the shoulder seam.

5. Join the sides, right sides facing, making continuous seams from sleeves to hem.

6. Measure individual neck size and round top of arms. Cut strips of fabric the same length, adding on 2 ins for turnings. The strips must be cut on the bias and should be 1 in wide. Pin binding to neck edge, right sides together, baste and machine stitch. Trim edge. Fold binding over to inside. Turn in edge and oversew neatly. Add a hook and eye fastening at back of neck.

7. Join ends of sleeve binding to make a bracelet shape. Gather fullness at base of sleeve and pin it to binding, adjusting gathers evenly, right sides together. Machine the two together and finish off the inside as for neck binding.

8. Turn up hem to suit individual size.

5 squares represent 4 inches

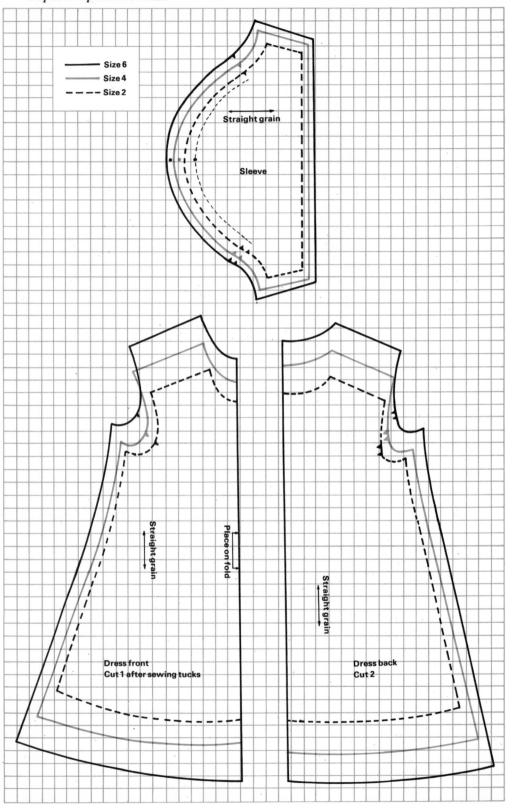

Size 6

Size 4

Size 2

Straight grain

Sleeve

Straight grain

Place on fold

Straight grain

Dress front
Cut 1 after sewing tucks

Dress back
Cut 2

Tucked dress

Dressing Gown

For something that is ultra quick to sew, try this practical pattern. With its warm towelling lining, the dressing gown is ideal for a child to wear after the bath or on the beach. The pattern is one large piece, with the addition of a collar and tab for front opening. With the minimum of seams, it is easy to make and illustrates how to make an original garment in a short time.

Materials

1¾ yds each of 36 in wide cotton and towelling
3 buttons

1. Cut out fabrics. Baste together, wrong sides facing and stitch round edge, following inner line drawn on pattern. Clip on curves.

Leave neck unsewn and use this opening to turn the fabric the right way out.
2. Baste round newly sewn edge to keep flat and machine stitch round edge again on the right side.
3. Cut out the two front tabs from cotton. Sew one edge of each tab, right sides facing to each side of the front opening. Fold tabs in half lengthways and turn raw edges under, slip-stitching into place inside the front opening. Overlap tabs at base of opening when stitching. On right side neaten lower and upper ends of tabs and oversew.
4. With right sides facing, sew along the upper edge and sides of collar. Turn collar right way out, baste and oversew with straight stitch round edge of join. Join collar to neck, using collar facing to neaten inside of neckline.
5. Join along underside of sleeves and sides of dressing gown by hand with oversewing.
6. Make buttonholes and attach buttons.

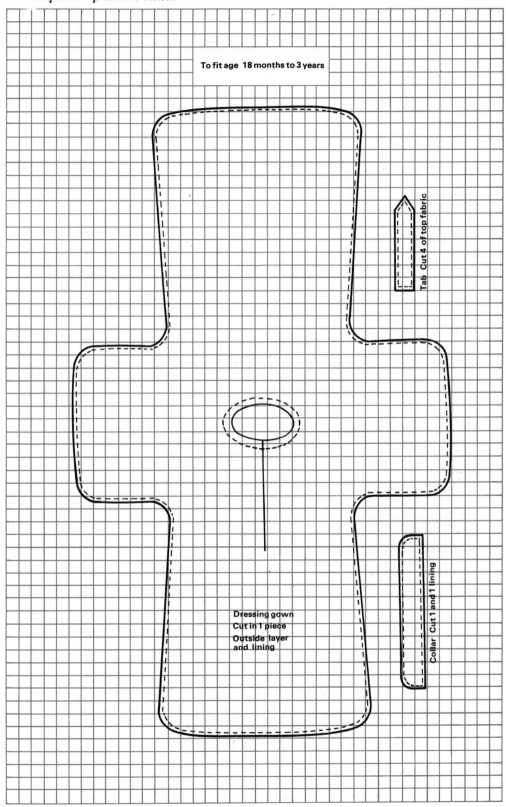

To fit age 18 months to 3 years

Tab Cut 4 of top fabric

Dressing gown
Cut in 1 piece
Outside layer
and lining

Collar Cut 1 and 1 lining

Dungarees Sets

These patterns are excellent money-savers because they are so quick to make. The tough denim dungarees are ideal for active children at play. The toddler's pair has an easy fastening along the inner leg seams for quick nappy changing. The appliqué initials add an individual touch. The stretch towelling sweaters would be relatively expensive to buy ready-made, but are surprisingly simple to make at home.

Materials

Denim for dungarees:
Smaller sizes up to 3 years
1¼ yds of 36 in or 1 yd of 45 in fabric
Sizes 4 to 6 years
1⅜ yds of 36 in or 1⅛ yds of 45 in fabric
Buttons and suspenders for fastenings
Velcro or strip of poppers (snaps) for leg fastenings on toddler's sizes.
Two small strips of sweater fabric for cuffs on toddler's sizes
Scraps of towelling and iron-on Vilene for initials
Stretch towelling for sweaters:
1 yd of 36 in fabric

Dungarees

1. Cut out pattern and overcast all edges using three-step zigzag. Pin facing to front, right sides together. Stitch upper edges and armhole. Trim seams and corners where necessary. Clip curves. Press facing to inside of garment.
2. Stitch centre back seams, re-inforcing seam at crotch. Clip curves. With right sides together, pin facing to back. Stitch along upper edges and armhole. Trim seams, corners and clip curves. Press facing to inside.
3. Join side seams and stitch from edge of facing to underarm and down to ankle. Press facing to inside, baste and sew a neat row of machine stitching ¾ in from top edge of dungarees all the way round.

4. Using the green stretch towelling, apply motif to dungaree front. First iron on Vilene to wrong side of stretch towelling, then draw out initial on a piece of firm tracing paper. Pin fabric in position with paper under dungarees. Sew round outline of initial with small straight stitch. Cut away excess towelling round this stitching, leaving a clear outline. Sew satin stitch all round raw edges to prevent fraying. (For a good satin stitch, use machine embroidery thread, stitch width 3, length about ½).
5. Fold straps in half lengthwise, right sides facing. Make a ⅜ in seam, leaving opening halfway down, wide enough to turn fabric to right side. Turn straps and press, then slipstitch opening. Machine stitch straps to outside of trousers at back with a square of stitching. Attach suspenders to other end of straps and sew on buttons at front.
6. **On larger sizes,** stitch inside leg, and hem at ankle.
On toddler's sizes, turn in small hem on front and back of inside leg. Fold ankle cuff in half, right sides together, seam at either end, turn to right side and press. Stretch towelling whilst sewing and use a machine stretch stitch to attach cuff to trouser bottom. If the machine is non-automatic, attach cuffs by hand with back stitch. Stitch Velcro along entire front and back inside leg opening—from cuff to crotch to cuff, front and back.

Stretch Knit Sweaters

1. Cut out sweater, making sure width of fabric goes round body of garment and length of fabric goes up and down; otherwise garment will be unwearable. Maximum stretch must be on width of garment so it's easy to put on and will keep its shape properly.
2. Join sleeves to body of garment by placing wrong sides together then seaming and overcasting in one operation, using Elna superstretch stitch, disc no. 152, or a similar

Dungarees sets

special stretch stitch on an automatic sewing machine. With a non-automatic machine, seams must be joined by hand, using back-stitch for elasticity. Then overcast cut edges by hand. Owners of automatic machines will score when they make this pattern, because it will take only about 15 mins to sew up the sweaters.

3. Seam from wrist to underarm and continue down side seam of sweater all in one operation.

4. Turn under $\frac{1}{2}$ in hem on bottom of sweater and on sleeves and again, (using superstretch stitch on machine, or overcasting, then backstitch for hand sewing), stitch turnings into place.

5. With *wrong* side of fabric facing, join neckband into a circle, again only leaving a narrow seam allowance. Fold band in half and with pins mark it into four equal sections. Mark neckline of sweater in the same way. Pin sweater and neckband together at quarter points. Then, using superstretch machine stitch or backstitch, seam sweater and neckband together, stretching neckband to fit garment as you sew.

5 squares represent 4 inches

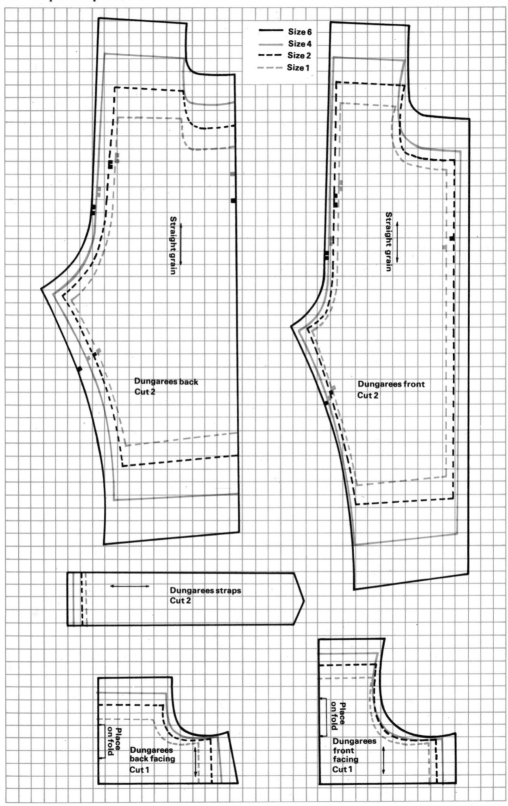

Size 6
Size 4
Size 2
Size 1

Straight grain

Straight grain

Dungarees back
Cut 2

Dungarees front
Cut 2

Dungarees straps
Cut 2

Place on fold

Dungarees
back facing
Cut 1

Place on fold

Dungarees
front
facing
Cut 1

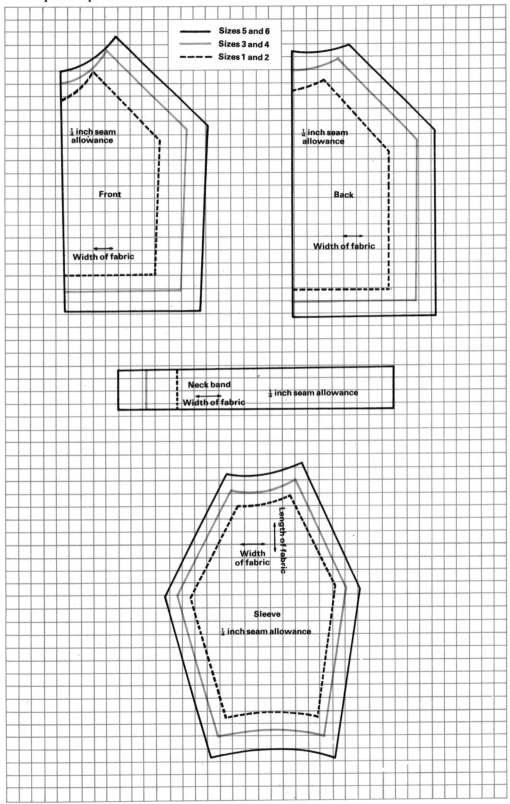

5 squares represent 4 inches

Sizes 5 and 6
Sizes 3 and 4
Sizes 1 and 2

¼ inch seam allowance

Front

Width of fabric

¼ inch seam allowance

Back

Width of fabric

Neck band
¼ inch seam allowance
Width of fabric

Length of fabric

Width of fabric

Sleeve
¼ inch seam allowance

Patchwork Robe

*An ultra-feminine dressing gown is something
most small girls long for. This one shows
an unusual way of using patchwork and the
finished result is something to treasure.
Making a complete patchwork skirt for this
dressing gown would take a long time, but
using the hexagonal patchwork as flower
shapes on the skirt takes much less time yet
looks lovely. The skirt and bodice are lined
with wadding for extra warmth. The dressing
gown is made in practical cotton, with cotton
patchwork and lining, and Terylene wadding
so it will be easy to wash. This pattern could
be adapted in several ways. Instead of the
patchwork flowers, cut out animal shapes
from cotton to appliqué round the skirt. If you
want a quick "make", use warm ready-made
quilting without the extra decorations.*

Materials

Pink gingham: 1 yd 36 in or ⅝ yd 45 in
Pink cotton: 2 yds 36 in or 45 in
Terylene or Courtelle wadding: 2 yds 36 in
or 45 in
Scraps of cotton for patchwork
Thread
Buttons for binding

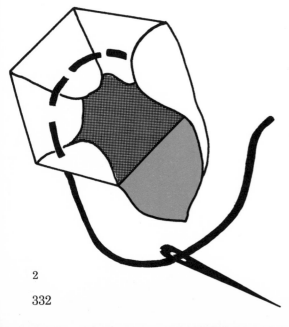

2

Patchwork

Use a one inch hexagonal template, or make
your own from stiff card, using our pattern
(diagram 1). Cut out a generous supply of

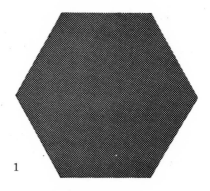

1

hexagonal patterns from old magazine paper.
Now cut out a supply of cotton scraps, each
one 1½ ins square. Place a paper pattern over
a fabric square. Fold cotton over paper to
make the hexagonal shape and baste securely
(diagram 2). Assemble the patchwork flowers.
Each flower is composed of one plain (for
the centre) and six patterned patches. Join
the patches along the folded edges, using
neat overcasting stitch. When shapes are
complete press firmly before removing basting
and paper. Trim away any bulky excess
material on underside. The flower shapes are
now ready for stitching to the dressing gown.

Dressing Gown

1. Cut out the pattern pieces and overcast all
cut edges, preferably using three-step zigzag
on machine.
2. Join shoulder seams of yoke on both lining
and garment.
3. Join side seams of both skirt and lining.
Join side seams of wadding by butting edges
and sewing with three-step zigzag so the join
is flat. Sandwich wadding between skirt and

lining and press front edge of skirt inside along fold lines to form facing. Gather in fullness along skirt top between notches.

4. Pin skirt to yoke, drawing up gathers to fit. Stitch yoke to skirt.

5. Mark where flowers and stems will be sewn on dressing gown skirt, using a free-hand design. Make stems. Either appliqué them in the form of green cotton, or, as in the illustration, use a cording foot on the sewing machine and sew on close rows of green pearl cotton, using a three-step zigzag (diagram 3).

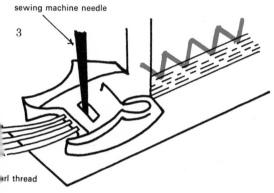

sewing machine needle

3

rl thread

This is the quickest way with an automatic sewing machine. Sew leaves at random, following design, using tapered zigzag stitch. Cut out circular pieces of wadding a little smaller than the prepared patchwork flowers. Place wadding under flowers and baste to skirt. Sew round edge of flowers with straight stitch, and again round edge of hexagon in centre of each flower. Remove basting.

6. Gather head of sleeves between notches (see useful stitches, page 10). Stitch underarm seams of sleeves, clipping curves. Make narrow hems on bottom of sleeves and insert elastic to fit. With right sides together, pin sleeves into armholes, matching dots to shoulder seam on each side. Ease fullness and stitch along seam line. Press sleeve edge towards bodice.

7. Cut out a strip of gingham for frilled collar, measuring 36×3 ins. Fold the strip in half lengthwise. Stitch down each end of the folded strip, right sides together. Turn right way out and press firmly. Gather base of strip (diagram 4). Pull up gathers and pin collar to yoke neck, right sides facing, starting one inch from yoke front edge on each side and adjusting gathers to fit

(diagram 4a). Pin lining to yoke at neck, right sides facing, so frilled collar is sandwiched between the two. Then pin lining to yoke from neck edge to base of yoke on

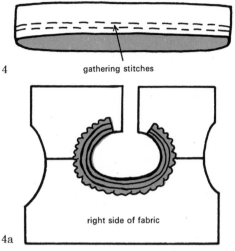

4   gathering stitches

right side of fabric

4a

both sides at front. Baste and stitch these layers together (diagram 5). Clip seams. Turn to right side, press. Turn under $\frac{5}{8}$ in seam allowance along both fronts, round armholes and along back of yoke lining and slip stitch into place.

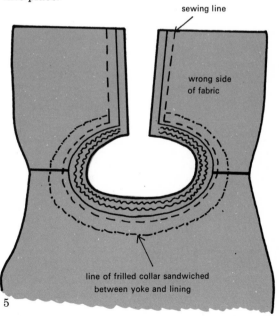

sewing line

wrong side of fabric

line of frilled collar sandwiched between yoke and lining

5

8. Turn up hem on lining and skirt and stitch into place.

9. Cover buttons in gingham. Stitch on to dressing gown. Make buttonholes.

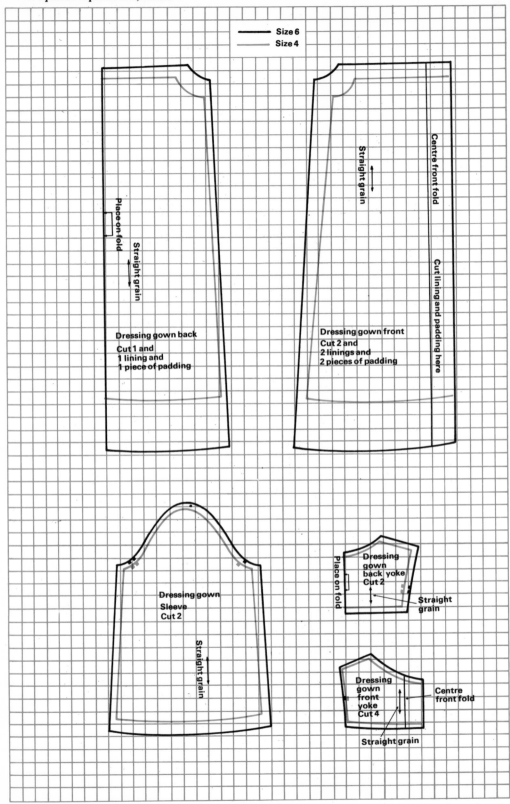

Size 6
Size 4

Place on fold

Straight grain

Dressing gown back
Cut 1 and
1 lining and
1 piece of padding

Straight grain

Centre front fold

Cut lining and padding here

Dressing gown front
Cut 2 and
2 linings and
2 pieces of padding

Dressing gown
Sleeve
Cut 2

Straight grain

Place on fold

Dressing gown back yoke
Cut 2

Straight grain

Dressing gown front yoke
Cut 4

Centre front fold

Straight grain

Patchwork robe

Nursery Accessories

Changing Mattress

Most mothers include one of these changing mattresses on their list of equipment for a new baby. It is easy to change a baby's nappies and to wash him when he is lying on a mattress like this one. The laminated surface makes it simple to wipe clean. The slightly raised sides will protect a young baby from draughts. However, an active baby may be able to roll off, so should not be left unattended if the mattress is on a table. The soft foam filling makes it comfortable for a baby to lie on. It is inexpensive and simple to make—the sort of job that can be done in an afternoon.

Materials

1¾ yds laminated fabric or PVC
Matching thread
1 in thick sheet of foam—15 by 24 in.
2 bags foam filling.
Sticky tape, and pattern or tissue paper
Size when completed—33 by 14 ins

1. Cut out the two pieces of fabric for the top and underside.
2. Place pieces of fabric together, right sides facing each other. Instead of pinning, bind together at intervals with strips of sticky tape. Machine round edge, leaving a ½ in seam allowance. Leave the base open and a 3 in gap for filling at the top end. Clip seam allowance on corners and turn mattress the right way out.
3. Place the foam sheet inside the mattress. With felt-tipped pen mark out the sewing line, ½ in from edge of foam. Pin carefully in three places along sewing line on each side. Remove foam.
4. Tape strips of paper over sewing line on both sides of mattress to prevent it from sticking when it is machined. Mark out the sewing line on the paper also and remove pins. Machine carefully, leaving base open. Remove paper and tape.
5. Slide foam sheet into place. Fill sides tightly with foam chips, using a rolling pin to help push filling into place. Fill top and neaten off seam with oversewing.

pattern or tissue paper

1   sticky tape   machining line

6. Secure the base with strips of sticky tape, so the top side is fixed to the underside. Place paper on both sides of mattress to cover sewing line. If necessary, mark sewing line with pen. Finish off base with row of zigzag stitch. Remove paper and sticky tape. Cut away remaining fabric below sewing line (diagram 1).

5 squares represent 4 inches

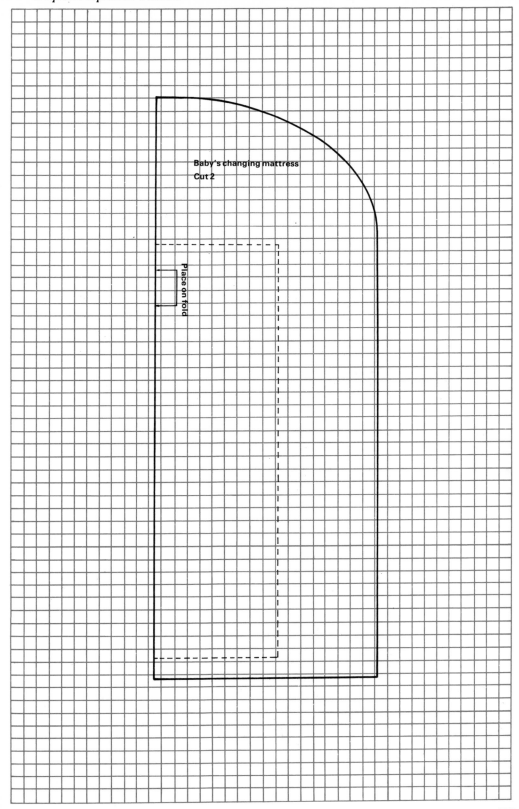

Baby's changing mattress
Cut 2

Place on fold

Wall Tidy

All the bits and pieces needed for changing or bathing a baby can be stored in this practical holdall. Use the big pocket for cotton wool balls. Other pockets are specially designed in an assortment of shapes to hold everything from baby lotions to cotton wool buds, nail scissors and medicaments. Later on the holdall can be used as a desk tidy, when it can be filled with homework equipment, like pencils and rulers. It is a good space saver because it hangs so neatly on the wall. This one is made in plastic-coated fabric so that it can be wiped clean. However, fabric of this type is quite awkward to sew and the pattern could be used equally well with a washable fabric like heavy canvas, or gingham backed with Vilene. When using a different fabric, sew pockets on with zigzag stitch and attach the holdall to the frame back with strips of strong poppers or Velcro so it can be removed easily for washing.

Materials

Hardboard square 22 in by 28 in with ½ in battens pinned around edges to make a frame (see diagram 2)
1¼ yds PVC coated fabric or material of choice
Squared pattern paper or tracing paper
18 in length of tape
Scraps of fabric for appliqué (optional)
Reel of sticky tape (to be used on PVC fabric instead of pins, which leave marks)

1. Cut out fabric for backing and pockets. Fold raw edges of pocket tops under and secure with short strip of sticky tape. The shiny side of the PVC sticks to the machine when it is being sewn, so fold strips of pattern paper over the area to be sewn and secure with strips of sticky tape. This helps the fabric to run easily through the machine. Machine pocket tops. Remove paper and tape.

2. Cut pocket shapes neatly from the middle of the backing pattern, then lay the backing pattern over the material so the pocket positions can be marked with faint pinpricks or felt tipped pen (which wipes off).

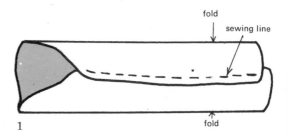

1

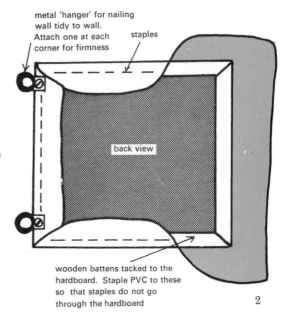

metal 'hanger' for nailing wall tidy to wall. Attach one at each corner for firmness

staples

back view

wooden battens tacked to the hardboard. Staple PVC to these so that staples do not go through the hardboard

2

3. Make neat knife pleats on both sides of each pocket. Secure pockets into position with sticky tape. Tape the pocket outlines (cut from the backing pattern) over each pocket to make the PVC easy to sew. Machine

Wall tidy and changing mattress

in place, using straight stitch. Remove paper and sticky tape. Complete one pocket before moving on to next. If the fabric shows signs of fraying, sew round edge of pockets with zigzag stitch.

4. Fold the paper roll holder in three, lengthways. Secure with tape and machine along centre to hold edges in place. Fold under the ends and machine. Machine one end on to backing fabric. Attach 9 in of the tape to the other end, and a further 9 in to the backing, so the holder can be undone easily when a new paper roll is needed (diagram 1).

5. Deal with safety-pin holder in the same way, machining it on to the backing at each end. Make slots to hold pins with short rows of stitching at half-inch intervals.

6. Tape appliqué into position (optional) under paper pattern, then sew—either with zigzag or straight stitch.

7. Pull holdall tightly over the hardboard square and staple tightly into position on the wood at the back (diagram 2).

1 square represents 1 inch

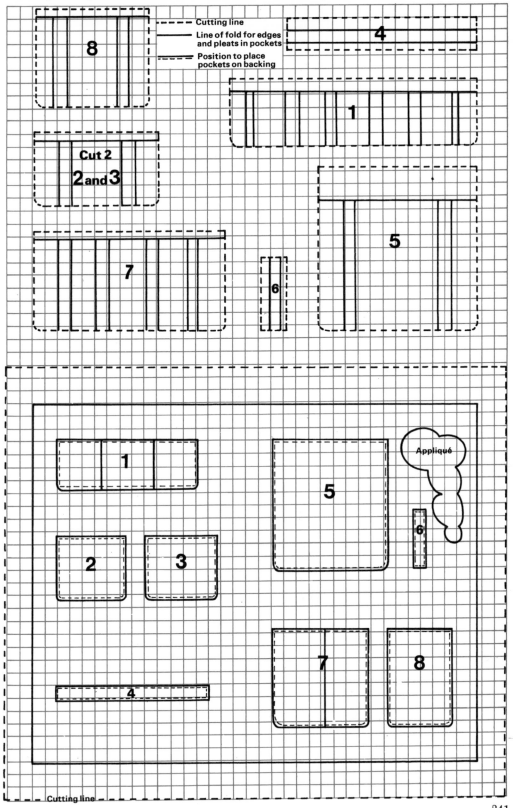

Cutting line
Line of fold for edges
and pleats in pockets
Position to place
pockets on backing

8

4

1

Cut 2
2 and 3

5

7

6

Appliqué

1

5

6

2

3

7

8

4

Baby's Cot

*Covering the cot is one of the most pleasing
preparations for a new baby. This pattern is
simple to sew. The broderie anglaise frills
and colourful ribbon bring a delicate finish.
The skirts can be removed easily so the
basket can be taken off its stand and used as
a carry cot. All the coverings are simple to
take off and wash. This method can be
adapted for either round or square ended cots.*

Materials

Cotton, Dacron or lawn for skirts (amount you
buy depends on individual cot size and shape).
For cot you need roughly 8 yds and for
canopy another $3\frac{1}{2}$ yds
Courtelle or Terylene wadding
Broderie anglaise frill trimming
Ribbon
Velcro
Brown paper

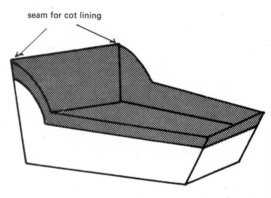

seam for cot lining

1

seam for cot lining

1. Use brown paper to make a pattern of the
inside of the cot. A rounded cot needs two
pieces to line sides and one for base. A
square cot needs four pieces to line sides
and one for base. When drawing up the
pattern (use a felt tipped pen and trace shape
of cot on to paper by feeling contours with
pen through paper), add 4 ins along top edges
so lining curves neatly over edge (diagram 1).
2. Cut out cot lining from covering fabric and
wadding. The two layers should be the same.
Pin, adjust fit, baste and stitch together with
wadding beneath covering fabric.
3. Measure round outside top of cot, 2 in
below edge. Cut a strip of fabric the same

length plus 2 ins for turnings. The side
measurement of this fabric should be 30 ins.
This covers the cot outside. Gather trimming
to go round top edge. This should be $1\frac{1}{2}$ times
or twice measurement round top edge of cot.

Baby's cot

Join it between cot lining and outside (diagram 2). Stitch these three layers together (diagram 3). Make a 1 in hem along bottom half of the Velcro. Neaten sides of skirts and attach to cot under frill by pressing Velcro strips together.

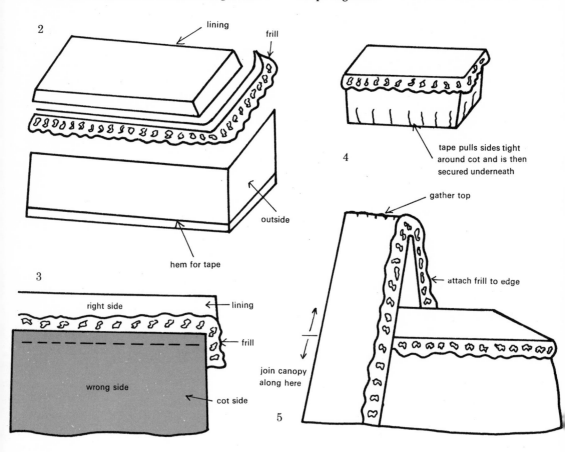

edge of cot side piece. Thread tape through this so sides can be pulled tight underneath (diagram 4).

4. Cut Velcro strip long enough to go round top of cot and sew velvet side of it under top frill.

5. Cut cot skirts—36 in wide and $1\frac{1}{2}$ or 2 times length of Velcro strip. Hem one long edge and gather the other on to the other

6. Make canopy by cutting a straight length of fabric twice the height of canopy. Fold length of fabric in half. Join it up one side. Sew trimming and ribbon to unjoined edge. Gather fabric along fold so it fits over canopy top (diagram 5).

Pram Toy

Five colourful felt teddy bears are designed to be strung across a young baby's pram or cot. As he kicks, they spring around on elastic and the bells round their necks jingle. When the baby is about six months old, the bears can be taken off the elastic and hung on the nursery wall or kept with the soft toys.

Scraps of felt in bright colours
Kapok or Dacron wadding
2 ft round elastic
Thread to match felt colours
Strands of embroidery thread for faces
5 brass bells (small)
Bag of colourful macramé beads
Scraps of fabric for skirts
1 yd narrow ribbon

The bears are 4 ins high. Trace and cut out the required number of patterns from the felt scraps. Each of ours is in the dark and light shade of a different colour to give a kaleidoscope effect as the baby pushes the bears round and round on the elastic.
Sort the cut-out Teddies into pairs. Oversew each pair together firmly round the edge on the right side, stuffing each limb firmly as it is sewn. Leave an opening in the side to stuff the body and head. Use a pencil to help. Finish off side. Using pinking shears, cut scraps of fabric measuring 4 in by 1 in for the skirts. Gather these and sew up the openings on the wrong side. Stay stitch on to bears. Sew faces with 2 strands of embroidery thread on the needle, using French knots for eyes and stem stitch for noses and mouths. Cut 5 pieces of ribbon 7 in long. Thread a macramé bead and a bell on to each piece of ribbon. Tie ribbon round necks so each

bear has a bead at the back of his neck and a bell at the front, knotted into the bow. Stay stitch the bell, the bow and the ribbon knot firmly in place on to the bear so the baby will not be able to pull it off. Thread

4 squares to the inch

cut 10

elastic through beads at back of bears' necks, separating each bear with 20 beads. Sew loops at each end of the elastic and stay stitch beads at each end so they cannot be pulled off over the loops.

Pram toy

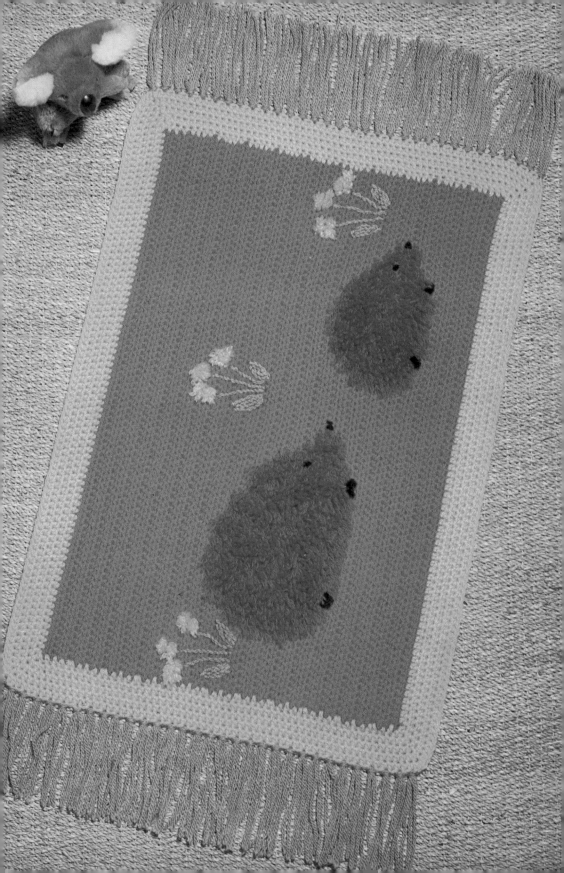

Crochet Rug

*The amusing tufted hedgehogs and dandelions
add an extra dimension to this little rug.
It shows how you can adapt crochet work for
furnishings. The pattern is especially simple
to follow and the rug is inexpensive to make
in a hard-wearing double knitting wool. For
added strength the rug can be backed with a
protective layer of felt.*

Materials

Monsieur Pingouin (Knitting Worsted), 50 gr
balls:

4 in orange, 2 in yellow and 1 each in rust
and green
A small amount of black double knitting wool
(knitting worsted) for the hedgehogs' face
and feet
A No. 5·50 mm (H/8) crochet hook
Strip of felt 18 in by 27 in for backing
(optional)

Measurements Approx 18 ins by 27 ins
(excluding fringe)

Tension 10 h tr (hdc) to 3 ins

Abbreviations and hook note
See pages 12 and 13.

To make

Using orange make 81 ch.
Foundation row 1 h tr (hdc) into 3rd ch
from hook, 1 h tr (hdc) into each ch to end.
Next row 2 ch, 1 h tr (hdc) into each h tr
(hdc) to end.
Rep last row until work measures about
14½ ins. Fasten off.

Border

Turn and work in yellow. Join yellow into
last st worked, 2 ch for 1st h tr (hdc), 2 h tr
(hdc) into same st, work 1 h tr (hdc) into each
h tr (hdc) until 1 h tr (hdc) rems, 3 h tr (hdc)
into last st. Now work 52 h tr (hdc) down left
side of rug to foundation edge, work 3 h tr
(hdc) into 1st ch (at ch edge) then work
1 h tr (hdc) into each ch until 1 ch rems,
3 h tr (hdc) into last ch, work 52 h tr (hdc) up
right side of rug, sl st into 2nd ch.

2nd round Sl st into next h tr (hdc), 2 ch,
2 h tr (hdc) into same st, work 1 h tr (hdc)
into each h tr (hdc) and 3 h tr (hdc) into
centre of 3 h tr (hdc) at rem 3 corners, sl st
into 2nd ch.
Rep last round 3 times. Fasten off.

Now Work Tufted Hedgehogs
First wind rust wool over a piece of stiff
cardboard about 1½ ins wide, then cut at one
side, thus having strands of wool about 3 ins
long. Now work from left to right from chart.
Insert hook under a h tr (hdc)—working in
line now with this h tr (hdc) from left to right
and work a knotted loop by folding one
strand of wool in half over hook and draw
through a loop, pass the 2 ends through loop
and tighten knot. Follow chart using 1 strand
for hedgehogs, but use 2 strands together for
dandelions. Using green single, work stalks
and leaves in stem-stitch. Use the black wool
double, work nose, eyes and feet as shown in
photographs. Cut green yarn into 10 inch
lengths and knot 2 strands through every
alternate st along short edges. Trim fringe.
Cut felt back to size and sew in place with
overcasting stitch (optional).

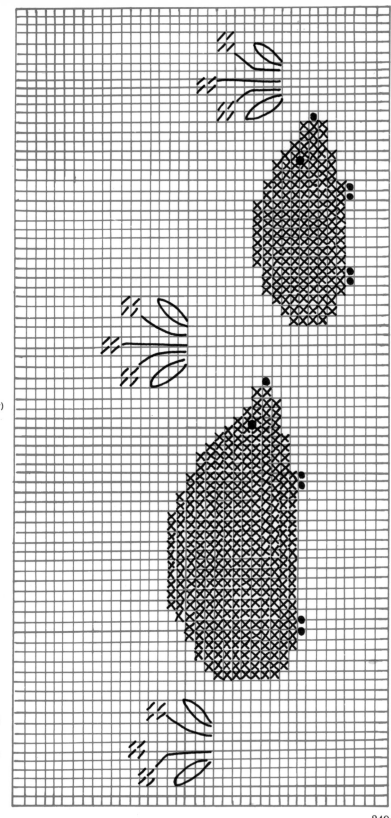

Centre of Rug (excluding Border)

X = rust
\ = yellow (use two strands)
● = black
ꝺl = stem stitch (embroidered)

Patchwork Bedspread

*This fresh-looking bedspread shows an
unusual and clever way of making patchwork,
using colourful cotton scraps. The circular
shapes are sewn in such a way that the
finished work has a nubbly three-dimensional
effect and does not need lining. The patchwork circles are joined to each other in four
places, instead of all the way round as in
traditional patchwork, which means it is
much quicker to sew. The method of joining
gives the bedspread a delicate cellular effect.
The nubbly side is the right side. The shapes
are easy to prepare at odd moments and the
patchwork can be used in several different
ways. Thin strips can be used as decorative
braid on curtains and long table cloths. The
patchwork would also make a colourful cot
or pram cover, or it could be used to cover a
drum-shaped lampshade, or even as a wall-
hanging.*

Materials

Plenty of cotton scraps
Thick piece of card for use as template
Thread

1. Make a template from thick card, the same
size as our pattern. Then cut out a good
supply of cotton circles (diagram 1).
2. Fold the cut edge of circle under and
gather fairly roughly, using double thread
with the ends knotted (diagram 2).

2

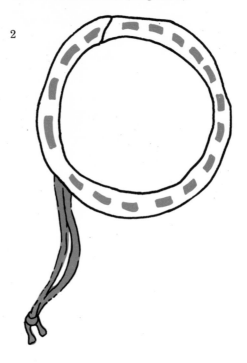

3. Pull up gathers tightly and tie off thread
neatly, passing it backwards and forwards
through neck of patch shape to make a firm
finish. This is important (diagram 3).

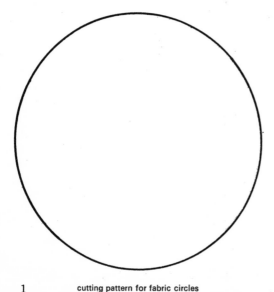

1   cutting pattern for fabric circles

3

4. Flatten the patchwork shape into a circle (diagram 4).

4   profile of patchwork shape

top of patchwork shape

5. Join patches in groups of 9 or 16. Sew patches together using overcasting stitches with about ¼ inch of stitching in four places round the now flattened circular shapes (diagram 5).

6. Arrange the prepared blocks of patches so colours mix well together. Carry on joining up blocks until bedspread reaches required size.

5